HOW TO HAVE THAT
DIFFICULT
CONVERSATION

Resources by Henry Cloud and John Townsend

Books

Boundaries (and workbook)
Boundaries in Dating (and workbook)
Boundaries in Marriage (and workbook)
Boundaries with Kids (and workbook)
Boundaries with Teens (Townsend)
Changes That Heal (and workbook) (Cloud)
Hiding from Love (Townsend)
How People Grow (and workbook)
How to Have That Difficult Conversation
Making Small Groups Work
Our Mothers, Ourselves (and workbook)
Raising Great Kids
Raising Great Kids Workbook for Parents of Preschoolers
Raising Great Kids Workbook for Parents of School-Age Children
Raising Great Kids Workbook for Parents of Teenagers
Safe People (and workbook)
12 "Christian" Beliefs That Can Drive You Crazy

Video Curriculum

Boundaries
Boundaries in Dating
Boundaries in Marriage
Boundaries with Kids
Raising Great Kids for Parents of Preschoolers
ReGroup (with Bill Donahue)

Audio

Boundaries
Boundaries in Dating
Boundaries in Marriage
Boundaries with Kids
Boundaries with Teens (Townsend)
Changes That Heal (Cloud)
How People Grow
How to Have That Difficult Conversation
Making Small Groups Work
Our Mothers, Ourselves
Raising Great Kids

DR. HENRY CLOUD
DR. JOHN TOWNSEND

HOW TO HAVE THAT
DIFFICULT
CONVERSATION

FORMERLY TITLED *HOW TO HAVE THAT DIFFICULT
CONVERSATION YOU'VE BEEN AVOIDING*

FORMERLY TITLED *BOUNDARIES FACE TO FACE*

ZONDERVAN
BOOKS

ZONDERVAN BOOKS

How to Have That Difficult Conversation
Copyright © 2003, 2005 by Henry Cloud and John Townsend

Previously published as: *How to Have That Difficult Conversation You've Been Avoiding*

Published in Grand Rapids, Michigan, by Zondervan. Zondervan is a registered trademark of The Zondervan Corporation, L.L.C., a wholly owned subsidiary of HarperCollins Christian Publishing, Inc.

Requests for information should be addressed to customercare@harpercollins.com.

Zondervan titles may be purchased in bulk for educational, business, fundraising, or sales promotional use. For information, please email SpecialMarkets@Zondervan.com.

ISBN 978-0-310-34256-4 (softcover)
ISBN 978-0-310-27437-7 (audio)
ISBN 978-0-310-34380-6 (ebook)

Library of Congress Cataloging-in-Publication Data

Cloud, Henry.
    [Boundaries face to face]
    How to have that difficult conversation you've been avoiding : with your spouse, your adult child, your boss, your coworker, your best friend, your parent, someone you're dating / Henry Cloud and John Townsend. — 1st ed.
        p.   cm.
    Originally published: Boundaries face to face. Grand Rapids, Mich. : Zondervan, c2003. With discussion guide.
        ISBN 978-0-310-26714-0
        I. Townsend, John Sims, 1952- II. Title.
    BV4597.53.C58C59 2006
    158.2 — dc22   2005027779

Published in association with Yates & Yates, www.yates2.com.

Interior design: Beth Shagene

Printed in the United States of America

$PrintCode

To all those who seek to make truthful conversations
a central part of all their relationships.

Acknowledgments

Sealy Yates, our agent, for his own commitment to truth and love.

Scott Bolinder, our publisher, for supporting and partnering with us in this work.

Sandy Vander Zicht, our editor, for her expertise and her genuine care about seeing people grow and mature.

Maureen Price, director of Cloud-Townsend Resources, for her appreciation for the value of boundaries face-to-face.

Denis Beausejour, director of Answers for Life, for his vision and commitment to the process of helping others find Christ and experience the life Christ designed.

The attendees of Monday Night Solutions in Irvine, California, for their faithfulness in seeking God and helping us develop the concepts that ended up in this book.

Contents

Part III
SEEING HOW IT'S DONE

Part IV
GETTING YOURSELF READY TO HAVE THE CONVERSATION

Part V
HAVING THE DIFFICULT CONVERSATION WITH PEOPLE IN YOUR LIFE

Confident Confrontations

We never foresaw how well our book *Boundaries: When to Say Yes, When to Say No to Take Control of Your Life* was going to do. Although we knew through our clinical work that many people identify with the need to regain control of their lives, we had no idea how widespread that need was. Almost everyone feels the need for better boundaries at one time or another.

Sometimes we need to deal with a difficult person in a relationship, such as a controller, a manipulator, or someone who is irresponsible or even abusive. At other times we need to figure out what demands of life to say no to so we won't overextend ourselves. At still other times we need to work out better patterns of intimacy and relatedness in a good relationship, or take a stand for our values in a difficult one. Still other times, we might need to keep someone from taking over more of our time, energy, and resources than we would like to give. There are many, many different contexts of life in which we need to exercise good boundaries. For people who care, setting those boundaries can be tough. So it really is no surprise that *Boundaries* has found such a ready audience.

As a result of the book's following, we find ourselves speaking to tens of thousands of people directly every year and literally millions through our radio program. When we talk to people, the theme of dealing with difficult relationships continues to surface. Resolving relational issues is always on the forefront of people's minds.

As we answer questions, we find ourselves continually telling people that they should have a direct conversation with the person with whom they have the problem. They repeatedly say either, "I've

tried that, and it didn't work," or, "How would I do that?" Either
they have tried and found themselves overpowered or outmaneu-
vered, or they just don't know how to broach such a conversation.
So we often tell them to role-play with us. We say, "You be him or
her and I'll be you. Now go." When we show them how to have such
a conversation, the lights go on for the first time. They often say
things like "I never thought about saying it like that. That makes
all the difference in the world. Now I know what to do."

Many people in the audience who observe the role-playing tell
us the same thing. Just hearing how to do it gives them a process
to follow, and they can go forward with more confidence that they
will be able to resolve a tough issue.

This book shows readers how to do that, how to have a "boundary conversation." Most people know that they need to set boundaries with someone or have a difficult conversation with someone,
but few know how to do it well. Some are so afraid, they never try;
others try and fail dismally; still others do it in a way that does more
harm than good. For that reason, people put off confronting, setting boundaries, or "facing into" difficult conversations. As a result,
their relationships suffer.

For many people, setting boundaries or confronting someone
has gotten a bad rap. Yet, both the Bible and research show that
confrontation is essential to success in all arenas of life. Successful
people confront well. They make it a part of the ongoing texture of
their relationships. They face issues in their relationships directly.
In fact, the Latin word for *confront* means just that: to turn your
face toward something or someone.

We hope this book will return confrontation to its proper positive role in the language of love and relationship. We will show
that setting boundaries, confronting, and having that difficult conversation you've been avoiding is not adversarial, but one of the
most loving things you can do. We will show that it is the only way
to have the relationship you desire, whether in marriage, dating,
friendship, family, or work. And if you learn to have those difficult

conversations in a loving, honest, and responsible way, your relationships can become better than you ever thought they could.

This book will show you the benefits and essentials of a good conversation, how to have that good conversation, how to prepare yourself before you have the conversation, and how to have it with the various people in your lives.

Our prayer is that this book will guide you toward specific conversations in both your difficult and delightful relationships. This will be a "how-to" guide to help you know how to have that difficult conversation you've been avoiding and, as a result, get more out of your relationships — and your life.

PART I

WHY YOU NEED to HAVE That DIFFICULT CONVERSATION

1

The Talk Can
Change Your Life

As we speak around the country at conferences on relationships, we will often hear some version of the following story.

A man will come up and say, "Thanks for your materials on setting limits and boundaries. They have changed my life and my marriage."

We will say, "Thank you, too. So what book did you read?"

"I didn't read a book," the man will say. "My wife did!"

He will go on to explain: "I was a crummy communicator with my wife. I controlled her, I had some bad habits, and I had no spiritual life to speak of. Then she read *Boundaries*, and she started applying the principles. That's when things started changing for both of us. It took some time and effort, but I'm really different now. We are closer, and we have more respect for each other and more freedom in the relationship. I'm doing a lot better with those bad habits, and I'm waking up to my relationship with God."

You would normally expect someone to talk about a book he has actually read. However, this man's unexpected response illustrates a reality: The person who has the problem in a relationship often isn't taking responsibility for his problem. This was bad news for the man's wife. She wanted to see change, but he either didn't see a problem, thought it wasn't a big issue, or thought his wife was overreacting. This can leave the wife who cares for her husband feeling helpless, discouraged, and less able to feel love in her heart for him.

YOU CAN CHANGE
THE RELATIONSHIP ALONE

But there is good news. Though the person with the problem may not be taking responsibility for, or "owning," the problem, the person affected by the problem can change things. You may be the motivated one, the one who is concerned, sees the problem, and feels discomfort from it, whether it be a bad attitude or a bad behavior. In fact, you may be feeling more pain and discomfort than the other person. In our example, the wife, before confronting her husband, most likely had to deal with isolation, lack of freedom, his bad habits, and the emptiness of not having a spiritual partner.

Things can change when the person experiencing the effects of the problem takes the initiative to resolve it. This wife took the first step. She became aware that her husband's ways weren't good for either of them and that nothing would change unless she did something herself.

That first step is often a conversation, a talk, a face-to-face confrontation with the other person. It is a conversation in which the two people discuss the problem and what can be done about it. It is a talk of truth. That single conversation may be all that's needed. But more likely, it will be the beginning of a series of conversations and events, as it was with the marriage in our example.

Things can change when the person experiencing the effects of the problem takes the initiative to resolve it.

We want to affirm and validate your decision to have "the conversation you have been avoiding." How to have that conversation is the core need this book addresses. *You need a caring yet honest and effective way to confront someone in your life.* The Bible teaches—and research supports the idea—that you can develop the skills and tools to be able to confront well.

WHAT IS A BOUNDARY?

Before we go further, however, we need to define a term that will come up a lot in this book: *boundary*.

Simply put, a boundary is your personal "property line." It defines who you are, where you end, and where others begin. It refers to the truth, to reality, to what is. When you confront someone about a problem, you are setting a boundary. You can set a boundary with your words when you are honest and when you establish a consequence for another's hurtful actions.

Boundaries help define who we are in our relationships. When we know what we want and do not want, what we are for and against, what we love and hate, what is "me" and what is "not me," we are setting boundaries. People with good boundaries are clear about their opinions, beliefs, and attitudes — in the way that Jesus taught: "Simply let your 'Yes' be 'Yes,' and your 'No,' 'No'; anything beyond this comes from the evil one" (Matt. 5:37). People without clear boundaries are unsure of their opinions, feelings, and beliefs. They find themselves easily controlled by the demands of others because they feel unsure of themselves when they need to take a stand.

Boundaries also help protect us from injury and harm. By setting boundaries we can take responsibility for the lives and gifts God has given us: "Above all else, guard your heart, for it is the wellspring of life" (Prov. 4:23). Boundaries protect our values, feelings, time, energy, and attitudes. When a person says to another, "I want you to stop criticizing me in public," he is setting a protective boundary.

God himself has boundaries. He designed them and lives them out. He is clear on who he is, what he is for, and what he is against. He is for relationship, truth, love, and honesty, and he is against oppression, injustice, sin, and evil: "For I, the LORD, love justice; I hate robbery and iniquity" (Isa. 61:8). (For more information on boundaries, please refer to our books *Boundaries, Boundaries in Marriage, Boundaries with Kids,* and *Boundaries in Dating.*)

In this book we deal with one specific aspect of boundaries: We tell you how to set them by having a helpful and effective "talk" with another person. We will sometimes refer to that confrontation as a *boundary conversation*, that is, a talk with someone in which you confront a problem you want to resolve with the person.

HAVING "THE TALK"

The last time someone said to you, "I need to talk to you," how did that strike you? Did you think, *Maybe she needs to tell me how much she appreciates me.* More likely you thought, *I'm in trouble.* When we consider having "the talk" with someone, it may create much anxiety and throw up many red flags. It may signal conflict, criticism, and even the end of the relationship.

Many of us live in two worlds when it comes to relationships. In one world we have friendly conversations in which we avoid all disagreements; in the other we have major conflict-type conversations that tear everybody and everything up. In the first world we have connection without truth, and in the second we have truth without connection.

> *Many of us live in two worlds when it comes to relationships. In one we have connection without truth; in the other we have truth without connection.*

God did not design us to live in these two worlds, having these two types of relationships. He wants us to live in the one world, where he lives and where truth and love coexist as allies, not adversaries. Our connections are best when they are truthful, and our truth is best when we are connected. The Bible calls this *truth in love*: "Speaking the truth in love, we will in all things grow up into him who is the Head, that is, Christ" (Eph. 4:15). Conversations work best when people both care for each other and tell the truth to each other. Good things happen. People get along, resolve issues, and still maintain the connection they need.

When people have had enough bad experiences in relationships, they begin avoiding conflict and confrontation altogether. They withdraw from truthful conversations. They fear the following things:

- **Losing the relationship**: They fear that the person will withdraw either emotionally or physically from them.
- **Being the object of anger**: They don't want to receive someone's rage or blame about being confronted.
- **Being hurtful**: They are concerned about wounding the person and hurting their feelings.
- **Being perceived as bad**: They want to be seen as a nice person, and they fear they will be seen as unloving and unkind.

These fears often prevent people from sitting down and having the necessary talks that would solve problems. If you identify with any of these fears, it would be worth your while to learn where they come from and how to resolve them. We don't have space to go into that topic now, but our book *Boundaries* is a good source for this information.

Right now we want to talk more about the major benefits of confronting others with whom you have a problem. Becoming aware of the benefits and advantages of a loving and balanced conversation will help you to get past the fear and have that talk. That is the goal of the next chapter.

2

The Benefits of
a Good Conversation

I (John) often think about all the people who have helped me grow in significant ways over the years. When they come to mind, I reflect on the many ways they gave me compassion, understanding, encouragement, and guidance. Not only that, but I am also thankful for these people's honesty, confrontations, and directness, which pretty much saved my life in many ways. I am the grateful recipient of the benefits of good confrontation.

For example, I remember years ago when I took on too many work responsibilities, and life started fraying at the fringes. I enjoyed all the things I was doing, and they were meaningful, so that's how I justified going too hard. An old friend, Carl, however, got my attention over lunch during that time when he said, "It's getting so that I don't know if I really know you anymore."

"What are you talking about? Of course you know me," I replied.

Carl proceeded to gently tick off several things he had been observing in me lately: self-preoccupation, a lack of emotional presence with others, distractedness, and unavailability.

I couldn't ignore his words, for I knew he wasn't bashing me. He really was concerned about my well-being. And his points truly resonated within me. That was a real turning point for me. I made some overdue adjustments in my work and relationships. Carl's confrontation may well have preserved me from some serious problems later.

We all need to know that the hard work of confrontation has a worthwhile payoff. In the rest of this book we will show the particulars of how to engage in a face-to-face conversation, and you will get examples, tips, and how-tos. But in this chapter we want you to see the seven benefits that come from "telling the truth," and why God has designed things this way.

PRESERVING LOVE

Probably the most important benefit of a good confrontation is that it *preserves love* in a relationship. This may seem counterintuitive to you. You may think, *This doesn't make sense. When I confront someone, they will either get mad or leave the relationship.* This can and does happen. But confrontation was not designed to make someone angry or chase him or her away. In fact, it was designed to do the opposite.

The Latin term for confrontation means "to turn your face toward, to look at frontally." It merely indicates that you are turning toward the relationship and the person. You are face-to-face, so to speak. In confrontation, people simply face the relationship and deal with an aspect of the connection that needs to be addressed. The intent is to make the relationship better, to deepen the intimacy, and to create more love and respect between two people.

That is why, to be an effective confronter, you need to understand that *confrontation works best when it serves love*. Boundary conversations are motivated and driven by love. They promote the purposes of love. They enhance a relationship, not end it.

How can confrontation preserve love? Basically by protecting the relationship from elements that would harm it. Love needs protection. It is like tending a garden. If you want your plants to survive and thrive, you need to do more than water and feed them. You also need to protect them from bad weather, insects, and disease.

In the same way, things like disconnection, defensiveness, control, immaturity, and selfishness have the power to infect an entire relationship and contaminate it. Unchecked, they can harm or even end a connection.

When I was in graduate school, I waited tables at restaurants. At one point I moved to a different restaurant closer to home. Scott, a friend of mine and also a grad student, was working there as a senior waiter. In fact, he knew I was looking for another place, and he had told me about the position at his restaurant.

One night Scott asked me if we could talk. We sat down for a cup of coffee after work. When we had settled in, he leaned toward me and said, "Ever since you came to this restaurant, I've felt as if you were competing with me for the senior spot. I wanted to let you know that's how it seems, and ask you what you think."

I thought over what he had told me and said, "I think you're right. I have been competing with you, and I haven't even been aware of it. I'm really sorry, Scott."

"No problem," he said. "I just wanted to get this cleared up between us."

I gave up competing with Scott and concentrated on doing my job. Scott's early intervention helped prevent a huge tear in our relationship. We worked together for some time after that, and we have remained friends to this day. A good confrontation can preserve a relationship: "Wounds from a friend can be trusted, but an enemy multiplies kisses" (Prov. 27:6).

RESOLVING ALIENATION

Healthy confrontations not only preserve relationships, but also bring disconnected people together. Think about someone in your life with whom you have an unspoken conflict or issue. Maybe he isn't emotionally available to you. Maybe she is critical of you. Maybe he expects you to solve his problems for him. Whatever the case, when an existing conflict is not brought into the relationship, it hurts the relationship. It disconnects and alienates you from the other person. *The extent to which two people in a relationship can* bring up and resolve issues is a critical marker of the soundness of the relationship.

Relationships are designed by God to be whole, and the more parts of you—such as strengths, weaknesses, vulnerabilities, passions, desires, and failures—that are connected to the parts of the other person, the greater the closeness, depth, and meaning of the relationship. Paul made this appeal to the hearts of the people at Corinth: "We have spoken freely to you, Corinthians, and opened wide our hearts to you. We are not withholding our affection from you, but you are withholding yours from us. As a fair exchange—I speak as to my children—open wide your hearts also" (2 Cor. 6:11–13).

The extent to which two people in a relationship can bring up and resolve issues is a critical marker of the soundness of the relationship.

Our hearts are to be open to each other. Where there is some unspoken, unaddressed, and unresolved area of conflict, our hearts can become closed. Many times in my marriage, my insensitivity or my not being there for Barbi has caused her to withdraw emotionally. The alienation I felt was painful. I wanted all of her to be with me, and part of her wasn't there. For example, a few years back I made a financial decision without consulting Barbi. At the time, I thought it wasn't important enough, but when I did tell her, she felt out of the loop, and she was hurt. For a time there was distance between us while she worked through her feelings about this.

Nothing is more miserable than to be in a relationship with someone, yet disconnected from her at the same time. It doesn't feel right, because it isn't right. God did not design us for disconnected relationships. It wasn't a lot of fun when either Barbi or I would bring up a problem, but at least we were talking. We would work it out the best way we could; but most important, the alienation was gone.

I cannot overstate the importance of this issue. It is at the heart of the way God designed relationship. Relationships are fundamentally about love, because God's relationship with us is fundamentally about love: "Dear friends, let us love one another, for love comes from God" (1 John 4:7).

Two people meeting to have the talk is a first step toward ending alienation. *A boundary conversation is, in and of itself, a connection.* The two are bringing their differences to the light of relationship and seeing what can be done. This might not be pleasant, but it is far better than a relationship that is a living death, where feelings of hurt, anger, conflicted love, and sadness never go away. Not talking about strong feelings doesn't make them go away; in fact, they become more pronounced in our attempts to live as though they don't exist. The two people in this kind of relationship try to get along by skirting issues, their emotions, and ultimately their deep love for each other, and they end up with a shell of a relationship. But when the timing is right and when both people's hearts are in the right place, the shell can again be filled with love, joy, and fulfillment.

Often a couple will remark on how connected they feel after even a poorly done confrontation. Though they may have said some things wrong or handled things badly, they were still able to sense the presence of the other person, and presence was preferable to the polite absence they had been feeling.

EMPOWERING

Confrontation also brings empowerment, the ability to make choices and changes in your relationship. God created all of us to be change agents for each other. We have a responsibility to influence the people in our lives to be the best possible people they can be: "Therefore encourage one another and build each other up" (1 Thess. 5:11).

When we encounter a long-lasting difficulty in a relationship, especially if we don't have the skills to confront, we feel helpless about seeing any change. We see the problem, we don't like what it's doing to the connection, but we don't know how to broach the issue or do anything about it.

This sense of helplessness often translates into resignation and passivity. We give up inside and accept that things will never change. You often see people who have been in a bad marriage for a long time take this stance: *He [or she] will never change, so I'll just have to live with it.*

While most would agree that we can't *make* someone change, it is also true that we can do much to *promote* change. When we learn to confront lovingly, directly, and effectively, we are often pleased in the change not only in our relationship but also in ourselves. We feel a sense of power that we can make changes and we have choices. We were designed to both connect and act. Confrontation puts the "act" into the connection.

> *While we can't make someone change, we can do much to promote change.*

I saw a man transform into another person after confronting his controlling father. Though he was in his forties, he had never been able to stand up to his dad. Finally, after a lot of work and preparation, he had a very appropriate and healthy confrontation with his father. He was direct, uncondemning, and caring. Dad didn't handle it well. He was defensive and critical, but the son was ready for that. Within days, I saw this depressed, burdened, stoop-shouldered man begin standing taller, becoming more creative and energetic, and reaching out to others. The conversation helped him own and integrate his personal power.

Often we will hear a person express her powerlessness in this way: "I've tried everything and nothing works with him, so I'm giving up." However, when we investigate further, we find that "trying everything" is often "trying the wrong things." She may have tried to confront, and either she was ignored or the conflict escalated. She did not know the best way to confront. When that person learns the tools she needs and employs them effectively, she will most likely gain a sense that she can be an agent of change in her relationship.

SOLVING A PROBLEM

Learning to have that conversation helps you solve problems. This seems obvious, but it's an important benefit of confrontation. Boundary conversations are geared toward addressing and resolving an issue that is keeping two people apart or is hurtful to someone. When things work well, a problem is solved and you can move on in the relationship. This can apply to all sorts of relational problems: your date's sexual advances, your wife's fiscal irresponsibility, or your boss's unrealistic demands.

The world just works this way. When you expose problems to the light of your relationship, it is far more likely that things will improve than when you ignore or deny them. Problems don't tend to go away by themselves over time. They often get worse. And that is the converse principle here: *What is ignored tends not to be solved.*

Alcoholics Anonymous has a great definition of how we change: *We change when the pain of remaining the same is greater than the pain of changing.* Confrontation can help solve a problem; avoiding confrontation can make a problem worse.

Part of the uniqueness of a boundary conversation is that it has a focus and an agenda. It is not generalized dissatisfaction with a person; rather, it points out some specific issue that is driving two people apart. People who confront well make a clear request for change from the other person: spend time with me, stop getting so angry, take responsibility for your addiction, and so on. The emphasis is not on renovating the entire person—which can be overwhelming—but on solving a specific problem.

A friend of mine has a son in high school. She knew her son was becoming more estranged and distant from her than was normal for a kid that age. She didn't know how to approach him. Then, by accident, she read an email he had written to a friend in which he had said some negative things about his relationship with her. She was upset.

My friend went to her son and told him what she had read. It was very difficult for both of them at first, but as it worked out, they both reached a greater awareness of the problems between them, and it gave them the focus and incentive to begin working on them. They are still in the process, but they are both good people, and I think their prospects for solving this relationship problem are high.

BUILDING GROWTH

Healthy confrontations help people grow emotionally, relationally, and spiritually. When you bring a problem to someone, something will probably change. Maybe you were wrong, and you will change. Or maybe the other person will change because of the conversation you had with him. But things will not stay the same. One or both of you gets stretched and helped to become a better person.

Good boundary conversations help us grow by making us aware of what we are doing and how our behavior affects others. This is often a springboard into looking at patterns and issues within ourselves that are a rich source of personal change and improvement.

Healthy confrontations help people grow emotionally, relationally, and spiritually.

You deliver the ingredients of growth to the people in your life. Part of the reason you are with whomever you are with is to provide those ingredients for those people. As the Bible says, you are an administrator of God's grace: "Each one should use whatever gift he has received to serve others, faithfully administering God's grace in its various forms" (1 Peter 4:10).

Your confrontation may be the wakeup call someone needed. It may affirm something she knew in the back of her mind, but was afraid to admit. It may bring relief to someone who has been hiding a problem.

In fact, without caring confrontation, there is little real growth. When a relationship has love but no truth, it either keeps the people too comfortable or even makes them more immature. Often, for example, a mother who has an out-of-control teen will try to be positive and encouraging all the time, hoping her child will get better. What is more likely to happen is that while the teen does benefit from the love, he gets further out of control since no one is confronting him, establishing firm rules, or enforcing consequences. Kids, especially, grow when they experience truth as well as love.

CLARIFYING REALITY

Good confrontations also help people to see the other person for who they really are. Often, when you are afraid to tell the truth to someone, you avoid or withdraw from them. The lack of real, face-to-face confrontation increases the distortions in your mind about the negative qualities of that person. The distortions grow when they are not modified and corrected by reality. You perceive that person as more dangerous, out of control, and powerful than he or she really is. It then becomes a vicious circle: You were afraid to confront anyway, and the more you avoid the talk, the scarier the person becomes, which increases your avoidance.

When people learn to confront the right way, reality comes back into the picture, and they see themselves and the other person in a much clearer light. They realize that they themselves are grownups with choices and freedom and that the other person is just another person. It takes the power out of the fear of the other person's responses.

A man I was counseling described his wife as a rageaholic, fire-breathing dragon. He talked about how intense her anger was and how out-of-control she was. I suggested he bring her to our next meeting so we could work on the marriage. He looked uncertain, but he brought her along the next week.

When his wife entered my office, I thought I was looking at the wrong woman. She was petite and soft-spoken—no scales and wings to be found. This wasn't to say that she didn't have an anger problem. He was right about that, and we did deal with it. But the more honest he became and the less he avoided confrontation, the less he saw her as a terrifying dragon. Good confrontations bring reality into the picture.

AVOIDING BEING PART OF THE PROBLEM

An old saying from the 1960s goes something like this: *If you're not part of the solution, you're part of the problem.* There is a lot of truth to this in relationships. Not only are there clear benefits to having that talk, but there is also a responsibility to confront. Even though you may be in a relationship with a person who has a severe problem or behavior, you may be helping the problem continue and hindering the solution.

When modern psychiatric and psychological researchers began studying addictions, they realized that most of the time, the addict does not live in a vacuum. Instead, he lives in a system of relationships, some of which serve to enable his behavior; that is, someone unwittingly tries to keep the addict from the consequences and effects of his addiction. In an attempt to help, the enabler instead rescues the addict from the discomfort that would drive him to face and solve his problem. As the enabling person becomes aware of this and allows the addict to feel his pain, good things begin to happen.

For thousands of years the Bible has named these realities. For example, see what God says about dealing with a rageaholic: "A hot-tempered man must pay the penalty; if you rescue him, you will have to do it again" (Prov. 19:19). Many people have experienced the frustration of finding the problem coming back the day after the rescue.

The Bible teaches that we have a duty to warn each other, that we are part of God's means of helping one another stay in the path of growth. It goes further than that, however. Not only should we warn each other, but if we avoid doing so, we must bear some responsibility for this as well:

> "When I say to a wicked man, 'You will surely die,' and you do not warn him or speak out to dissuade him from his evil ways in order to save his life, that wicked man will die for his sin, and I will hold you accountable for his blood. But if you do warn the wicked man and he does not turn from his wickedness or from his evil ways, he will die for his sin; but you will have saved yourself" (Ezek. 3:18–19).

Sobering words, but profoundly clear. When you confront a person the right way, she always has a choice, and she may ignore your warning. Sad as that might be, you will still know that you have done what you could and that you have not participated in that person's self-destruction.

Sometimes all it takes is a little nudge. As a youth, I was a Boy Scout. Scouting was a big part of my life, and Troop 4 was a very active troop, with lots of camping and activities. During the latter years of my scouting experience, I was in my teens and getting close to earning my Eagle rank. As a teen, however, I was also experimenting with becoming an individual, which involved some rebellious attitudes. During one weekend campout, when we were putting up our tents, I used some pretty rough language to make my buddies laugh. It was the wrong time to do this, as our scoutmaster, Mr. DeKeyser—whom we called "DK"—was walking by.

DK pulled me aside, looked at me, and quietly said, "You're too close. Don't mess up."

That was all it took.

DK's six words were enough. I knew what he meant. He knew I knew. No more was needed. He never brought it up again. From then on, I curbed my tongue — as much as a teenager can anyway — and stayed pretty much on track until I got the Eagle.

Six words were enough. I knew what he meant. He knew I knew.

Now, this wasn't about me being on drugs, being violent, or ditching school. My language wasn't a huge thing as problems go, but at the same time, it's very possible that eventually it could have been, had not DK said those six words to me. He helped me become aware of what I was doing and its possible effects. And he did it right: He was on my side, he was direct and noncondemning, and he let it go to see how I would handle it. I have always been grateful to DK for the little nudge of correction that helped keep me on the right path.

OUR OTHER MOTIVES

As you have read these benefits of confrontation, we hope you are more motivated than ever to learn the skills. At the same time, be aware of any darker motives you may feel about confronting someone, such as wanting to fix or change the person, or to punish and get revenge. Let those motives go, and stay on the higher road.

In the next section we will deal with the specific elements of all good confrontations.

PART II

The
ESSENTIALS
of a GOOD
CONVERSATION

3

Be Emotionally
Present

Being emotionally present and connected while we are confronting another person is the first essential of a good conversation. It truly requires a work of grace in us.

Being present refers to being in touch and in tune with our own feelings as well as those of the other person. This is an important skill, because when we are "there"—that is, emotionally present—we are available to the other person. He is not shut off from us while we are telling him a difficult reality about himself and the relationship. It is hard for anyone to absorb a confrontation. Presence and connection help to make it tolerable.

A boundary conversation is very difficult because it feels unnatural—and it is unnatural, in that the natural person within us does not think this way. On our own, we seek to protect ourselves from discomfort because we are "weak in [our] natural selves" (Rom. 6:19). We don't want to be vulnerable and emotional in a confrontation, as we might be hurt. That is why we need grace for this essential.

Also, when you are present and connected to the other person, you are doing something very important for the relationship: *You are providing what you are requesting.* You want the other person to be "there" with you. This is why you are confronting a problem in the first place; the issue has caused a rift in emotional presence. In the same way that God takes initiative to reach out to his alienated children, you are being with the person who is not with you.

Because you have taken the first step, this helps him be emotionally present with you.

Here are ways to help you "be there" in your boundary conversation.

Be Warm

Remember that although confrontations can be uncomfortable, this does not mean you need to be angry, detached, or distant from the other person. As much as you are able, be warm and available to him. What you say is highly colored by how you are with the person. If you are warm, he is much more likely to receive what you have to say. If you are not present, he can't be sure of your intent, motives, or your heart, and you run the risk of failure.

If you think you are too afraid to be present, don't have the talk yet. Take those feelings somewhere else before you get into the conversation and deal with them in a safe context. Better to do that than to come across as cold and distant.

Be in a Conversation, Not a Lecture

Being present also means allowing the other person to respond. You have a side to present, and so probably does she. Be there with her feelings as well as your own. Listen to her heart even when you don't agree with her stance.

In extreme circumstances the talk may be not a conversation, but an announcement, as in a formal intervention, for example. But even if you are doing an intervention, the more present you can be, the better your chances are of being received.

Connect Even with Differences

Staying present means being "there" not only when you agree with each other, but also when you disagree, when there is tension, and when you are confronting. We tend to connect when people are on our side and draw back when they are not. However, as much as possible, be safe enough to be present with the person even when he resists or gets angry.

Discomfort versus Injury

We need to be willing to suffer discomfort—to a point. The limit here is the limit of injury. If you get in a bad situation with a person who can truly injure you because of where you are emotionally, or because of how powerful an influence she currently is with you, you will need to guard your heart (Prov. 4:23) to avoid having wounds that would set your spiritual growth back. Sometimes you may need to not let the person in too deeply, or even end the conversation until a better time to protect yourself. At the same time, if the talk is more discomforting than injurious, you may want to press on toward reconciliation.

Observe Yourself

Be aware of how present or absent you are in the talk. Monitor what makes you shut down and what makes you open up. When you are aware of yourself, you have more choices and options available. I remember one boundary conversation I was having with a friend. I thought I was pretty present until he said, "Look at your arms." I looked down, and I had wrapped my arms around myself protectively. Some presence! That made for a more interesting talk that day.

4

Be Clear about
"You" and "I"

Any good confrontation takes into account that two people are involved. This sounds obvious, but it really isn't, and it is an essential part of an effective boundary conversation.

One reason you have a problem in the first place is that you and the person you want to confront are not of one mind; you aren't the same person. You don't see things the same way nor feel the same way, and you have different ideas on what to do about it. This is not a bad thing, in and of itself. The differences between you can help both of you grow and enjoy life.

The problem arises when you don't clearly distinguish your feelings and opinions from the other person's, especially when having the talk. The process of problem solving and reconciliation can quickly get bogged down. You see this when people say things like "You need to change this" rather than "I need for you to change this." There is an "I" who has a desire and a request, and there is a "you" who is being asked to change something. That is clear.

A friend of mine had great difficulty with this issue in her marriage. When she was tired of cooking and wanted to go out to dinner, she would say to her husband, "You haven't taken us out for a while," or, "You probably need a night out to dinner." Her husband was suspicious of these sorts of statements, because he would feel blamed or manipulated. When she said instead, "I don't want to cook tonight, and I would like to go out to dinner," she clarified whose desire it was to go out to dinner, and he responded much better.

If you are not clear about "you" and "I" in your confrontation, the other person may feel controlled by you, you may assume feelings he doesn't have, or he may balk at whatever you want. Here are some suggestions to clarify your communication.

Look at It Empathically

Reflect on how you don't like it when people try to put their words in your mouth. Think about how you disconnect from another person when she tells you what you are feeling when it is really what she *wants* you to feel. Reflecting on your own experience will give you empathy for the other person's situation and will help you be clearer about your own opinions and emotions. Remember that even though confronting is hard, so is receiving a confrontation. Therefore allow the other person the grace to have her own responses to your opinions.

Be Clear in Your Own Mind

The more clear you are *ahead of time* about what you want in this relationship and what you are asking the other person to do, the better things will go. Write out, or talk through with a friend, exactly what the "I" and "you" parts are. Then, when it is time for the conversation, you will have a road map in your head for what you want. I have seen many breakdowns happen when the person being confronted says, "So what do you really want?" and the confronter gets flustered. Have a specific answer for that question before you begin the conversation.

Speak from Your Need, Not His

Tell the other person, "I really need more commitment from you in our dating, or I don't think I can move forward." This is much better than "You need to be more committed to me." He may not experience that need, and he is likely to resent you for telling him what he needs. Speaking from your own need helps you avoid being seen as the "parent" in the relationship, a position that never helps.

When people say, "We need to talk," for example, they are confusing their wishes with those of the other person. It's much better to say, "I need to talk to you."

Deal with Any Fears of Separateness

Often, a person who avoids clearly saying "I need" and "I want" has a problem with experiencing herself as a separate person, with her own set of values, desires, dreams, and feelings. Saying what she needs and wants makes her feel very isolated and alone; her difficulty in expressing wants and needs indicates that she is not comfortable with being an individual.

If this is your situation, get some help from knowledgeable people on how to become more established in your own identity, so that you are not so afraid. (Our book *Boundaries* is a good resource for this process.)

Be Humble

You have no control over the person you are confronting. More than that, you are asking for something you need from him. This is a humble position, and it helps to accept it. Saying "I want" and "I need" is a way of letting the other person know that he is important to you, that you do need him, and that you are aware he might see things differently. While this is not a very comfortable position, it's the best position, because the other person knows he is free to choose and he is not controlled by you. The Bible refers to God's attitude toward this: "You save the humble but bring low those whose eyes are haughty" (Ps. 18:27).

As much as possible, stay away from the "we need to" and "you need to" traps. Speak from your own experience, your own heart, and your own needs. This increases the likelihood that your side will be heard, because it has been clearly identified as your side. No one likes to be told who he is or what he should think.

5

Clarify
the Problem

In the previous chapter we urged you to be clear about what is yours and what is the other person's. Now we encourage you to be clear about the nature of your problem with the other person. Many people run into logjams when they attempt to confront, because they are not clear about the problem. Their inability to focus on the problem itself can end up in confusion, distance, alienation, and lack of resolution.

Don't lose focus and end up going over a whole list of offenses that overwhelms the person being confronted. Don't start with "It seems you don't pick up after yourself as regularly as you should" and end up with "What about the time you forgot the kids at the mall last year?" You may have so many unconfessed issues with the other person that in the momentum of the conversation, you bring up everything else you have a problem with. Holding problems inside in an isolated fashion makes this worse. In these cases, unburden yourself with some friends who can empathize with you and help you think through and process these problems. Then you can settle on the one subject you want to deal with in the problem relationship.

Let us look at the three important elements of the problem itself and what you would like to see happen.

Clarify the Nature of the Problem

Be clear and focused as to what the problem is really about. Make the issue as understandable as possible to the other person. You want to have your terms clear between you so that you are both on the same page and can work toward resolution together. Furthermore, the other person may be unaware of the problem, so you need to shoulder the responsibility of stating the problem clearly.

This step may have more than one level to it. For example, a husband might say to his mother, "Mom, I've noticed that you are pretty critical of Laurie's cooking and parenting. You put her down a couple of times in front of everyone at the party last week. I don't know what this is about, but it seems you are seldom pleased with how she does things." Notice the two levels: the specifics, and then an observation about the nature of the specifics. This gives the other person clear information about what you are concerned about.

Clarify the Effects of the Problem

Include not only the facts and realities about the problem, but also what it does to you and the relationship. Obviously, it must affect you at some important level or you would not be bringing it up. It helps to talk about the effects for two reasons. First, the other person might not be aware of what he is doing to you, and becoming aware often helps him see how important the issue is. Second, talking about the effects lets him know that he is not being judged and criticized as an imperfect project you are working on, but that his behavior is hurting you.

The husband talking to his mother might say, "Laurie gets discouraged, because she knocks herself out for you. The kids are confused about why you are so mean to Mom. Dad is embarrassed because he feels caught in the middle. And you and I get disconnected, because even though I love you, Laurie is my wife, and she's getting hurt. So it makes things worse for me, you, and all of us."

Clarify Your Desire for Change

Avoid the mistake of stopping with the negative aspects of the problem. Doing that can make the person feel as though she just got dumped on, with no way to resolve the problem, or feel that there is no way to please you, that you are insatiably critical. Instead, let her know what you would like to see that would change the situation and solve the problem. This gives her hope, a structure, and a chance to do something to make the relationship better.

In our example, the husband might say, "Here's what I would like you to do. If it's a small matter, drop it. I don't bring up little things you do. If it's a big thing, pull Laurie aside quietly and tell her your concerns. She is very open to constructive feedback. And finally, notice the good things she does, and talk about them in front of everyone. I would really appreciate it. It would bring me closer to you, and I think the whole family would be happier."

At the heart of the problem is usually a relationship that matters to you. As you keep the issues and your desires clear, you don't attack or diminish the relationship and you preserve the connection.

6

Balance Grace and Truth

A successful confrontation will always involve balancing grace and truth. Grace is your being on the side of, or "for," the other person as well as the relationship. Truth is the reality of whatever you need to say about the problem. This balancing combination is referred to as being *neutralized*.

Being *neutralized* doesn't mean being *neutral* about the problem—not taking a side or expressing an opinion. In fact, the clearer you express your opinion, the better your chances of success. Instead, being neutralized means that having grace and truth together counters the bad effects of having one of these by itself. In other words, grace alone or truth alone can have a negative effect in a confrontation, but having the two together neutralizes the negatives.

Jesus was the perfect combination of these two elements of growth. Jesus' approach was superior to that of the law of Moses: "For the law was given through Moses; grace and truth came through Jesus Christ" (John 1:17). People need both grace and truth in relationships with God and with each other.

Think about a time when someone told you the truth without love. You probably felt attacked, judged, or condemned. No matter how accurate the truth, it hardly mattered, because the hurtful feelings erased the truth in the confrontation. In good boundary conversations, truth needs grace for the person to safely receive and digest the information.

Now reflect on a time you received grace without any truth. Grace comforts us and keeps us safe and loved, but it doesn't provide reality, structure, direction, or correction. You may have come away from that encounter feeling refreshed and encouraged, but without the path or insight to know what to do next. Truth neutralizes that problem and provides the way we need.

Here are some ways to keep both aspects in balance when you are having the talk.

Keep in Mind That the Other Person Needs Both Just as You Do

Remember that even though you might be upset with someone, his ability to take in truth will also require love and grace, just as yours does. Your intent is not to fix, straighten out, or punish. It is to provide enough amounts of truth and grace to reconcile and solve the problem.

Lead with Grace

It is always best to start with grace, as it sets the stage for the other person to be able to tolerate the truth. Tell the person, "Before we get into the topic, I want you to know I really care about you and about us. I want us to be better, and I want us to be on the same team. I hope I can convey that to you even when we talk about the problem." Don't assume that she automatically knows these things. In fact, in a confrontation the other person often needs more reassurance of the grace, because the situation may access her own unloved and condemned parts.

Keep Both Elements Present at the Same Time

Keep grace and truth integrated and woven together in your talk. As much as possible, avoid the tendency to have a "grace" part and then a "truth" part of the talk; otherwise, it could seem like two different, and even inconsistent, talks. When you are confronting, sprinkle in your care. When you are caring, sprinkle in the truth. For example, you might say, "While I want us to be close again, this problem is getting in the way, and I need to resolve it between us. I can't dance around it or ignore it. But it's hard, because I don't want this talk to distance us even more."

Be Aware of Your Imbalances

None of us are totally in the middle here. Some of us lean toward grace and are too soft on the truth. Others may be very clear about an issue and can come across harsh and critical. Work on developing whichever part of grace and truth you are weak on, so that you can stay neutralized in the boundary conversation.

When in Doubt, Go for Grace

If you are unsure at a given point in the conversation, lean toward grace. The damage done by a lack of grace is more severe than the converse. With grace alone, you stand a chance of being able to have another conversation later. With truth alone, the judgment could possibly rupture the safety of the relationship so much that things fall apart.

For example, if the person resists your point, you may want to press it to see if there is another way he can receive it. However, if he becomes increasingly unresponsive, defensive, or angry, this is probably not the time to keep pressing home with truth. Back off, try to reestablish the connection with grace, and try again later. In our parenting book, *Raising Great Kids*, we refer to those times in which you are totally lost in a conflict with a kid. At those times, drop back to the relationship and get reattached. Otherwise, nothing good happens.

In your effort to stay neutralized, keep grace and truth friends with each other, not adversaries. Look to God and his example of keeping the two aspects of life together: "Love and faithfulness meet together; righteousness and peace kiss each other" (Ps. 85:10).

7

Stay on Task

Here is a common crazy-making script in confrontations:

> **You:** "Sharon, I'd like to talk about a problem in our relationship."
>
> **Sharon:** "Well, what about all the things you do?"
>
> **You:** "Like what?"
>
> **Sharon:** "You never call when you're going to be late, you work too much on the weekends, you don't spend enough time with the kids, you don't help around the house...."

This little script illustrates a common problem in having the talk: the inability to stay on track and on task. A good confrontation has a specific and clear focus. It can be reduced to one or both of two things: You want the other person to start doing something you want or to stop doing something you don't want. If all goes well, each of you understands the other's view and feelings, and you agree on how things will change. This is how the conversation above could be kept on track.

> **You:** "Sharon, I'd like to talk about a problem in our relationship."
>
> **Sharon:** "Well, what about all the things you do?"
>
> **You:** "I know I do things that irritate you, but I want to focus on my concern right now."

47

Sharon: "Sure, it's always about you."

You: "I'll be glad to talk later about what you want to talk about, but for now, I'd like to talk about how we can stay within our budget."

Often, what complicates things is the other person's defensiveness. In other words, the other person doesn't want to be faced with either the problem or the problem's effects on you.

It is important to deal with defensiveness because it is often related to why you have had problems confronting this person in the first place. When people are open about receiving feedback and truth, issues tend to be resolved fairly easily and quickly. But very often, *people who have long-standing patterns of negative behavior and attitudes have also developed character patterns that help maintain those problems.* That is, they have some internal resistance to seeing themselves as being wrong, flawed, or responsible. So, in the face of all reality, feedback, and circumstances, they turn a blind eye to their immaturity or hurtfulness. The problem either doesn't exist or it's not as bad as you think or it's your fault.

And that is how the script we started with, as well as all its variations, begins to happen. The other person wants to deflect and divert the attention anywhere away from what she is doing. Then you find yourself sidetracked and lost. I remember one relationship in which the other person was so adept at defensiveness that almost every time I had a problem with him, I ended up apologizing for causing the problem! Needless to say, confrontation was not a very productive strategy.

But there are some helpful things you can do. Before you tear your hair out, here are some tips for staying on track.

Be Prepared

Chances are, defensiveness and deflections have caught you unaware before. Don't be surprised or upset. Accept this as part of that person for now until he decides to change. Anticipate that you will be received not with open arms, but with resistance. When you have accepted the defensiveness, you can more readily deal with it. In sports you have a backup move for whatever you think your opponent will try. While confrontation should not be adversarial but as much as possible an alliance, it is nevertheless wise to know what to do next, which we cover below.

Hear Them Out to a Point

In the main, it is always best to give the person a chance to be heard and understood. You cannot go wrong with that stance, as you're giving grace before moving in with truth. The other person may have a legitimate point you need to understand. You may have been provocative or uncaring and contributed to the problem, or an accident on the freeway might have made her late. As the Bible says, "Judgment without mercy will be shown to anyone who has not been merciful. Mercy triumphs over judgment" (James 2:13). You might say, "I didn't realize that you feel so nagged by me. I really want to look at that, and if I am doing that, I want to change it."

Note, however, that we said "to a point." When a person is open to feedback, she needs her point to be heard, and then she is ready to hear yours. When you are dealing with a character problem, it is different. After you have heard her out, she may still not be open to hearing you. She always has another excuse, or she blames you again. It is not good for either of you for this to go on indefinitely.

Make Several Attempts to Get Back on Track

Again, using grace, simply listen, empathize, and get back to the issue at hand. Say things like "I really will take a look at my part there; I don't want to make the problem worse. But I'd like to get back to what I was saying about your drinking...." Don't give up quickly in this. Many people try to stay on topic a little, but then feel it is hopeless and they shut down. The message they are sending to the other person is that a little resistance will end things. Be persistent and let him know you will keep bringing this up because it is important to you and the relationship!

Make the Defensiveness an Issue

If the person has a pattern of diverting things, bring that to the light. Don't keep getting sidetracked by excuses. Say, "I have noticed that every time I talk about our problem of how to allocate the chores, it seems you get angry or change the subject. I really do want to own my part, and I will be glad to when we deal with your part. But it's hard for me because you keep diverting things. Can you tell me what goes on when I bring up problems, or how I can give you feedback in a better way?" Don't blame; inquire. The person may be feeling judged or put down, and simply reassuring her that you are on her side will be enough to get back on track.

Practice with Others

There is nothing like experience to help you deal with a defensive relationship. Role-play most common-excuse scenarios with a good friend. Have them coach you on when you get flustered, discouraged, or angry, so that you get used to the process and can smoothly get back on track. This will help you get less emotionally invested and be more in charge of your part of the talk. It will also help you know when to back off and when to take a stand.

Remember that in all likelihood, you may be the only person focused on the goal. Take responsibility for that focus, and stay graciously zeroed in.

8

Use the Formula,
When You Do "A," I Feel "B"

One of the most powerful and effective ingredients of a good confrontation is explaining to a person how her attitudes or actions influence you: "When you do 'A,' I feel 'B.'" In other words, you show how what another person does affects your emotions.

Few actions are more vulnerable than letting someone know how much she matters to you, how much she can hurt you. Opening your heart can often get through to another person, because it accesses the love and care she has for you. When you show her how you are affected emotionally, she is drawn into the very core and basis of all God-designed relationships, which is love: "Love one another deeply, from the heart" (1 Peter 1:22). It helps her reconnect to her own heart and to her feelings about you. It helps her move away from winning an argument and into being involved in the relationship.

This ingredient is also very important because it avoids blame and assault. Telling how you feel describes an internal reality of which the other person might not be aware. This is the opposite of the "blame barrage," in which a person runs through the list of all the other's infractions. Not many people can remain open and undefensive when hit with that. They become more invested in protecting themselves from all the badness, guilt, and condemnation being thrown at them.

Keep the following tips in mind as you bring your feelings into the conversation.

Concentrate on Feelings, Not Thoughts

Be clear about the feelings you feel, not the thoughts you think. This is a hard task; it is easy to use the word *feel* and then say a thought. For example: "When you negate my words, I feel like I shouldn't say anything." It would be better to say, "When you negate my words, I feel hurt and disconnected from you."

Identify Your Feelings

Knowing what you are feeling is not a natural ability, and it may take a little work. Know the difference, for example, between being hurt, sad, angry, frustrated, afraid, and anxious. One mistake many people make is identifying angry feelings as hurt feelings. Sometimes they do this to avoid their own aggressive parts; other times they do this because they identify with being a victim, fearing that their anger may provoke others to hurt them. Have friends help you know when you are hurt and when you are angry.

Stick to Your Experience

In the same vein, stick to your own experience, not what you think the other person is doing. It is very easy to slip into focusing on the other person, and it can sound as though you are blaming him. Practice and role-play with friends to avoid this. For example, instead of saying, "When you negate my words, I feel like you don't care about me," say, "When you negate my words, I feel alone and unloved."

Avoid the Statement "You Make Me Feel ..."

Though it is true that the other person highly influences you emotionally, convey to her that this is about your reaction to her rather than about her power and control over you. Avoiding this kind of blaming statement keeps the other person from reacting to being blamed: "I made you frustrated? How can I do that? Those are your feelings. I can't control what you feel." Making an association for her solves a lot of problems. Instead of saying, "You frustrate me," say, "When you are constantly late, I feel frustrated and unimportant."

Own Your Part of the Feelings

Your emotions do belong to you, and you may need to admit when you are oversensitive so that not all of the weight falls on the other person. Remember, you are not ascribing fault as much as opening a window into your heart so the other person can be drawn into your world. You might say, for example, "I know sometimes I get hurt too easily, and that's not you, that's me. But last night, when you made fun of my dress at the party, I really felt attacked and embarrassed."

Be Specific, Specific, Specific

Identify the behavior or attitude specifically so that the other person understands what you are talking about. Give him a description of what he really said or did, or what tone of voice he used, so that he has a picture of the situation. "When you teased me about my weight at the dinner table last night, I felt hurt."

Saying "When you do 'A,' I feel 'B'" is, at heart, not only a way of confronting, but also a way of reaching out to the other person. Allow yourself, as much as it is safe, to let him or her see this part of your heart.

9

Affirm
and Validate

I (Henry) remember being shocked. Not only did I have no idea I would do such a thing, but I also had no hint I did it enough for people to invent a term for it. Here is what happened.

One day, a number of years ago, we were discussing some issues with our financial controller, Mary, in her office, and we needed a particular report from someone in the department.

"I'll run down to Susan's desk and get it," I said. "Then we'll know exactly what we're dealing with."

"No, don't do that," Mary said. "I'll get it."

"No, that's silly! It'll only take me a minute. Be right back."

"No!" Mary retorted. "Let me do it. I'll be right back."

I got the feeling that Mary was volunteering to do this errand for some other reason than just being nice. I decided to check out my hunch. "Is there some reason why you don't want me to go down there?" I asked.

"No, it's okay, really," she said. "I'll be right back."

"Mary," I pressed. "It's not okay, is it? Something is up, and I want to know what it is."

"Well, okay. If you really want to know. I don't want you going down there, upsetting everyone, getting them off track, and leaving a mess I'll have to clean up."

"What makes you think I would do that? I won't upset anyone; they're my friends. I'll just get the report, say hello, and come right back." I was relieved to discover that this was just about Mary's unrealistic fears.

"No, that's not what will happen," she said. "You'll upset them. That's what you do with things like this."

"What? What do you mean?" I didn't have a clue what she was talking about.

"When you are bugged about something, you just walk in and tell people. It's easy to see you're bothered with them, and it gets to them. Then you just leave after telling them, and I, the mother hen around here, have to go pick up the pieces."

"I do that? When I tell people something is wrong, I upset them?" I could not believe what I was hearing.

"Yes, you do. When you confront people about something, you do it in a really curt and critical way. We even have a term for it," she said. "We call it 'the wrath of Henry.'"

Now I was really bothered. Not only did I have a problem, but it was so bad they had a term for it. You don't make up terms for random occurrences.

I asked Mary to tell me more about how I confront others. Then I talked to the other people in the office, and they validated her perception. Although we shared good working relationships, they affirmed that I had a hurtful pattern of confrontation. They said they didn't mind being confronted or being told they needed to change, but they did not feel affirmed by me at those times. Instead, they felt criticized.

> *Affirm and validate the people you confront so that they know they are valued.*

These conversations made me very sad. The last thing I wanted to do was to criticize. I thought I was solving problems; instead, I was creating them. I needed to learn how to make people feel validated when I confronted them.

The principle here is: *Affirm and validate the people you confront so that they know they are valued.*

What I had been doing wrong was bringing up a problem to people in an isolated context, and it felt as if a bomb had hit. Not only that, but the tone with which I confronted others was even worse. They said I seemed irritated, bothered, and critical. Pretty crummy stuff! In terms of the Golden Rule, I had failed miserably.

How to Affirm and Validate

Affirmation and validation of a person is not brain science. The basic message you want to convey is that you care about the person; you notice things he is doing well, or you let him know you are on his side. The key phrase is this: *Be on his or her side.* Otherwise, your words become meaningless flattery, which is ugly and manipulative. Real affirmation comes from your genuine care for the person and your desire for things to get better. It is *grace* before *truth*. Grace means "favor." Establish your favor, care, and belief in the person before "facing the issue." Here are some ideas for affirming and validating in two different situations:

1. In ongoing problem solving where there is no big issue, you need not utter some big proclamation of your love and commitment. You are merely correcting a problem. Here are some examples:

"Sara, I love going to the movies with you. I really enjoy our time together. One thing that would make it better for me would be if we could leave on time. When we are late, I feel rushed, and I want to enjoy the time we have together."

"Joey, I like how you have been trying to do your chores. Would you look a little harder at the way you leave the den before you go outside to play? I end up picking some things up for you, and I don't want to do that. Thanks."

Validate other people with language that lets them know you are with them and not against them.

2. In situations other than the moment-by-moment corrections, where you want to sit down and talk through a problem, a little more proclamation is needed.

> "Sara, you know that I am your friend and that I am with you a hundred percent. You know how much I value our relationship. Because of that, I need to share something with you that would make things better for me. You are late a lot. The time we have together means a lot to me, and your lateness robs me of what I really desire — to have good time with you. So I wanted to talk about it."

> "Jay, I like how much you care about the work we are doing. It is really contagious, and it helps me. But I want to make sure we look at an issue that is getting in the way of our working together effectively."

> "Joe, you know how much I love you and how you are the most important person on the earth to me. I am your biggest champion. But something you do sometimes makes my heart sort of go away, and I want to talk with you about it."

> "Sam, I want you to know that the reason I'm bringing this up is because I love you and am committed to our relationship. I love and value so many things about you. In fact, that is why I have to talk about this. I miss seeing those things because your drinking is getting serious, and we have to do something."

With significant confrontations, it is really important to firmly declare your *favor*, or grace, for the people you are confronting. It reestablishes that you are for rather than against them, and it establishes the connection that serves as the bridge for the truth to pass over to their heart and mind.

Be Genuine

People used to be taught the following formula for correcting someone: Say a positive, then the negative, and then another positive. It was called a "correction sandwich." It was probably created to affirm and validate. This might be helpful at times, but it can also seem manipulative. This is *not* what we are talking about here.

In good confrontation, we are "turning our face toward" something together. Take the appropriate effort to make sure that the other person knows that you are "together," that you are on the same side, looking at the issue as allies and not enemies. Let him know this in whatever way is appropriate. Affirm him, the relationship, or his deeds. And let him know that the negative is not all there is, nor is it the biggest thing. His value to you and your relationship with him are the most important things. The confrontation is in the service of both of those. Let him know that.

10

Apologize for Your Part
in the Problem

One of the most powerful things ever said on confronting someone's problems came from Jesus. This message should be in every psychiatry and psychology book ever written about relationships: "Why do you look at the speck of sawdust in your brother's eye and pay no attention to the plank in your own eye? How can you say to your brother, 'Let me take the speck out of your eye,' when all the time there is a plank in your own eye? You hypocrite, first take the plank out of your own eye, and then you will see clearly to remove the speck from your brother's eye" (Matt. 7:3–5).

When we want to talk to someone about something difficult in a relationship, we often cannot even see the person clearly because of our own hurt and fears and projections. It is very important that we deal with what is going on inside of us first. (We will talk in greater detail about this in part 4, "Getting Ready to Have the Conversation.")

But this passage speaks to another important dynamic in confrontation: being humble, looking at what we have done wrong in the relationship, and owning it first—before we talk to the other person about what she did wrong. The principle is this: *When confronting, do not do it from a deficit balance. In other words, don't confront someone if you owe her an apology first.*

When you talk to someone about a problem, it is tougher for her to listen to you about her part of the problem if she is aware of how you have hurt and failed her. She has thoughts like "Well, how can you judge? You do such and so...." It is easier for her to be defensive, and she may actually have some evidence to back that up.

But if you begin with owning and apologizing for ways you have failed her, or for poor ways you have dealt with this failure, your humility paves the way. Here is what it does:

1. It lets her know you care.
2. It lets her know you are not there to lord it over her or be judgmental.
3. It lets her know you are not there to "win."
4. It models for her what humility looks like and takes away the shame she might feel.

The good things humility brings are tough to overestimate. Therefore, if you are going to confront someone, make sure you have a clean slate before the person. If you have so much to apologize for that you cannot do it in the same conversation as the confrontation, delay the confrontation (if there is no danger in doing so) and just have an apology session first. Bring up your issue at a later time.

Don't confront someone if you owe that person an apology first.

In most situations, you can do both; in fact, doing so often creates a good rhythm. You apologize, then she listens and does the same. It is very common for an apology to open the door for the other person to see what she has done. Here are some examples:

"Mary, I want to talk to you about the argument we had the other day. I did not like how it went, and I thought I needed to begin by telling you that I'm sorry. As I thought about it after I cooled off, I could see I was way out of line in the way I responded. It was wrong, and I'm sorry for how I behaved, and also for how that must have felt to you. Will you forgive me?"

"Joe, I want to talk about what's been going on between us. I want us to look at the ways we have been interacting and at some things that have happened, but I want to begin by telling you that I've reacted to you in very hurtful and inappropriate ways. I've been angry and judgmental much more than I've been helpful. I've nagged, been bitter, and even punished you for some things. I was wrong. I'm sorry for how that must have felt to you. Will you please forgive me?"

"Sam, as you know, I've been upset by some things you've done, and I want to talk about them. But I want you to know something first. I'm just as wrong as I've said you are. I've not held up my side of our relationship in some ways. I've come down on you way too hard and not really been your friend or ally in trying to resolve things. I lose it, and I'm not very helpful. I want to be more helpful and loving, and let you know that I'm on your side. But I can see how you could not feel that way at times because of how I have acted, and I want to apologize for my behavior and my failure to be what you need."

There is no hard and fast rule on how to do this. You can apologize and then go right into your issue. You can tell the other person you want to talk about the issue right up front, and then say, "But first I have to apologize for some things." Each situation has its own chemistry, and there is no "right" way. Nor should you have to begin every confrontation with an apology; if one is not needed, don't apologize. But if you are aware of ways that you have failed the person, deal with that first. It will do a lot of good, and it may give the confrontation an entirely different tone.

11

Avoid "Shoulds"

You should have thought about this beforehand, because then this never would have happened. You should plan better. You should write it all down. Then we wouldn't be in messes like this."

When you hear these statements, how do you feel? Guilty? Ashamed? Angry? Or do you think, "Wow! What helpful input. I wish that person could follow me around and evaluate everything I do"?

Chances are, when someone says you *should* do something, you feel more of the former than the latter. People who use many "shoulds" fetch less helpful outcomes and reactions from other people than those who don't.

The word *should* feels very parental and judgmental to people. That's sad, for the word itself has a great meaning. According to the dictionary, it connotes an "exhortation." It expresses something that would be good for us. It encourages us to go the "right way." So in its purest form, *should* isn't a bad thing.

But the word has at least two problems. First, it is not always said in "pure form"; instead, it is said as a shaming tool or a command. It comes across as an obligation—"You 'must' do this"—which is actually another meaning for the word. When we tell people they "must" do something, it sounds as if they don't have a choice; it feels controlling and dominating. It can fail to communicate what we are trying to get across.

Second, many people have been in relationships in which others have tried to control them, dominate them, and tell them what to do. So at times, even though you mean it purely, it is not heard that way. And if your goal in the confrontation is to solve a problem, it makes sense not to put any unnecessary stumbling blocks in the way.

If you are talking about the past, saying "You should have" doesn't give the other person many options other than to see how he blew it. He will often feel, "Okay, fine! Now I feel awful. What do you want me to do about it? It's done! I should have done better, but I didn't. So you are right: I am pond scum." That might be extreme, but you get the idea. It reinforces his feelings of failure and shame.

Likewise, if you are talking about the future, "must" sounds like a command, and the other person feels as if she has no choice. "You should do this" or "You should choose to ..." puts her in the bind of feeling as if she "has to." Humans will fight for their freedom, and they may resist what you are telling them more than they would if it were said another way.

> *In its purest form, should isn't a bad thing. But the word can be used to shame or control.*

We don't mean to split hairs here or be nitpicky. We wish everyone could hear things and say things from a totally guilt-free place. But that is difficult for many people to do. When someone says, "You should," people feel their choices going away. Instead, you want the other person to freely choose to do what you are suggesting, to feel good about it, not forced into it.

Joshua preserved the freedom of the people of Israel when he said, "If serving the LORD seems undesirable to you, then choose for yourselves this day whom you will serve, whether the gods your forefathers served beyond the River, or the gods of the Amorites, in whose land you are living" (Josh. 24:15). Joshua told them to serve God and be faithful to him, but he also said that if it were disagreeable for them to serve the Lord, then they were free to choose whom they would serve. He preserved their choice. He was clear about what he thought was the right choice: "As for me and my household, we will serve the LORD." But he did not try to force them to choose what he had chosen.

Therefore watch your use of *should* in situations where it could be heard the wrong way. Are you using it as a command? Are you using it to control or to make someone feel guilty for what she has already done? Or are you using it to be helpful and let her know what would be best?

In good relationships, where it does not get in the way, using *should* is fine. "You should do it this way, and it would work better" can sound like "Here, let me help you get out of that bind. Turn the handle to the right, and you can get out of that basement you are locked in." But it can also sound like "You idiot! If you were turning the handle the right way, you wouldn't be stuck down there in the dark." To the pure, all things are pure.

HOW TO SAY IT BETTER

Not so good: "You should have called me and told me you were going to be late. Now you have ruined the whole night for me. I could have used the time to do something constructive instead of waiting for you."

Better: "It would have really helped me if you had called when you knew you were going to be late. Please do that next time so I can make use of the time."

Not so good: "You should get up early, read the paper about new jobs, and get ahead of the game. You should also be making more calls. You are sitting around so much that you are never going to get a job. You should have been out there looking all this time, and you have just wasted your time."

Better: "Things would go better if you made some changes. You would have more success, I think, by getting an early start and using the days to find the work you agreed to seek. It seems as if you are letting really valuable time slip by."

Not so good: "You shouldn't hang around with those kids. You should be finding better friends, and you should not be out anyway. You should be here doing your homework."

Better: "I don't think that that group of friends is good for you. Some of the things they are into are things I don't want you doing, and it is tough to avoid falling into things when you are around kids who are doing them. Let's talk about what is going on, why you are there, and what you think about it all. Also, I want you to do your homework first before going out, no matter who you are with. So finish that, and then let's talk."

Not so good: "You shouldn't be drinking so much. You should focus more on me and the family. You like your beer better than us."

Better: "I am concerned about your drinking. It is becoming a problem, and we miss you. When you drink, the kids and I lose you, and we don't want that."

Good relationships preserve someone's dignity, choice, freedom, and equality as a person. When someone is confronted well, in the context of a caring relationship, he feels as if he is being helped, not caught or controlled. Watch your use of *should* to make sure that it is being heard correctly, as helpful. If it is used or heard as punitive, condemning, or controlling, you might want to find another word.

12

Be an Agent
for Change

In a certain way, you could categorize how people confront each other in three different ways. First, there is the "you got me, now I am going to get you" type of confrontation, in which the confronter unloads wrath and hurt, and leaves it with the offender. It is "an eye for an eye and a tooth for a tooth." These confrontations give the confronter a sick, victorious feeling of "he had it coming to him" or "I gave him a piece of my mind." We have all heard people, after those kinds of conversations, almost gloat or feel proud of "letting him know. . . ." It has been a dumping-ground experience.

The second kind of conversation is the "wipe the slate clean" type, in which the confronter seeks to clear the air in a more loving manner so as not to have something lingering between her and the other person. "Now that we are past that, let's go on." This is a "getting back to where we were" approach, or a return from a negative to a neutral position. No one owes anyone anything anymore. This kind of conversation can be helpful.

The third kind of conversation is, we think, the most redemptive because it represents the spirit with which God approaches us. The confronter enters into the conversation with an attitude to help, be an ally, and be an agent for change. She takes on the role of helping the other person to the best of her ability. As Paul says, "Do not be overcome by evil, but overcome evil with good" (Rom. 12:21). Even when bad things have occurred, the confronter tries to make the situation one in which good things can happen for the person and for the relationship.

Earlier chapters have already talked about two things that go into being an effective agent for change. First, get the log out of your own eye so you can see clearly to help the other person (Matt. 7:3–5). Second, go in with a humble attitude that identifies with the other person's imperfections. The more we see the ways in which we don't always treat others perfectly either, the less we will approach these situations judgmentally, and we will be more gentle and humble (Gal. 6:1).

Another characteristic of an agent for change is an attitude of helpfulness and support. It is the ability to let the person know outright that you don't want to bring this up to dump on him or even just to clear the air, but you want to help him in any way you can and also improve the relationship between the two of you.

The third kind of conversation brings out this important characteristic.

REDEMPTIVE CONVERSATIONS

Here is an example of how to begin this kind of conversation:

> "I don't want you to feel I'm here just to dump on you or make you feel bad. That's not my intention at all. I want us to talk about how we can make this better, and I want to know if there's anything I can do to help you. I'm on your team here."

Another way to approach this conversation is to share your own failures in similar situations:

> "I don't want you to think I'm coming at this from a 'better than you' place. I don't like what you did. But I have done the same thing [or similar, or worse, or hurtful things] also. At those times what I needed was, first of all, to know that it was going to be okay, and, second, to feel as if someone

wanted to help. I want you to know that this is how I feel. I want to talk about how to make it better and grow past this."

There is something very powerful about the one who was hurt being the one who wants to help. It is this humble approach that Jesus brought to the world. The world sinned against him, and yet he came to befriend, forgive, and help the very ones who had turned against him. Our taking this same approach has a powerful melting effect on the offender. It is humbling in the best of ways, because we submit to love, not to our tendency to get even.

Many times, besides just offering to help and be "for the person," you can come with suggestions the person can implement or you can implement together:

"When I was struggling, I found counseling to be really helpful. If you want, I will help you find a counselor."

"I know that this was tough for both of us, and I want us to do better. I would like for us to go together to see a counselor or pastor and learn how to do better."

"We didn't communicate very well in this thing. Let's go to that workshop on communication at the church and work on it together."

"I will help you find an addiction group and even go with you if you want."

The list is endless, as there are many different kinds of problems and solutions. If "confront" means to "turn our face toward," then let's do that. Let's turn toward this issue or problem together, look at it for all its worth, and both do the best we can to make it better. This is the high road — and the one with the best possible destination.

Certainly there are situations where this is neither practical nor advisable. Where there has been so much hurt, where there is ongoing hurt not being owned and turned from, or where you might be in danger, you can't do this. Things have to change. So don't let this suggestion put you under a pile of guilt and make you feel as if you have to do this in all situations.

But in many relationships, it is the way we all get better. Becoming "change agents" for each other is the best kind of confrontation there is. It is confrontation in the highest service of love.

13

Be Specific

I (Henry) was doing a seminar on healthy confrontation not long ago and asked for a volunteer to role-play a conversation with me. I asked if anyone in the audience was in a relationship where they wanted something they were not getting. Quickly a woman raised her hand. I called on her and asked what the issue was.

"It is with my boyfriend," she said.

"What do you want from him?" I asked.

"I want more connection with him."

"More connection?"

"Yes. I just want to feel more intimate. Closer."

"Okay, so what do you mean by that?"

"It means that I just want more connection. Just to be more connected."

"So what do you tell him?"

"I tell him that. I tell him I want to be more connected."

"Wait a minute! That is what you tell him? A man? You tell a man you want to feel 'more connected'?"

"Yes, that's what I tell him."

"Let me get this right. You just say to this guy, 'I want you to connect more with me.' That is what you say."

"Yes."

"Does it work?"

"No, it doesn't. He doesn't get it."

"Imagine that!" I said.

Now the audience was laughing, and even the woman got the point.

When the laughter died down, I asked, "Have you ever seen the cartoon of a man and his dog, in which the man is standing over the dog with his finger in the dog's face? In the balloon above the man in the first frame, it says, 'Blacky, don't chew that shoe; Blacky, don't pee on the rug, don't jump up on people, don't lie on the couch....' The next frame shows what the dog hears: 'Blacky, blah blah blah; Blacky, blah blah blah blah blah....' When you say to your boyfriend that you want him to connect more, he probably hears, 'Blah blah blah blah blah blah....' He might nod and say 'Okay' or wag his tail, but I doubt he knows what you want or what he might do differently to give you what you want."

"What do you mean?" she asked.

"Asking him to be more connected is much too global, especially for a guy! He needs something specific that he can understand and do. How about these?"

"Honey, I want to go for a walk with you, and I want you to tell me what is going on at work and how you are feeling about it."

"Marty, I want us to sit down and talk about our dreams and where we want to go from here. When can we do that?"

"I want to know how you are feeling lately. I want to know what you think and feel about us. I want you to tell me what it is that makes you feel good about us and what makes you feel not so good."

"See what I mean? Those are specific things he can do. 'Connect more' is too big and sweeping. He probably doesn't know where to start. But tell him some specific things he can do, and the two of you will have something to work on."

I could see the lights go on for this woman. She had hope in her eyes. My hunch is that if she follows this advice, her boyfriend might also get some hope of making her happy in ways he would not have known before. As it was, he probably thought this was impossible.

Specificity is a big issue. We hear this problem when people talk about recurring conflicts within significant relationships. Not only do they describe the other person in global, sweeping terms, but they also are not specific about the problem. They use words like *never* and *always*. They say things like, "You never communicate love to me." Global statements in all-or-nothing terms do little to solve a problem. When you talk to someone, instead of giving big-picture descriptions, give her specifics about the problem, what it is that you want to be different, or what she can do to resolve a problem.

HOW TO BE SPECIFIC

Global: "You are so irresponsible. I need for you to be more responsible around here."

Specific: "I feel as if there are a lot of times when you leave things undone. I want to talk about your paying the Visa bill on time and taking care of the car insurance payment like you promised. Let's talk about how to resolve this."

Global: "I want to feel more loved."

Specific: "I wish you would tell me you love me at times other than when we have sex."

Global: "You're so mean to me. I am tired of your verbal abuse."

Specific: "When you get angry at me and yell like you did last night, it hurts. I want to know that you can see how hurtful that is."

Global: "You treat me like an idiot. You act like I am so stupid."

Specific: "When you don't talk to me about our finances, like the refinance application the other day, I feel as if you think I'm too dumb to understand. And when I don't understand something and ask you a question, like about the insurance claim, you didn't answer me. You grabbed it out of my hand and said I was dense. I want you to talk to me about specifics, and if I don't understand something, answer my questions without putting me down. Please treat me like a partner, even when I don't know everything you do."

Global: "You always do this. You promise me you are going to do something, and then you forget about it and leave me hanging. This happens every time I try to depend on you."

Specific: "I need to know that if you tell me you're going to do something, it will get done. Yesterday you promised me you would get my prescription filled, and you didn't. Now I am without my antibiotic, and I fear I'm not going to get over this infection before our vacation. It also happened the other day with the form I asked you to mail. I want to talk about what we can do to make this better. I love you, and I want to trust that you will do what you say you will do."

Almost any confrontation can deteriorate into labeling the other person, such as "You're irresponsible" or "You're so mean." These adjectives may be helpful and appropriate, but only when they are backed up by specific instances that illustrate both what they mean to you and what the other person can do to solve the problem.

So avoid sweeping, global complaints. Be specific about the problem, and you are more apt to get better solutions.

14

Differentiate between Forgiving and Trusting

I know I'm supposed to forgive," a woman at a recent seminar said, "but I just can't open myself up to that kind of hurt anymore. I know I should forgive him and trust him, but if I let him back in, the same thing will happen, and I can't go through that again."

"Who said anything about 'trusting' him?" I (Henry) asked. "I don't think you should trust him either."

"But you said I was supposed to forgive him, and if I do that, doesn't that mean giving him another chance? Don't I have to open up to him again?"

"No, you don't. Forgiveness and trust are two totally different things. In fact, that's part of your problem. Every time he's done this, he's come back and apologized, and you have just accepted him right back into your life, and nothing has changed. You trusted him, nothing was different, and he did it again. I don't think that's wise."

"Well," she asked, "how can I forgive him without opening myself up to being hurt again?"

Good question.

We hear this problem over and over again. People have been hurt, and they do one of two things. Either they confront the other person about something that has happened, the other person says he's sorry, and they forgive, open themselves up again, and blindly trust; or, in fear of opening themselves up again, they avoid the conversation altogether and hold onto the hurt, fearing that for-

giveness will make them vulnerable once again. How do you resolve
this dilemma?

THE PAST, THE PRESENT, AND THE FUTURE

The simplest way to help you to organize your thoughts as you confront this problem is to remember three things:

1. **Forgiveness has to do with the past.** Forgiveness is not
   holding something someone has done against her. It is
   letting it go. It only takes one to offer forgiveness. And just
   as God has offered forgiveness to everyone, we are expected
   to do the same (Matt. 6:12; 18:35).
2. **Reconciliation has to do with the present.** It occurs when
   the other person apologizes and accepts forgiveness. It takes
   two to reconcile.
3. **Trust has to do with the future.** It deals with both what
   you will risk happening again and what you will open
   yourself up to. A person must show through his actions that
   he is trustworthy before you trust him again (Matt. 3:8;
   Prov. 4:23).

In reality, you could have three different kinds of conversations,
each one dealing with one of these themes. You could have a conversation only talking about the issue and offering forgiveness. In
this conversation you would deal only with what happened and let
the person know that you forgive her and want to put this behind
you. If "where do we go from here?" comes up, you could say, "I want
to talk about that at another time. Right now, I just want to know
we are clear with each other about what has happened. I don't want
you feeling as if I'm holding it against you." Obviously, when there
is a great deal of hurt, getting to the point of true forgiveness can
take time, so it does not always happen immediately.

By contrast, you could have a conversation that deals with two
of these issues, or all three. In some good boundary conversations

you forgive the other person for the past, reconcile in the present, and then discuss what the limits of trust will be in the future.

The main point is this: *Keep the future clearly differentiated from the past.*

Keep the future clearly differentiated from the past.

As you discuss the future, you clearly delineate what your expectations are, what limits you will set, what the conditions will be, or what the consequences (good or bad) of various actions will be. As the proverb says, "A righteous man is cautious in friendship" (Prov. 12:26).

In some situations you may forgive someone and reconcile with him but desire no future close relationship. Forgiveness and reconciliation do not dictate the future structure; they only wipe the slate clean. Forgiveness and reconciliation are important requirements, inasmuch as they depend on us. But future relationship involves more. If you desire to continue the relationship and you need to work through significant issues, your conversation may sound something like this:

"I want to talk about the way our relationship is going to be for a while. First, I want you to know I accept your apology and forgive you for the deception and the stuff that happened. I want us to be close again, and the past is past. So, I don't want you to think that I am holding on to anything. I want this to work out.

"But we have been here before, where things happened, you apologized, we got right back together, and nothing really changed. So this time, I want us to figure out a way to work toward getting back together when I feel as though you are doing something different I can trust.

"I only want to talk about it with a counselor present, and then I want to decide how much time we should spend together until I know it is safe for you to move back in. And

I will consider your moving back in only if you are getting some help and sticking with a program. I forgive you, but I have to learn to trust you again, and that has to be based on your actions."

Differentiating between forgiveness and trust does a number of things. First, you prevent the other person from being able to say that not opening up again means you are "holding it against me."

Second, you draw a clear line from the past to the possibility of a good future with a new beginning point of today, with a new plan and new expectations. If you have had flimsy boundaries in the past, you are sending a clear message that you are going to do things differently in the future.

Third, you give the relationship a new opportunity to go forward. You can make a new plan, with the other person potentially feeling cleansed and feeling as though the past will not be used to shame or hurt him. As a forgiven person, he can become an enthusiastic partner in the future of the relationship instead of a guilty convict trying to work his way out of relational purgatory. And you can feel free, not burdened by bitterness and punitive feelings, while at the same time being wise about the future.

PART III

SEEING *How* *It's* DONE

15

Telling People
What You Want

Peter was sad over his recent breakup with Jan. He really liked her spunk, energy, and passion for life, and at one point even thought they might marry. I had thought she might be the "one" for him as well, so I was surprised when he told me he had broken up with her.

"What happened?" I (Henry) asked.

"I just couldn't deal with her demandingness," he said. "She wanted everything her way, and she was so pushy. I thought about a lifetime of that and got a headache thinking about it. I know I liked her, but in the end, she was just too much."

I understood what he meant, because I thought she was pushy too. I remember thinking that if he married her, he would be a very busy boy. She made you feel that you needed to dig in. But I felt for him in the split up. He was sad and would miss her.

Not too long after that, he began dating Marla. At first, he was in absolute heaven. She was so "easy to get along with, not like Jan at all," he said. "She is not pushy; she's up and positive so much of the time. It feels like I have emerged from winter."

About five months later, something happened. "I broke up with Marla," he said. "It just wasn't working out."

"What happened?" I asked. "I thought she was the answer to all of your 'woman' issues. Not demanding, not pushy, not controlling. You were so into her."

"I know. It's weird! In the beginning I really liked that she was not like Jan, always wanting something and so demanding. She was like a breath of fresh air. But as time went on, I noticed a couple of things. First, I could never figure out what she wanted. I would ask her what she wanted to do, or where she wanted to go, or how she felt about something, and she would always defer to me. Even though that felt good in the beginning, I think I was just gun-shy from Jan. Over time, I got bored with Marla's flexibility. There was something missing. I don't know exactly what it was. Second, I started to see another part of her that drove me a little batty."

"What was that?"

"I don't know the right word for it. *Pouty* is a little strong. She wouldn't really pout, but she would be sad, or quiet, or something. I would feel like I had done something wrong, but I didn't know what it was. So I would ask. At first, she would say, 'Nothing,' but I knew that was bull. So I would have to pull it out of her, and then I would find out that she had wanted me to do something I hadn't done, or that she was bugged about something she hadn't told me about. I felt like I was letting her down, but I couldn't read her mind. I was frustrated not knowing when things were okay and when they weren't. I think I need someone more up front with what they are thinking and what they want."

"Like Jan?" I asked.

"Oh, no!" he said, startled. "Maybe, but no. No. I don't really know." He looked confused and a little sad. At that moment he didn't have a lot of hope for a good relationship.

WANTING WELL

Peter's problem is not hard to understand. He wanted a woman with passion and desire, but he didn't want to be controlled by her. He wanted to give freely, but he didn't want to have to figure out what someone wants.

As I told Peter later, he *wanted someone who wanted well*. On the one hand, Jan wanted strongly, and he liked that, but she expressed her desires in a way that ultimately drove him away. She did not want well, or at least communicate her wants and desires well. On the other hand, Marla wanted weakly; her wants were almost invisible, until Peter didn't meet them. Only after disappointing her did he know what they were. Jan's and Marla's inability to communicate their wants left Peter looking for something else.

Sadly, Peter probably could have worked it out with either Jan or Marla had he understood at that time what the issue was. Committed married people do that all the time. And later he did figure it out with another woman. But married or single, in romance, family life, friendship, or business relationships, many people can identify with the problem of getting what they want in their relationships in a way that is good for both parties. How do you communicate wants in a way that gets your desires met and doesn't drive someone away? That's the topic of this chapter.

YOU CAN'T ALWAYS GET WHAT YOU WANT, BUT YOU'D BETTER TRY

Solomon said it well: "Hope deferred makes the heart sick, but a longing fulfilled is a tree of life" (Prov. 13:12).

Your heart's desires and longings bring life to your life. If you don't have ways of making them known, they won't be met, and you'll feel "sick at heart." Wanting is key to feeling alive in a relationship, key to keeping the relationship vibrant for both people. If only one person is getting his or her desires met, the relationship suffers, intimacy lessens, and sickness of heart results.

Many people do not get what they want in relationships where they could if they knew how to communicate their desires.

Unfortunately, many people do not get what they want in relationships where they could if they knew how to communicate their desires. Jan had that problem, and ultimately she lost what she wanted. Marla had the same problem in a different way. And although he didn't know it, Peter did too. Had he been able to tell either Jan or Marla what he wanted from them, things might have turned out different. Instead, he just reacted to them, and left.

Wanting is difficult in the best of scenarios. Many things can get in the way. But in the end, wanting is the only way to live fully, and if that is true, then we need to learn how to communicate our wants in ways best for us and best for our relationships. Let's look at some ways to do that, some ways not to, and how to handle what can happen when we want well.

KNOW WHOSE WANT IT IS AND WHO IS RESPONSIBLE FOR IT

Many people, when they think of "boundaries," think of them only as setting limits, saying no, or trying to stop something destructive from happening. But having good boundaries is more than stopping bad things from happening to you. *It is also taking responsibility for the good things you want to happen.*

When you take responsibility for your desires and communicate them well, a relationship has much more chemistry, connection, and mutual fulfillment. You know about and negotiate any issues; there is give and take. And no one is walking around resentful and depressed.

Think about Marla for a moment. She had desires she wanted fulfilled in her relationship with Peter. But she thought Peter was responsible for knowing what her desires were and for taking the first step toward fulfilling them. She shifted the responsibility for what she wanted from her to him; she thought her "wants" were his problem, not hers. When he did not solve her problem, when she felt sad or resentful, she saw it as Peter's responsibility to figure out what she was feeling and do something about it. Ultimately, this proved too much for him to do.

To have a relationship that works well, Marla first should communicate her wants not outwardly, but inwardly. She should have a "responsibility" talk with herself before she has a "talk" with another person. Here are some of the things she will need to do:

- Own her "want"—be honest with herself about what she wants and be aware that her desire is her responsibility
- Own the feelings that occur when her desire is not getting met—if she is sad, she needs to tell Peter, not wait for him to figure it out
- Choose to communicate and move toward Peter to let her wants be known
- Communicate desire, not demand

If Marla approaches the process this way, she will be off to a much better start. She will be getting "the log out of her own eye" first. We always have to look at ourselves first to make sure we are doing our part correctly. This is particularly true with wants and desires; others do not magically know what we want, and they need to be told in ways they can accept. So the first conversation has to take place inside. Here is how the conversation would sound inside the old Marla and then inside the new one:

The old Marla: "I want to go to a good thought-provoking movie tonight. I don't want to see another action movie. Peter always chooses those. I wish he would be more considerate and do what I want for once. I hope that happens, but it probably won't. He knows I like deeper movies, so maybe for once, he'll ask me. I doubt it. I'm bummed. He isn't going to do that. I don't know why I even hope for it. This feels really crummy."

The new Marla: "I want to go to a good thought-provoking movie tonight. I bet Peter is thinking about another action movie. If I don't say something, I'll end up being bummed out again. I'll end the evening in a crummy mood and want to eat five gallons of ice cream. It would be nice if he asked me what I want to see, but I doubt he will. I'd better call him to let him know what I'm thinking. Wait, what if he doesn't want to see a thought-provoking movie? Well, we'll just talk about it. I'll tell him the movies I want to see, and I'll ask him what he wants to see. That's fair. Oh well, if he doesn't want to see one of the movies I want to see, I'll deal with it then. He's free to say no. It won't be the end of the world. Maybe I'll go with Jill if Peter doesn't want to go. I'll see how it goes."

The big difference between these two internal dialogues is that in the second one, Marla is taking ownership of her desire. She is thinking of how to actively communicate what she wants to Peter. It starts with how she handles her desire inside of herself long before she gets to the conversation with Peter. It starts with her realizing that her desires are *her* responsibility.

PRESERVE THE OTHER PERSON'S FREEDOM

Ask yourself this question: "What do I do when I hear no to something I want?" Here are some not-so-good reactions:

- I get mad, either inwardly or outwardly. I have an internal or external temper tantrum.
- I judge the other person, thinking that she "should" do what I ask; I think she is selfish or doesn't care about me.
- I go further than judging. I see the other person as really bad; I don't see him as good at all. All I see is bad.
- I emotionally or physically withdraw from the person.
- I feel hurt and unloved.
- I try to make her feel guilty, either to punish her or to get her to do what I want.

- I become cynical about ever getting what I want in life or the relationship.
- I turn into a judge, prosecutor, and salesperson. I object to every reason he has for saying no.
- I smile on the outside and hide my real feelings, going along as if it's okay when it's not.

Freedom is essential to a good relationship. If we're not free, we can't love. If people feel as though they can't say no to us and if they do things for us out of compulsion, guilt, or feelings of obligation, they will resent doing those things. If we ask for things we want in ways that make someone feel as though no is not okay with us, the relationship turns into a control battle. Freedom and love suffer, and even fulfilled desires can't fully satisfy because they are not given in love.

Mostly this has to do with our attitude. There are no magic words to show someone she is free to say no. You need to tell her. Here are some suggestions on how to do that:

"I don't want you to feel like you 'have to' do this, but could you give me a ride to work tomorrow?"

"I want you to feel totally free to not do this, so tell me if you don't want to. Will you help me move this weekend?"

"I don't want you to feel any pressure about this, so I want you to know that going in. Feel free to tell me no, okay? So here it is — I want you to join this committee with me and help me organize the Fall Festival."

People who find it difficult to ask for things may find it helpful to say things like this to put the other person at ease. If you have controlled someone in the past or have been demanding, or even if that person *feels as if you have*, you may want to preface your request with statements like this to remind the person that he or she can say no to you now.

Another way to preserve another person's freedom is to avoid the word *need* when it is not accurate. A "need" is something we must have for survival. If we do not have what we need, we suffer injury. We need air, water, food, safety, and connection. It is rare that only one person can provide something we need. Most of the time we are talking about "wants," not "needs." When we use the word *need*, it smells more like an obligation than a request. Who feels free to say no to someone's request for air, water, or food? So when you are talking about what you *want* from someone, beware of casting it in terms of a *need*.

When a relationship becomes close, the stakes go up in terms of the distress one may feel when one doesn't get something. For example, if a woman is going to have a close relationship with a man, she needs to be able to trust him. But even then, she needs to talk about what she wants him to do. For example, here are two different ways of making the same request:

> "I want to be close to you. And to be close, I need to feel like you are committed to me. So I would like you to spend one of the weekend days with me and see your buddies on the other day."

> "I need for you to be with me on one of the weekend days. You can't expect me to be close to you when you are gone both days."

The first request expresses vulnerability; the second feels more like a demand.

Communicating wants is very touchy, and the words we say are not always the issue. The real issue may be the attitude we take when we communicate our desires. So, no matter what you say, observe your attitude when you talk. Make your request in a way that shows you are not implying that the other person "should" do whatever you want, but instead shows that you realize you are not "entitled" to what you are asking for. Don't remind the other person of all you have done for him or her, or some other form of manipulation that communicates that he or she "should" do what you ask.

Observe how you respond to another person's choices. Don't punish or react. If he or she says no, don't come back with one of the following rejoinders:

"Fine. Excuse me for wanting something."

"It seems like the least you could do."

"That will be the last time I ever ask *you* for anything."

"It seems like after all I have done for you, the least you could do would be...."

"See? It doesn't do any good to ask you for what I want."

Look at your reactions and see how much freedom people really have to say no to you.

BE CLEAR, AND BE DIRECT

The best way to ask for what you want is to be clear and direct. Do this by using "I" statements, not "you" statements:

"I" statement: "I would like it if we could talk more than we have been doing. I would like to know more of what is going on with you. I feel out of the loop."

"You" statement: "You don't ever really talk to me very much. You leave me in total darkness. Seems like you would want to tell me things if we were really close."

"You" statement: "It seems like you don't care, judging from how much you talk to me."

The "I" statement is very clear and responsible. Talk about *yourself*, not the other person and his or her failures to provide for you.

The "you" statements judge, interpret, and globalize. "You" statements accuse the other person.

Be specific instead of global when expressing wants. When a husband says, "We never have any intimacy," he is not being specific. Here is how he can be more direct in stating what he wants:

"I want to make love with you."

"I want to take a vacation with you."

"I want to take an afternoon and spend some time talking about our goals together."

The use of "I" statements seems simple, but it is especially important in communicating your wants and desires. Remember the slogan "Just say no"? Well, the rule here is "Just say":

"I want to go out to eat tonight."

"I would like you to call if you are going to be late for dinner."

"I would like you to pick up your clothes off the bathroom floor."

If you are going to use "you" statements, use them in requests, like the above, instead of accusations:

"Would you please pick up the dry cleaning for me on the way home?"

"Would you dance with me?"

"Will you be willing to take care of the kids so I can go out with my friends?"

All of these requests preserve the freedom of the other person. They do not bind the other person into some "no choice" position, and they decrease the possibility of his or her becoming defensive.

WHAT CAN HAPPEN, AND WHAT DO I DO THEN?

When you ask for something, several things can happen. You can receive an unqualified yes. A yes is not too difficult to deal with, unless you have trouble receiving good things, but that is a different book! The harder times are when you get a no, an objection, defensiveness, or a personal attack just for asking.

In dealing with responses when you have asked for something, remember the principles we talked about for asking. They also apply for responding.

First, take ownership of your desire. It is your desire, not that of the person who just said no.

Second, don't punish, retaliate, or use counterattack. Try one of the following alternatives.

1. Accept the No and Move On

One of the biggest problems with the "Jans" of the world is that no "no" is acceptable to them. Peter felt as though if he did not do whatever Jan wanted, he was going to be in trouble. So make sure you do not have a "have to have" attitude about everything you ask for, and don't see a no as something bad. After all, you wouldn't want to have to say yes to everything everyone ever wanted from you, either. In addition, some things are not that important.

But this does not mean that you won't have feelings about not getting what you want. The "free" response — and the response that will also leave you free — is sadness. Instead of becoming angry and trying to control the situation, accept the fact that we don't always get what we want; that is part of life and part of love. So, be sad for a moment and say to yourself or the other person, "Rats! Bummer! That's sad. I really wanted that. Oh, well. Onward!" Or something like that. It denotes that you are taking responsibility for your own wants and not having a temper tantrum when you do not get your way. Then the relationship can go on in its normal ebb and flow.

2. If the Want Is Really Important to You, Accept the No, but Dialogue

Sometimes what you want may be really important to you and to the relationship itself. It is much bigger than a ride to the mall or how you will spend a particular vacation or where you will go on a date. It concerns your core values or signals a change of direction in your relationship. The request from the woman who wanted one weekend day of her boyfriend's time is a good example of that.

Just because your wants are your responsibility doesn't mean you should roll over and play dead when they are not granted. How boring! Persistence can be a great quality, but there are good ways and bad ways to be persistent. Sometimes the person might not even be aware of how important something is to you. Also, his or her no may come from some other reason you will need to explore. Sometimes, just giving up is not the answer.

> *Persistence can be a great quality, but there are good ways and bad ways to be persistent.*

So, if you are going to take responsibility for your wants and desires, yet take a strong stand for them, how can you do that? Let's look at some ways:

Communicate the Importance of Your Request

Here are some illustrations of how you can communicate to the other person how important your request is to you:

"I understand that you don't want to give up a day with your buddies. I know you enjoy that, and I want you to have time with friends. But maybe you don't know how important the weekend time together is for me. Let me describe it to you. During the week we are both so busy I really miss you. Then, if we miss each other on the weekends as well, I go into the next week feeling really disconnected. I want more from our relationship than that. To you, it may just seem like an

CHAPTER 15: TELLING PEOPLE WHAT YOU WANT

afternoon. To me, it sets a pattern for an entire week. Do you understand that?"

"When I asked you to swap schedules with me, did you understand what was behind that? If it seemed like something small to you, I might have not made myself clear. It really is important. I don't want to put pressure on you, but at the same time, if you are going to say no, I want you to know what you are saying no to."

Even an "Are you sure? Please ... I really want to do this" can communicate how strongly you feel about your request. Timidity never got anyone anything. We are not opposed to strong requests and good assertiveness. Even God says he responds to that when he sees how much someone really wants something he has previously said no to (for example, see Gen. 18:20–32). Make your case known. Persist. Present a good argument. This is important in every relationship, from the hostess at the restaurant who says they have no openings to a spouse or a business relationship. Every good salesman knows how to deal with objections and to be bold. Listen to what Jesus says about asking:

> "Suppose one of you has a friend, and he goes to him at midnight and says, 'Friend, lend me three loaves of bread, because a friend of mine on a journey has come to me, and I have nothing to set before him.'
>
> "Then the one inside answers, 'Don't bother me. The door is already locked, and my children are with me in bed. I can't get up and give you anything.' I tell you, though he will not get up and give him the bread because he is his friend, yet because of the man's boldness he will get up and give him as much as he needs.
>
> "So I say to you: Ask and it will be given to you; seek and you will find; knock and the door will be opened to you. For everyone who asks receives; he who seeks finds; and to him who knocks, the door will be opened" (Luke 11:5–10).

Many times the other person, who has already said no, will "get" it: "Oh, I understand now. I didn't know it was such a big deal to you. I can see why this is so important."

It is true with God, and it is true with each other as well. Sometimes we just have to make the case for what we want and be persistent. Again, attitude is important. Don't persecute, judge, or react. Don't make the other person feel bad, and let him know he is still free to say no. Then, if you get the picture that the no is firm, deal with your sadness and move on. Even in moving on, you might also say that you would like to revisit the issue at a later date.

Seek to Understand the Reason for No

Sometimes someone says no, not because of the request, but because he or she is resisting something else in the request. If what you want is very important to you, try to find out the reason for the no, and see if you can help solve that problem for the person. Inquire further without being controlling:

Sarah: "Help me understand why you don't want to go to the ballet."

Bob: "I had planned to go to the library that night and do some research about my fishing trip in the spring. It's the only night I can do that."

Sarah: "So you are not against going to the ballet with me. You want to go to the library and do research."

Bob: "Right."

Sarah: "Okay, is there another night you can go to the library?"

Bob: "No, because I have to go to class on Tuesday, and the other nights you have your meetings."

Sarah: "Well, what if I skipped my meeting on Monday, and we went that night instead? Would you be willing to do that?"

Bob has a reason that he can't go to the ballet. When the reason is explored, new possibilities open up. This seems simple, but it is amazing how couples and friends often do not get to a workable solution because of either control issues, reactivity, or the inability of the one who wants something to take responsibility for finding a workable solution.

Empathize and Re-ask

At times, a person's no is reflexive or not very well thought through. Sometimes it is a reaction to longstanding control issues, and he or she simply says no to assert his or her autonomy, much like a toddler. Without being controlling, angry, or demanding, just empathize and re-ask:

"It sounds like it seems like a lot to you, huh? I understand that. Still, I really want to do this."

"I realize this would mean some effort on your part. I know that. But I really want it. It is important to me. I wouldn't persist if it weren't."

"I can see that this is going to be hard on you. Still, I think it's an important thing."

Connecting and empathizing with the initial difficulty someone feels is often enough to build a bridge of understanding. It allows him or her to see how important it is to you.

Closely akin to this is listening to a person's objections. When the other person objects, inquire more. Listen. Ask for more information:

Tom: "I can't do that. It would cause me so much trouble with my schedule. No way."

Ellie: "Really? That sounds hard. Tell me more. I want to get it."

Tom: "Well, it means that I would have to go to the boss and change things around."

Ellie: "Yeah, I understand. That would be uncomfortable, especially with the way he can be. What do you think he would say?"

Tom: "There's no telling. He might blow up. How can I know?"

Ellie: "Brutal! What do you do when he does that? That sounds like a lot of pressure."

Tom: "You're darn right it is. I hate it!"

Ellie: "Okay, I can see that this is no small thing. And it's going to be a sacrifice. I understand that even better than I did. But I still want you to go forward for me in this."

Remember, this is not a tug-of-war. It is two people trying to come together and know that they are understood. Even if the person says yes, you would want to fully understand what is being given so you can be properly grateful. Thus, inquire if you need to.

Deal with Defensiveness

Sometimes the person may get defensive with you in his reflexive no or invite you to an argument. If this happens, just remain centered on what you want. Empathize, then go back to your desire. State it plainly and clearly, and do not try to justify it or answer the person's defensiveness:

Tom: "What? You are always wanting something from me. I can't believe you want me to go to that. Can't you see I'm busy? Do you think I don't have anything to do myself?"

Ellie: "I understand you have a lot to do. But I want to do this."

> **Tom:** "See, there you go! Just thinking about yourself again. What about me?"
>
> **Ellie:** "I know it seems like that to you. Sorry! But this is something that I really want."

Tom is sending Ellie a lot of invitations to get off track. But Ellie does a good job of empathizing with his defensiveness and not getting sucked in. If she had, she would indeed have gotten off track and gone down the wrong road. Consider this response:

> **Ellie:** "That's not true! I don't always want something, and I try all the time to help you when you are busy. Just the other day. . . ."

Or another response:

> **Ellie:** "When do I think about myself? Just give me an example. I think I am very giving around here. What do you mean by that?"

Instead of giving either response, Ellie just stayed clear, kept in touch with what she wanted, and stated it. The person is free to say no, but not free to get you off track or into an argument.

Emphasize Real Consequences

Tom and Sandy were in a demanding season of life with his work and rearing three small children. He was an attorney who had taken on a tough case that required many nights at the office and much weekend travel for the better part of a year. Although it was one of those "have to do it" seasons of work many professions require, the strain on him was showing. When he had decided to go to law school, Sandy and Tom both understood the future demands of the job, but together they committed to it. They were willing to make sacrifices because they both enjoyed the fruits of his work.

But when Tom worked, Sandy was stuck with three young children all of the time they were awake. She had little time either to herself or with Tom. She was weathering it well, however, because she knew he was suffering too.

The problem arose when Tom got some unexpected time off. Every now and then someone would cancel, and he would not have to work that day. When this happened, Tom would go fishing to "get away from it all." Sandy did not mind his fishing, and she even wanted him to have relaxation time. But while he was getting his time, she was getting none.

Several times, when he got time off, she had asked him if they could do something as a family or if he could keep the kids so she could do something for herself. Each time, he said, "No, I have to go fishing and get away."

After this had happened a few times, Sandy decided to do something about it. Until then, she had communicated in noncontrolling ways. She had understood his need for time to himself, and she had provided ways for him to have that. At the same time, she had persisted in making her case for why it was also important for her to have time to herself and time with him. Still, Tom took only himself into consideration. So she accepted his no, but she let him know that his actions were having real consequences:

> **Sandy:** "Tom, I understand you have a lot of work, and I know you don't get much time off and need some time to get away. But I think I have been pretty gracious about giving that time to you. Whenever you've had a day off, you've taken it for yourself. I've been happy for you, but I would like some time for me and for us. Each time I have asked for that, you have gone fishing anyway.
>
> "I don't want to punish you for that, but I want to let you know the effect it's having on me. I used to ask you for time because I wanted to spend it with you. I desired it. I felt a warm longing for you. But since you have been denying me time, my

feelings are changing. I have started to feel more distant from you. I'm feeling far away from you and not like we are partners in this together. I'm not trying to get on your case, but I am trying to let you know the truth of what's happening inside me as you continue to choose to use all of your free time for yourself. I'm not here to argue about this. It's just true. And I want you to know that it's a serious issue."

Tom: "But you have no idea how hard I'm working. I'm doing this for us, and it's killing me. You don't understand how hard it is on me."

Sandy: "I understand how you feel. I feel for you as well. What I am telling you is what is happening inside me. I can't be close to you on an 'on call' basis unless I'm feeling that you are showing some desire to move toward me too. I don't want you to respond right now. I have already talked about it enough to let you know how it is affecting me. I would like you to think about it. I want you to commit to our getting some counseling together. If you won't either change things or go talk to someone with me, I'm going to have to do something for myself. I'm not doing well the way things are. If you won't join me, I'll have to begin to take care of me by myself."

Tom: "What does that mean? What are you going to do, leave?"

Sandy: "I don't know what I am going to do. I'm not going to talk about that right now. What I am telling you is that this is getting serious, and I want you to either change or go to counseling with me to find a solution to this problem. If you won't do

either, I will deal with that when it happens. I'm
just telling you the way it is with me. I love you
and want this to change."

Notice that Sandy didn't get hooked into Tom's defensiveness
or his invitation to get off track. She persisted in letting him know
that, although he was free to continue to say no to her requests,
he would experience consequences if he did. These consequences
would be different in different situations, but the main point is that
she let him know the situation was serious and would affect their
relationship. The consequences of being ignored in a relationship
for a long time were real.

If one spouse's relationship "wants" are not fulfilled, the other
spouse will reap a loss of intimacy and closeness in the marriage. If
a husband like Tom never gives time up from his hobbies or work to
be with his wife, he risks losing intimacy with her. These are real
consequences.

FIND A BALANCE

Every good relationship has a balance of yeses and nos. If you never
said no to anything, you would be a puppet. If you never said yes,
you would be a dictator. In the middle is the give and take of a good
relationship, in which you negotiate and persist when something is
important to you.

When trying to find a balance, remember that there is a difference between wants and needs. Both are valid. Both are important.
(In a paradoxical way, we "need" both.) There are some things we
need, things we can't live without. Things we need are different
from things we want—things that would make life better or more
enjoyable. We naturally have to take a stronger stand on asserting
needs and getting them met.

What's the difference between a need and a want? Recall how
we defined this earlier: When a need is not met, we suffer injury.
Here are some needs worth standing up for:

- Our need for connection
- Our need for freedom from control
- Our need for unconditional love
- Our need for equality and mutuality
- Our need for physical safety
- Our need for emotional and mental safety
- Our need to express talents and interests
- Our need for rest
- Our need for pleasure
- Our need for healing

These needs are worth fighting for more than wants that only make life or a relationship better or more fulfilling. Relationships are, at times, going to fail to make us happy and fulfilled. At those times, people commit to doing without while they solve those problems. So don't act as if everything you want is a need and that your relationship should be providing your every want. Reserve that stance for serious infractions.

But remember, even serious infractions by your partner are still your responsibility. If, for example, you are in a marriage where there is no connection or in which your spouse has an addiction that is making things emotionally unsafe, it is still your responsibility to deal with things appropriately. Go get support for your need for emotional stability, safety, and healing. Don't be a victim.

When you go outside the relationship to have those needs met, have them met in *a way that will support the healing of the relationship.* If your spouse has an addiction, for example, and that is why your needs are not being met, get support and connection from a co-dependency or co-addicts support group or counselor, not a relationship that could potentially lead to an affair. Choose the *redemptive* way of getting your needs met: "Do not be overcome by evil, but overcome evil with good" (Rom. 12:21).

In the arena of preferences, be "sad" when you don't get what you want instead of making someone "bad." Don't make yourself bad for wanting things, and don't make the other person bad for not granting them. Be proactive about getting your needs and wishes met inside the relationship, and if that does not happen, get them met somewhere else. But again, don't do it in a way that is destructive to the relationship. Keep yourself free from bitterness, and keep the other person free from control. In the long run you will get more love and satisfaction, and you will get what you want.

Sometimes it is more than something you want. There is a real problem to be brought into the open. In the next chapter we will see how to do that.

16

Making Someone Aware of a Problem

Many years ago our (John's) family spent a lot of time with another family who lived nearby. Our kids were about the same age, and the grownups all got along well. Our lives intersected around birthday parties, school events, and backyard barbecues. During this time I also got to know the wife's mother, Fay, who was at many of the family events we attended.

Although Fay was pleasant, she was also very intrusive, inappropriately inserting herself into other people's spaces. When chatting with a small group, she would sometimes interrupt and change the topic to herself. At other times she would break in on private conversations. Most times she would stand uncomfortably close to others, so that they found themselves backing away from her to get some space. I could tell she was totally unaware of her effect on other people. She thought she was fitting in fine with everyone and everybody was enjoying her company.

It might seem funny in a way, but actually it was sad. I could tell that the family was annoyed by Fay's behavior, but nobody would talk to her about it. They would avoid her, roll their eyes, and joke about her behind her back. I once asked Jayne, Fay's daughter, why no one said anything to her mom. She looked embarrassed and said, "I don't know. I guess we don't want to hurt her feelings." Yet I often thought that it might have been worth it for Fay to suffer some hurt feelings in order to be aware of how she was putting people off. At least then she could have had an opportunity to change.

I even thought about talking to Fay myself. But when I asked Jayne about it, she said she'd prefer that the family handle the matter in house. I don't know whether that ever happened.

If someone in your life behaves in a way that causes problems but he doesn't know his behavior is a problem, you are dealing with unawareness. It can be something bothersome but not dangerous, as with Fay. Or it can be something life threatening, as with a prescription pill addiction.

Like Fay's daughter, you may be acutely aware of the issue yourself, much more so than the person with the problem. You may want to address it with the person for his sake and yours. At the same time, you may be at a loss on how helpfully to approach him. This chapter gives you a hands-on guide to helping that person come to awareness and finding a solution to the problem.

AWARENESS 101

Awareness means "knowing" something. It implies a knowledge beyond thinking, a knowledge that comes from *experience*. The Hebrew word for being aware is the same one used to describe Adam and Eve's sexual intimacy. It is a knowledge that involves the whole person.

In order to solve a problem, a person must be aware of it. She must know that it exists and that it is important to her and to you. This awareness is not an on-off process like a light switch; it is more of a continuum. People have varying degrees of awareness of their problems. For example, a person who is, in reality, argumentative and combative may honestly think she is the most easygoing person in the world. Or she may think she is a little opinionated at times. Or she may be very concerned about and working to resolve the issue.

Becoming aware doesn't solve the issue by itself, but the issue cannot be solved without awareness. Until the person becomes aware, you will experience the problem more than she does. And that puts you in an impossible situation, as you are then attempting to correct a problem only she can correct. *Only to the extent that someone becomes aware of a problem is she able to take responsibility for the problem.*

Only to the extent that someone becomes aware of a problem is she able to take responsibility for the problem.

The Bible has a hard teaching: Even when we are not aware of our problems, we are still culpable for their effects. God is more negative about our defiant rebellion than he is about our unintentional mistakes, but we are still answerable for both:

> "But if just one person sins unintentionally, he must bring a year-old female goat for a sin offering. The priest is to make atonement before the LORD for the one who erred by sinning unintentionally, and when atonement has been made for him, he will be forgiven. One and the same law applies to everyone who sins unintentionally, whether he is a native-born Israelite or an alien.
>
> "But anyone who sins defiantly, whether native-born or alien, blasphemes the LORD, and that person must be cut off from his people. Because he has despised the LORD'S word and broken his commands, that person must surely be cut off; his guilt remains on him" (Num. 15:27–31).

This makes sense when you see someone who ruins relationships by a trait she is not aware of or can't succeed in business because of a deficiency others see but she doesn't. Lack of awareness does not mean a lack of suffering, either for the person or for those around her.

On the one hand, a person's lack of awareness may cause you to feel compassion for her. It may be causing serious problems in her life. She may be suffering and knows neither why nor what to do about it. This requires a mature level of love from you, especially when the problem affects your relationship with her and your life in other ways. On the other hand, you may find it hard to feel compassion for someone when her behavior or attitude disrupts your life.

At times like these, look at the most profound example in the universe of compassion for the unaware: "Father, forgive them, for they do not know what they are doing" (Luke 23:34). At a moment of deepest suffering, Jesus felt concern for our blindness even though that blindness was part of the reason for his pain.

Furthermore, as we said in chapter 2, we may have an obligation to help the person in our life "know" what the problem is (Ezek. 3:18–21). She may need you to shed light on the issue before it ruins your relationship. In fact, that may be one of the reasons God put you in her life. Bringing awareness is all part of how we care for each other. Remember that compassion does not mean you are to be soft on the issue. Directness, clarity, and truth are necessary. But keep the balance of love and grace, too.

This chapter gives examples of specific conversations that model how to help the person in your life who is not aware of a problem that must be addressed. We also show the wrong way to go about this so that you can be "aware" of your own possible pitfalls in confronting someone on her unawareness.

HOW TO HAVE THE CONVERSATION

Take a "Presumed Innocent" Approach

Until you know better, assume a person is innocent of bad motives or intents, and approach him accordingly. If, like Fay, the person truly does not know what he is doing, he needs compassion and gentleness from you. *Being innocently unaware is a far cry from being resistant, defensive, or blaming* (see chapter 18). The other person may simply be unable to comprehend the problem. Perhaps he is afraid to see it or does not possess the tools to look at himself. In other cases he may simply not know the full extent of the severity of the issue—how it may be ruining his life as well as your relationship with him. Or he may not want to know something about himself because it would interfere with his concept of his own goodness and perfection.

Presuming innocence also means giving the person a chance to show that his heart is in the right place. You are hoping that all he needs is a nudge to deal with the problem; that is, when you come alongside him and inform him of the issue, you anticipate that he will be open to the feedback and will want to take responsibility to resolve the problem.

Given more time and experience, you might conclude otherwise about his heart, character, and motives. You may find that, knowing the truth, he still doesn't care enough to change. Even so, until you know this about him, love requires that you begin with this approach: "Love does not delight in evil but rejoices with the truth. It always protects, always trusts, always hopes, always perseveres" (1 Cor. 13:6–7).

Sometimes the confronting person will interpret a problem as stemming from a lack of love for her. For example, a wife whose husband does not remember to ask her about her day may feel that he's not interested in her. She might judge him prematurely, saying, "Why don't you care enough about me and my feelings to ask me how I'm doing?" or "When you don't ask me how I'm doing, it makes me feel like I am not interesting to you anymore." However, it may simply be that her husband does not know how important this is to her. The wife's quick judgment may alienate him from her so that it becomes more difficult for him to give her what she wants.

Also, you may need to come to terms with your own wishes that the other person "should" know what you need or want. *Often an unaware person will be unjustly accused of not caring because the confronter expected him to read her mind.* For the confronter to have to tell the other person what she needs and wants makes her feel unloved. Taking responsibility for making known what she wants will often help: "But everything exposed by the light becomes visible, for it is light that makes everything visible" (Eph. 5:13–14).

Here is an example of how to confront a person who is unaware of an issue:

"I wanted to let you know I have noticed something in our relationship that could end up being a problem. Sometimes it seems that when we talk, you aren't really listening to me. You say the right things, but you look around and don't make eye contact. It even feels at times as if you are waiting for me to finish so that you can talk about whatever is on your mind. I don't know if you are aware of this, but before it becomes a big deal, I wanted to bring it up. What do you think?"

Here the confronter starts with the stance that all the person being confronted needs is some basic information, and she gave him room to give his own input on the question. When a person genuinely is not aware, often making him aware is all the "nudge" needed for change to take place.

Be Humble

Approach the person and the situation humbly. Humility is not about perceiving yourself as *lower than you are*. It has to do with *perceiving yourself as you really are*, with both weaknesses and strengths.

"Do not think of yourself more highly than you ought, but rather think of yourself with sober judgment, in accordance with the measure of faith God has given you" (Rom. 12:3).

All of us have our blind spots. This is why the Bible often teaches about our responsibility to speak truth to each other. We need the feedback of others to bring light to a situation: "Therefore each of you must put off falsehood and speak truthfully to his neighbor, for we are all members of one body" (Eph. 4:25). So come to the person not as someone who has it all together, but as someone who has also failed and also needs grace and support.

Without humility, you may take a superior or patronizing tone: "I want to make you aware that sometimes you control the situation in our relationship and others. I can tell you that because I used to be that way, and I can remember the days before I really grew in that area. That's why I can help you with this." This tone creates a sense that you are looking down at the person from your high position of growth, and it can cut her off from wanting to pursue the issue with you.

Humility has to do with perceiving yourself as you really are, with both weaknesses and strengths.

A better approach might be this: "I want to make you aware that sometimes you control the situation in our relationship and others. Please don't misunderstand where I'm coming from here. This isn't about putting you down or saying that I'm better. I have many things I've been working on for some time, so I'm in the same position you are. My intent is to let you know about the control problem, not as a judge, but as a friend."

Empathize

When you make someone aware of a problem, empathize with him. Empathy is the ability to identify with the feelings of another person. Think of times when someone was unloving or harsh with you, when he told you about a problem you had that you were unaware of. Think also of those occasions in which someone made you aware of a problem and you were able to receive it well. Most likely the second person gave you empathy and warmth along with the truth.

When we are out of touch with our hearts, we often cannot give the person the empathy he needs. We may say things like "I can't believe you don't know you are doing this" or "Are you that clueless?" These approaches hurt people and keep them from receiving feedback.

When you are aware of your own needs for empathy and kindness, the dynamic between you and the other person changes: "I want you to be aware of your financial irresponsibility, because if

I were in your position, I would want someone to tell me. I would hope someone would care enough about my situation to take a chance and approach me on it. That is how I feel about you. I'm on your side, and I know that hearing about this is not easy for you. Hang in there with me."

Find Out How Unaware Is Unaware

Understand how aware a person is about herself and her effect on others. Some people, for various reasons, have little self-awareness; they possess little ability to look at themselves and perceive what they are doing or why they are doing it. They have often not had many relational experiences in which they had to look at themselves. This type of person has usually suffered from her lack of awareness. She may have lost romantic, relational, or career opportunities due to her inability to check and correct herself.

You may need to shepherd a person like this into the world of awareness. She may not fully understand what you are telling her. Don't be impatient with her. Say something like "I want to let you know that what you do affects me for good and for bad. When you are kind to me, I feel loved and close. But when you snap at me for giving you directions, you hurt my feelings, and I shut down." This clarity and specificity gives the person some association between her behaviors and her relationship with you.

Another type of person, however, may be acutely aware of himself and his faults and mistakes and may also be quite self-critical. At the same time, he may possess a blind spot. He may not be aware, for example, that he shuts people out emotionally or that he can be controlling.

With an otherwise aware person, you probably do not need to say much for him to understand. In fact, you may need to be careful not to join with any critical voices in his head by saying, "You are really weak in this area." This can make a self-critical problem worse. Instead, you are likely to get awareness and even gratitude from this type of person by gently pointing out what you know: "I want to make you aware of a problem. First, however, I want you to know I realize that this is not all of you. There are so many more good parts of you. And even this part is not as bad as it could be." Thus you help preserve his grounding in love and help him correct himself without self-hatred.

Another type of person has an investment in not being aware of her behavior. She may be afraid to look at herself out of a concern that she is a very bad person; she may carry a sense of entitlement leading her to think she should not have to be aware of herself; or she may attribute what she does to people to other things, for example, blaming her tardiness on the traffic instead of on not leaving early enough to get to her destination on time.

With this person you may need to not only attempt to make her aware of a problem, but also make her aware that she has difficulty being aware. If this is not brought into the open, you run the risk of finding yourself never able to get into the heart of that person.

If you find that the person shies away from awareness, you might approach him in this manner: "I want to talk to you about your job instability. I think it is a serious problem, but I don't know how to approach you with it, because you tend to dismiss my feelings and opinions about something when you don't think you have a problem. It makes it very difficult for me to bring things up to you, and it distances me from you. I'm concerned that you're also hurting yourself. I would like for you to be open to my thoughts about this." If the person has the capacity to feel safe enough to listen to you, this direct but relational approach can often work.

Be Direct

When you need to make someone aware of a problem, the best approach is always to be loving but direct.

If a person does not know what he is doing, it is no favor to him to hint around or be indirect about what you know is true. Remember that he is blind to this behavior, so he has no context for understanding it. The clearer you are, the better his chances of seeing what you are saying about him. That is how God is with us. Though God is full of grace, he does not leave room for confusion or misinterpretation about his confrontations. As Jesus says to his

church about its shortcomings: "I have a few things against you" (Rev. 2:14).

> *To make someone*
> *aware of a problem,*
> *the best approach is always*
> *to be loving but direct.*

We often are indirect out of a desire to be kind or to not hurt the person's feelings. Yet, sparing feelings now can lead to injuries later. It is certainly possible that you will cause the person you are confronting discomfort or pain. This is one of the effects of the truth: It makes us uncomfortable as it points out a problem. However, your directness can also give life to someone who needs it.

Try to avoid the following examples of indirectness and the pitfalls they entail:

> **Indirect:** "Do you think you might want to pick me up on time tonight?"
>
> **Better:** "Please pick me up on time tonight."
>
> **Indirect:** "I really like it when you put your dirty dishes in the dishwasher."
>
> **Better:** "Please put your dirty dishes in the dishwasher, not in the sink."
>
> **Indirect:** "Doesn't that bother you when you are so mean to me?"
>
> **Better:** "Please don't correct me in front of our guests."
>
> **Indirect:** "Are you sure you want to buy this DVD player?"
>
> **Better:** "Please don't buy that DVD player. We can't afford it."

The person being confronted can interpret these approaches as suggestions or ideas, not as problems you want him to be aware of.

He could easily listen to and appreciate the statements, yet not give them the weight of a true problem.

Rather, in a clear and undistorted fashion, present the person with the reality you want him to be aware of:

"I want you to know that when I try to bring up a problem, you dismiss me."

"Your drinking hurts you and gets in the way of our relationship."

"When you make promises and don't keep them, it causes a real problem, and I think it could get worse."

"I have noticed a behavior pattern in you that really concerns me. You lash out at me without thinking."

These confrontations are more likely to bring the person the awareness you seek.

Be Specific

Using specific examples can help a person become aware she has a problem. If it is a significant problem, you will in all likelihood be able to come up with many examples that can illustrate both that the person does have the problem and that it negatively affects her life and relationships.

Specifics add substance and meaning to your presentation of a problem. They flesh out what you are trying to convey and clarify the point you are trying to make. The Scriptures contain many instances of how God gives specifics to make his people aware of what they are doing: "The people of the land practice extortion and commit robbery; they oppress the poor and needy and mistreat the alien, denying them justice" (Ezek. 22:29).

When you use specific examples, approach the person anticipating that at first she is likely to be open to what you have to show her. Give her the benefit of the doubt. Often a goodhearted person will be surprised at seeing evidence of a problem. Sometimes she will even be remorseful, feeling bad about the effects of her actions. These types of responses are good indicators that the person is taking the specifics to heart and will do something to resolve the issue.

Even if the person proves to be more resistant, however, don't avoid giving specifics. Specifics can help break through defenses. But if he is invested in not realizing or admitting his problem, you will need not only to use specifics, but also to address the underlying resistance (see chapter 18).

Specifics can be objective, verifiable information, or they can be personal and emotional in nature. Objective information—times, dates, and descriptions of events—can help bring the picture into focus for the person. Emotional information such as feelings and impressions can reach his heart. Here are some examples of using specifics in making a person aware of a problem:

"Thursday I asked you to pick up Dylan from soccer, but Pam had to bring him home because you never showed up."

"At the restaurant, you were so rude that the Thompsons told me they don't want to go out with us again."

"You got so angry last weekend that you hit the wall in the living room."

"Three times in the last month, when I disagreed with you on where to go out to dinner, you withdrew and were surly for a couple of hours."

"The last time I remember you taking any initiative to connect with me and our relationship was in November, when you went for a walk with me."

"Your work attendance and performance dropped significantly last year. Here are the numbers."

"When I wanted to be with you last night, you changed the subject and turned away from me."

Avoid the use of global or vague examples and terminology that do not convey the clarity you need. They may also communicate that the person and problem are worse than they truly are:

"You never show any interest in me."

"You have no respect for other people's feelings at all."

"Every time we talk, you don't try to work things out."

"You can't go shopping without overspending."

Spend some time thinking through and selecting the examples that can best provide the "aha" experience for the person in your life.

Making a Person Aware of the Effects

Part of helping someone know what he is doing is making him aware of the effects of his behavior. This approach helps to change your confrontation from an abstraction to something more personal and real; the problem does not exist in a vacuum. Often, when a person finds out he is hurting himself and others, it touches him at a heart level. You are showing him what he is doing in the context of his life and relationships. This might include your concerns about both the present effects and also what could happen in the future if things do not change. There are three areas of effects you can bring up:

The Effect on Him

Tell him what you see as the results of his behavior or attitude in his own life. You care about him and do not want the problem to hurt his quality of life, his goals and dreams, his health, and so on.

Be careful you do not bring up effects on him that only you care about. If these are not pertinent to him, you are less likely to make him aware: "You may not be able to be stable enough to get a wife and family and settle down." If he enjoys being single, this confrontation might not convince him to become more career-oriented.

Instead, bring up what means something to him: "I want to make you aware that you seem to be off track in pursuing your job and career path. This could have a bad effect on your life. I know you have dreams and passions about doing something meaningful and interesting with your talents. But I'm concerned that if you continue to ignore a career track, you may lose the opportunities you would like to have for your work."

The Effect on You

Often, when you show a person how what he is doing is affecting you, it can help him become more aware of the problem. Many people avoid being aware of some issue by employing the mentality that says, *I'm not hurting anyone but myself, and that's my choice.* However, more often than not, others are being compromised.

God created us to matter to each other. The nature of relationship is that our lives and hearts intersect with one another, even in suffering: "If one part suffers, every part suffers with it" (1 Cor. 12:26). When you show the person how you are being affected, the care and connection he has with you can help him understand that this is an important issue.

Do not make the mistake of overstating the effects of his actions. This distortion can lead him to either feel guilty or simply negate what you are saying. Talk about the effects of his behavior on you. Avoid confrontations with tones such as "You spend so much time with your buddies away from the family. This is devastating to me, and I do not know if I can survive" or "I can't be happy or complete in my life if you continue being negative with me."

Rather, make the person aware realistically and directly of his effect on you:

"Your lack of interest in spiritual matters distances me from you."

"You hurt my feelings when you are critical."

"You tend to overrun my opinion, and when you do that, I get angry with you and don't feel as if you care."

"When you try to be the life of the party, I feel disconnected from the person I know and love."

The Effect on Others

You can also increase a person's awareness by providing information about the problem's effect on other people. This approach accesses the care he feels for those in his life who matter to him. This can include relationships such as

- Spouse or date
- Friends
- Children
- Parents
- Other relatives
- Neighbors
- Coworkers

For example, I have known many addicts who only became aware that they had a problem when they found out how miserable they were making their children. Their love for their children made it safe to look at what they were doing. A powerful example of this is a formal intervention, used in situations such as alcoholism or addiction. (See the first type of awareness situation below.)

Request Change

When helping a person become aware, make sure you make a request for change. Since she has not realized until now that her behavior or attitude is a problem, she may also not know what to do about it or even if she should do anything. Requesting change helps clarify what is expected and gives her a structure for reestablishing any connection between you and her.

A request for change is specific. It also preserves freedom. In other words, it is not a demand; you are aware that the person has a choice. Also, a request should originate from your heart; it needs to be based on your care for and about the person. Here are some ways to ask for change:

"I would like for you to start attending my church small group with me."

"I want you to work on doing what you say you will do, so that I can rely on you. Maybe we can establish a cookie jar fund that we both contribute to when we don't follow through."

"When I am talking, I would like for you to let me finish my thoughts and sentences before responding."

"I need for you to work on your anger; it scares me and the kids. There is a counselor I want you to see this week."

TYPES OF AWARENESS SITUATIONS

When you want to help a person become aware of a problem, know what sort of situation you are in because different contexts require different approaches. Below are three scenarios, with ways to approach each.

1. For the Other's Own Good, with No Self-Interest on Your Part

In this scenario you see a problem you want the other person to become aware of, but it does not directly affect your life. For example:

- You are the adult child of an alcoholic in denial. You are not dependent on your parent any longer, but you are concerned.
- You have a married friend who appears close to having an affair.
- Your teenaged son is hanging out with a rough crowd, and his grades are dropping.

In situations like these, make sure that you orient your confrontation toward the person's welfare, not your own. He is the one who is hurting himself. While you certainly suffer through your empathy for him and you want him to know how the problem affects you emotionally, the purpose of the confrontation should be more structured toward his getting help for himself.

"Your drinking is causing problems for your health, your relationships, and your work. I want you to get help."

"I am concerned about what is happening in your relationship with Bill. I know you care about him, but I want you to be aware of all the risks you are taking with your marriage, your family, and your faith."

"I know you don't think there is anything wrong with your friends and your grades, but there is a lot wrong. I want you to make choices, but the choices you have been making are affecting you in very negative ways. I am going to have to insist that we deal with this as a big problem."

A serious example of this type of situation is a *formal intervention*, in which a person has a problem that could ruin his life, yet he is not aware of what he is doing. In the intervention process, things are arranged so that a surprise meeting is set up in which those closest to him (family, friends, neighbors, etc.) show up where he is. They have him sit down, and they sit in a circle around him. He is asked not to talk or respond.

Then each person in the circle individually tells him, sometimes from a prepared statement, how his behavior has affected her or his life. A daughter will talk about how she felt when her dad showed up drunk at the prom. A co-worker will tell him how his drinking impacts the company. A mother will talk about her sadness at seeing her son wreck his life. These statements can often help a person break through his denial and admit to himself that he actually does have a problem. Then they ask him to go get treatment for his problem. Sometimes his luggage is packed and the taxi to the rehab center is waiting outside.

The group may also tell him that if he refuses, they will disengage from their relationship with him and will stay disconnected until he agrees to get help. Interventions are a powerful last resort to deal with someone who is in danger of doing serious harm to himself. They are emotionally intense. Often the person with the problem will have strong reactions, ranging from rage about being exposed to deep remorse over what he has done and gratitude that people care so much about him.

Interventions are complex and are backed by much research. They are often run by professionals who have specific training in intervention approaches and who then train the family and friends in what to do. If you are in this situation, find an intervention specialist and let her take you through the process. Your chances for success are much better with a professional.

2. For the Other's Good, with Self-Interest on Your Part

In other instances, a person's problem has a direct impact on your life. That is, the person you are confronting needs to be aware for herself and for the relationship you have with her. Here are some situations that have direct impact on the lives of others:

- A husband whose emotional self-interest is so severe that you can no longer feel the love you had for him, and you worry about your marriage's survival.
- A date who becomes highly angry and critical when you disagree with her. You care about her, but she hurts you deeply.
- A co-worker whose irresponsibility has led to poor performance, and his performance affects evaluations made about you.

In these scenarios you are concerned for both your sakes; therefore confront the other person with both of you in mind. You want her to be aware of what is going on from the standpoint of both her own interest and her care and attachment to you:

"You are responsible and a good provider. But you have a serious problem with not being able to get outside of yourself. The kids and I can't relate to you anymore because you won't look at anyone else's point of view. I am concerned that you are losing them and that they are withdrawing from you more and more. I know it is affecting your work and friendships. And I am starting to lose the love I have for you. I can't overstate how afraid I am about our marriage and my own feelings toward you. I want you to get some help with me very soon."

"When we don't see things the same way, a part of you I don't know comes out, and I'm not sure even you know it. You get enraged, you put me down, you even seem to lose control. This can't be good for you—emotionally, spiritually, or relationally. And it really hurts me inside. I feel like you hate me and want to put me down. I have to recover from being with you after one of those sessions. It is starting to make me question if we should keep seeing each other. I need for you to be aware that this is a real problem."

"I want you to be aware that you have a serious problem getting reports in on time. I know this has impacted your evaluations, and that has got to be hard for you. At the same time, since we are on the team together, your performance affects me. I have received bad evaluations myself, due to your lateness with reports. This is irresponsible of you, and it is really bad for both of us. I want us to brainstorm together about a way you can become timelier. I want to stay on the team with you, but if this doesn't improve, I will ask to be transferred off this team."

These confrontations maintain a balanced focus on the person's situation as well as yours. This approach can open her eyes to the seriousness of what she is doing.

3. The Person Is Aware, But Sees No Need to Change

The final goal of awareness is *repentance*. In other words, the person truly changes his mind about what he is doing and subsequently changes his life. John the Baptist said, "Produce fruit in keeping with repentance" (Matt. 3:8). That is how issues are best solved and relationships reconciled.

In some situations, however, the person may realize what he is doing, be aware that you think it is a problem, and even know that it is a problem, but he experiences no need to change or repent.

This can be a serious issue, as you can't rely on his awareness alone to reach his heart and move him to change. Something else may be broken inside him, such as distortions in his perception of how bad a problem is, an inability to feel empathy for others, or self-centeredness. What often happens then is that *someone else begins experiencing the effects of a problem he should be owning.* This can be disastrous for lots of people. Here are some examples:

- A husband with an Internet pornography problem. You have discovered it and have confronted him, but he says it is not really a problem.
- A wife who overspends. You fear the financial repercussions and want to solve the problem, but she laughs it off and says you need to lighten up.
- A friend who puts you in the middle of her problems with others. She avoids telling other people how she feels, but goes to you. You don't like the position you are put in, but she keeps doing it.

Though these problems can be discouraging, you can do things to help. You will need to structure your confrontation with the person in a way that addresses their lack of concern.

- Make sure you are unambiguous about your concern. You do not want him to be confused or uninformed.

- Address her lack of concern as a problem in and of itself. Bring up how her lack of interest in changing makes you feel and how it affects the relationship.
- If she persists in doing nothing, establish limits and boundaries to protect yourself and others from her problem and to make her responsible for the problem.

These elements give you the best possible chance for helping the person. Here are some examples of what to say:

"I know you think the pornography is not an issue, but that's not true. It's a major problem. I am concerned about your own emotional and spiritual well-being; I am afraid you are addicted. And I am afraid for myself; I am devastated inside. I feel betrayed, unloved, and deceived. I don't even know how I feel about us anymore. This has turned my world upside down. Yet you persist in thinking it is not affecting me or us. I am going to insist that we deal with this, and deal with it now. I want to be clear with you on this: I will not tolerate pornography in our home. If you don't agree to stop now and get help, I will take some serious steps to deal with this."

"The reality is that, though you think I am just being cheap, I have examined your spending with our accountant. We are running the risk of not having enough money for our kids' college education or for our retirement. It is becoming serious, and I want you to take it seriously. When you shrug it off, it angers me and makes me feel that my opinion doesn't mean much to you. I want us to be financially accountable to each other. But if you insist on going your own way, I will have to start protecting our family's finances from your spending, until you change."

"I'm sorry for the problems you are having with Nancy and Beth. But as I've mentioned before, I should not be the person you go to about them. You need to go directly to them. I am very uncomfortable with being in the middle, because it involves both of us in gossip, and I don't want to have anything to do with that. It bothers me that you don't seem to think gossip is a problem and you keep bringing these matters to me. I am afraid that if you don't stop, I will have to limit our time together until you can solve this."

These are hard lines to draw, but they are often the most effective approach. If this is your situation, make sure you have the support of others behind you so you can say and do what you need to. Remember, also, that all of us need to repent at many, many points in our lives. God is intimately involved in helping us change our minds about many things: "I have not come to call the righteous, but sinners to repentance" (Luke 5:32). Ask the God who calls us all to help you with the person you are confronting.

FAY REVISITED

Let's return now to Fay, who probably could have benefited from a loving confrontation. Here is an example of how someone could have confronted her:

"Fay, we love seeing you at our get-togethers. You add so much to our lives. But I wanted to mention a problem that happens. It's not a huge thing, but it is significant enough that I would like to clear it up.

"There are times when, during people's conversations, you change the topic to something about yourself. We love hearing about your life, but sometimes it makes it hard for others. I would really like it if you would stay more with what people are discussing and share about yourself at about the same rate others do.

"I really don't want to hurt your feelings on this, and I always want you to feel welcome. Are you okay with this, or does

it cause a problem for you in some way? I'd like to know,
because I don't want this to cause you difficulty."

If Fay could hear this in the spirit in which it is meant, it
might make for much more enjoyable connections at the family
gatherings.

Another important situation is when a troublesome behavior or
attitude continues, with no sign of resolving. In the next chapter
we will provide an approach to confront this situation construc-
tively so that things can improve.

17

Stopping
a Behavior

Linda called our radio show upset about her husband. When we asked what the problem was, she said that whenever she and her husband went out, he would stare at other women. If a pretty woman walked by, he would all but fall out of his chair, following her with his eyes. Linda would feel ignored. When Linda mentioned to him how uncomfortable his behavior made her feel, he tried to make it seem normal and sometimes even blamed her for it. "What are you talking about?" he would say. "I don't do that. Besides, if you would get into shape, maybe I wouldn't notice other women. Have you thought of that?" Linda ended up feeling sad and hopeless. Trying to talk about the problem ended up nowhere, so she had stopped bringing it up.

But the night before she called us, something else had happened that brought the problem to the surface again. She had awakened in the night, and her husband was not in bed. She decided to go see what he was doing, and she found him at the computer looking at pornography sites on the Internet. Now the "looking at other women" had gone too far. She felt she had to do something, but with their history of blow-ups she didn't know how to proceed.

"What did you do?" we asked.

"I told him that he was a pervert and that this is what I've been saying all along. I just told him I couldn't stand to be around him and went to bed and cried the rest of the night. I have been awake all night and don't know what to do."

"Have you talked to him since last night?"

"No, and I don't know what to say, either. I don't know if I am more sad or angry. I just feel lousy inside. What should I do?" We could hear the desperation in her voice.

Think for a moment about this question: Is anyone in your life doing something you would like him or her to quit doing? It is probably easy to think of someone who does something that bothers you. In fact, given enough time, you could think of more than one person. For most people, there are several situations in life where a relationship would go better if someone would stop doing a particular thing. For others, it goes beyond "things would go better" — it could mean a relationship or even a person's life would be saved.

Generally, behavior you would like stopped falls into one of four categories:

1. If he stopped doing it, you would stop being bothered or hurt.
2. If she stopped doing it, your relationship would improve.
3. If he stopped doing it, he would be better off.
4. If she stopped doing it, other people would stop being hurt or be better off.

Not all things are as hurtful as what Linda's husband was doing. Some things that require talking about can be quite small. Consider the following possibilities, large and small, ranging anywhere from annoying to life threatening:

- Tardiness
- Hurtful attitudes
- Addictions
- Verbal or physical abuse
- Irresponsibility
- Controlling behavior
- Betrayal or unfaithfulness
- Dishonesty
- Abusing a friend or family member's generosity

- Messiness
- Overspending and financial problems
- Insensitivity
- Passivity or lack of follow-through on promises
- Disrespect

The list could go on and on. There is no shortage of ways people hurt each other. But we have all avoided confronting some people when we should have, and when we have mustered up the courage to broach the subject with someone, the conversation has not gone well. In this chapter we look at principles to apply to that difficult conversation when the issue is that person's behavior. It can be one of the stickiest situations you ever have to deal with, but it can also be one of the most redemptive.

PREPARE BEFORE YOU CONFRONT

Linda told us more about her situation as we continued to talk. She told us the ways she had confronted and not confronted her husband over the years. He sounded like a real problem character. But as she talked, I had two feelings I often have in situations like this. First, I was sad that things had gone the way they had, and second, I was hopeful that things might work out differently with a different kind of confrontation, one in which she was better prepared. One thing that reduces the chances of a good outcome is a lack of preparation, which we discuss in chapters 19 and 20.

We want to emphasize just one of those principles here. One of the best maps for confronting another person about his behavior comes from the book of Micah: "He has showed you, O man, what is good. And what does the LORD require of you? To act justly and to love mercy and to walk humbly with your God" (Micah 6:8).

If you prepare before the confrontation and remember this stance as you go in, the chances of a helpful outcome are much greater than if you just "fly by the seat of your pants" or react and confront "in the moment," as Linda had done over the years. Let's take a look at this three-pronged approach to confrontation.

1. Act justly
2. Love mercy
3. Walk humbly with your God

One thing "act justly" means for our discussion is that justice, or what is right and good, is important. In other words, when something is wrong, we should move to address it. In the realm of relationships, we need to "judge" each other in the good sense of the word, the way Paul uses it when he tells us that we are responsible to judge each other's behavior and speak the truth to each other in love (1 Cor. 5:12; Eph. 4:15). Paul says we will grow if we do that. And, as the proverb reminds us, "whoever heeds correction gains understanding" (Prov. 15:32). Obviously, this requires that someone do a confrontation.

So, when you prepare to confront someone's behavior, remember that it is a good thing for you to do. It is the right thing, and it is a helpful thing. This will keep you honest in the confrontation and will help you avoid the tendency to minimize the problem or the issue or to not take a firm enough stand against whatever is wrong. Remembering this will help you to "go all the way" and not hold back.

To "love mercy" primarily signals kindness and compassion. It means to bow to someone in kindness, favor, and good deeds—in other words, to be "good" to them, showing understanding and love. It is very easy to be "mean" in exercising justice, since the truth can be tough on people. But to "love mercy" says that in administering truth in confrontation, we must be kind and compassionate as well as honest. In our "judging" we don't judge in a condemning way. We do it in an "evaluative" way without condemnation.

When you put these two qualities together, as God suggests, there is much greater possibility for things going well than if you were only administering justice or only giving mercy. We all need the integration of the two. If someone is going to be able to use confrontation, he must know that the confronter is "for him" and not "against him." The best description I know of this combination came from a friend of mine who said

Go hard on the issue and soft on the person.

he does it this way: *Go hard on the issue and soft on the person.*

If you stay firm on the issue and go soft on the person's feelings and heart, you are more likely to get a good outcome. Then add the third side of the triangle: Walk humbly with God.

This means that you do not assume the role of God the Judge, condemning the person or meting out punishment. Instead, in your "evaluating," you identify with the person you are confronting as a fellow imperfect struggler and do not "lord it over him." You remain an equal.

Also, to be humble before God means you are answerable to him, open to correction by him about your attitudes, and "fearful" of him in the good sense that he is "chaperoning" the process. If we are hurt or angry, we might be tempted to deal with those feelings destructively if we did not have God telling us to "be nice." It helps us when we desire to walk in God's ways and be like him.

So put this attitude into action when you confront, and you have a better chance of a good and redemptive outcome.

KNOW WHEN TO CONFRONT AND WHEN TO LET GO

One thing some people don't do very well is evaluate the appropriateness of a confrontation. In today's culture of people growing and learning how not to "enable," some are like kids with a new toy. They feel as if every behavior they do not like should be confronted, or that every behavior that is not okay should be confronted all the time. This can be a problem.

There is a time for confronting and a time for letting go. Some people have expectations out of line for where a person is in his spiritual growth or maturity cycle. Suppose, for example, that a woman's husband is uninvolved in spiritual growth and leadership in the family. It turns out that a depression has paralyzed him and kept him from taking on this role. It would be wiser at this point for the wife to talk to him about getting help for his emotional problem than to confront him for not being a leader. In addition, a person might be stopping a behavior on his own, and we would do well to be patient and thankful for his being on the path.

So before confronting, ask yourself, "Is this the proper time for this? Are there other issues this person needs to understand first? Does she need to feel safer before I bring this up?" Evaluate carefully both the person and the relationship to know whether or not this is the time to confront.

Some things are not worth the fight. Remember that the relationship is what is important, and if a particular stand will win you a skirmish but cause you to lose the war, then you might do well to wait. As Proverbs says, "A man's wisdom gives him patience; it is to his glory to overlook an offense" (Prov. 19:11). Sometimes a person can be offensive, but there is a larger issue to work on, so we just let it go.

CLARIFY YOUR MOTIVES

We have a lot more to say about motives in chapter 20, but here we want to emphasize that when you clarify your motives—the "why" or the purpose of the confrontation—you can really affect the outcome. In general terms, here are good motives for a confrontation in which you want someone to stop doing something:

- You confront to help yourself—the person's behavior is causing a problem for you.

- You confront to help the relationship — the person's behavior is causing a breakdown in intimacy or the workability of the relationship.
- You confront to help the other person — stopping the behavior would be good for him or her.
- You confront to help third parties — the person's behavior is hurting others.

When you know why you are confronting, it helps you stay focused on the issue.

I (Henry) was doing a seminar one night, and during the question-and-answer session, a woman raised her hand and said she wanted to talk to her dad about his attitudes. When I asked her why, she said she wanted him to experience the kinds of growth she had experienced. I suggested that we role-play her conversation with her dad. She played herself, and I was her dad.

She opened by saying how much she cared for her dad and how she wanted him to learn and experience the good things she had experienced. That is why she wanted to talk to him. It sounded good. But as she went on, she talked almost exclusively about herself — how she had been hurt by him, how critical and mean he was, and how she wanted him to change.

Before long, I stopped her and asked, "Wait a minute! Who is this for? I thought you were trying to help your dad here. It sounds to me like you're trying to get a lot of things off your chest. I as your dad am not experiencing a lot of help!"

We talked about what she had said, and she could see that her conversation was confused in intent and purpose. She had said that the conversation was supposed to be for the good of her dad, but it was really focused on her good, not his. I told her it was perfectly legitimate to talk to her dad about her hurt in the relationship and to seek understanding, forgiveness, and reconciliation. But don't act as if that is a mission to help him.

When you clarify inside yourself the purpose of the confrontation, you will be much clearer and more focused in the talk itself.

UNDERSTAND
THE THREE POSSIBLE REACTIONS
TO CONFRONTATION

We began the book with a positive vision of the value of confrontation. We looked at all the good things it can produce in life and in a relationship. In fact, there is no such thing as a good relationship without confrontation.

Remember that confrontation doesn't always go smoothly, and it may not even end "well" — if you define "well" as everyone singing "Kumbayah" and in a love feast. But even when it does not, confrontation can have great value as a start, or even as one of many in a series of conversations a person may receive over time. When she hears the same song over and over again, one day she may experience a breakthrough. And you will have been a part of that "chain of truth." So don't be dismayed if a confrontation doesn't go smoothly or end "well."

Basically three things can happen. First, you can be received well, the person gets it, and it all ends well. As the proverb says, when you rebuke a wise man, he will love you (Prov. 9:8). He even may thank you for it, if he has King David's attitude:

> Let a righteous man strike me — it is a kindness;
> let him rebuke me — it is oil on my head.
> My head will not refuse it (Ps. 141:5).

Or, take Matthew 18:15, which refers to situations where we need to confront someone who has sinned against us. Jesus says, "If he listens to you, you have won your brother over."

Second, you may face resistance, defensiveness, or some other form of opposition. Here is the way Proverbs describes this:

> "Whoever corrects a mocker invites insult;
> whoever rebukes a wicked man incurs abuse.
> Do not rebuke a mocker or he will hate you;
> rebuke a wise man and he will love you" (Prov. 9:7–8).

> A mocker resents correction;
>> he will not consult the wise (Prov. 15:12).
>
> A wise son heeds his father's instruction,
>> but a mocker does not listen to rebuke (Prov. 13.1).

Third, you may face not only resistance, but also retaliation. If this happens, the only thing you can do is protect yourself and take appropriate action. Sometimes, in extreme cases, because this scenario can't be resolved through further confrontation, you may need to hire an attorney or call the police. For example, a person may have repeatedly tried to work with a spouse who is having an affair and is also making moves toward divorce. In these cases, depending on what is going on, the individual could need legal and financial help and, sometimes if there is physical abuse, even protection.

So be prepared for the different possibilities when you confront someone about his or her behavior.

CHOOSE THE RIGHT TIME AND PLACE

Many people make the mistake of confronting an issue with someone when they are in the middle of experiencing it. In tougher conflicts, this may not be the time to have the talk. Too many sparks are flying for it to work well.

Choose another time when things are going more smoothly. At those times, when both of you are less reactive, there is a greater chance of things going well. At a later date, your emotions may not be confused, and you can observe the conflict itself. Cooler heads might prevail.

REACT WITH SHADES OF INTENSITY

A toggle switch is a switch with only two positions: off and on. There are no shades of intensity. There is no increasing speed, as with the gas pedal of your car. A toggle switch is more like a missile; it is either at rest or firing full speed.

Some people react to others' faults like a toggle switch. No matter what has happened, they come on full strength or not at all. They react the same to a small thing as to a big thing. Someone being late for a date incurs the same amount of wrath and distress as if the person had had an affair.

Remember, there are levels of faults, hurts, and transgressions. It is not true that "all sin is sin." As Jesus said, there are "more important matters of the law—justice, mercy and faithfulness" (Matt. 23:23). In other words, there are spiritual and relational felonies as well as misdemeanors. Check yourself to see if you are having the appropriate level of concern for what is happening. Don't confront smacking one's lips at the dinner table with the same force you would lying or stealing. And don't minimize lying and stealing as if it were merely smacking.

I saw a good relationship between two people break up because the woman did not have the ability to react with different levels of intensity to the man's imperfections. No matter what he did, large or small, she came at him full force. Finally he grew tired of having a nuclear war over small issues. It was sad to see, and if she had understood this concept, they might have made it.

DISTINGUISH BETWEEN
WHAT YOU PREFER
AND WHAT'S WRONG

Before you talk to someone about changing his behavior, figure out if what he is doing is really a "bad" thing or just something you don't like. I refer to this as the "God and the Beverly Hillbillies Would Agree" test. Some things are just things you don't like and want someone to change, but that person is not really doing anything wrong. Depending on where you come from, it may be acceptable or not. What is fine to Jed Clampet might be very distasteful to you. He might keep a raccoon inside the house, and if your spouse did that, it would really bug you. It is all a matter of taste.

But mistreating people or not taking responsibility for one's actions or morals, both God and even most hillbillies would say is wrong. There is little disagreement about those behaviors. Before you proceed, figure out if what you are bugged about is in the "preference" category or in the "wrong for civilized humans" category. If it is just your preference, realize that you don't have a "higher moral ground" from which to speak. Instead, you are really asking for a favor.

Failure to make this distinction commonly happens in a relationship in which one person is more structured than the other. One may be more orderly, time-conscious, budgeted, or organized than the other. The less structured one is looser and okay with things being more "unraveled." Typically, the structured one feels that her way is the "right" way and approaches the conversation in that fashion. This is usually a disaster. Instead of demanding better behavior from her spouse, what she should be doing is asking to negotiate a compromise — just asking the other person to come her way a bit.

The rules here are similar to those in chapter 15 on telling people what you want. Remember, ask as though you don't have a "right" to what you are asking for; preserve the freedom of the other person to say no or to disagree; and do not judge. You will have a greater chance of getting what you want.

Avoid the Line "We Need to Talk"

Have you ever gotten a voice mail or a message from someone important to you, or with authority over you, and it said, "We need to talk. Please call me?" How did that feel? Did you think you had won the lottery? Or did you have some angst inside, wondering what was up or what you had done to make him angry? Depending on what your experiences in life have been, you can have some pretty anxious anticipation to a line like "We need to talk."

When you are going to confront someone, remember the anxious position in which you are putting her. Put yourself in her shoes, and remember that hearing about one's faults is very unpleasant and may evoke fear. Her past experience with being confronted may have been hurtful, and she may be expecting the same from you. Or she brings a lot of guilt and shame to the table. So, when you are inviting another person to have the talk, try to make it as palatable as possible:

"Can we go for coffee tomorrow? There are some things I think will help our relationship, and I would like to discuss them with you."

This is a lot better than "We need to talk" unless you have the kind of relationship where the other person will take that statement positively.

Sometimes the person will want to know what you want to talk about, but you may not be ready to tell. Men seem particularly eager to know what the topic is and move toward closure. He may push to know: "What's it about?" If you do not feel it is good to go into it then, just tell him you don't want to talk about it until later, but offer some reassurance if appropriate: "It's just some things about how we relate. It's nothing we can't work through, just some stuff. Don't worry."

At other times it is not appropriate to put someone at ease other than to empathize with how it must be for her. For example, if you have had multiple confrontations over the issue or it is very serious, it is not true to say that it is no big deal or that she shouldn't worry. Just empathize and say, "I understand it might be frustrating for me not to go into it now, but I need to wait until tomorrow [or whenever]. I don't feel comfortable talking about it right now, but I'm sorry if that's hard for you."

AFFIRM SOMETHING GOOD

As we mentioned earlier, when you confront something negative, remember the importance of affirming something about the intended outcome or desire for the person, the relationship, or you. The person you are confronting needs to know that you intend good and not evil. Beginning with assurance will help:

> "Joe, I love you and I am committed to our relationship. That's why I want to talk about this issue. I want it to help us get closer."

> "Susan, I want to talk to you, and I want you to hear what I have to say in the spirit in which I mean it. Some things have been concerning me about you, and I mention them in the hopes that they will help you. I am doing this *for* you, not to hurt you."

> "Terry, I don't want you to think I am down on you or on your case. I just want the best for you and for us, and there are some things getting in the way of that."

> "Sam, the reason we have called you here is that we are worried about you. We want the best for you, and we think you are at risk and in danger, so we want to talk. We want to help."

> "Jerry, I want you to know something right off the bat. The things I'm going to say to you may not be easy to hear. I have some serious things to talk about. My hope is that you can listen with an open mind and we can work together toward a good resolution. I want to end up today with our being closer and having more understanding, not less."

There is no right way to give assurance, and in some instances you may not even need to do it. Yet you probably know when affirming and validating would be a good idea. The words are not as important as getting across the message of desiring something good for the person and the relationship. State your end goal of wanting things to be better.

GET SPECIFIC AND BE CLEAR

After setting up the conversation appropriately and affirming the other person, it is time to talk about the issue you want to confront. Be as specific and as clear as possible, using "I" statements when you are talking about yourself and clear "you" statements when talking about the other person. Do not confuse the two. Then there is the issue itself. *Always remember that there are three things on the table: you, the other person, and the issue. Speak appropriately to each one.*

> *There are three things on the table: you, the other person, and the issue. Speak appropriately to each one.*

One way to do this is the old formula of "When you do 'A,' I feel 'B,' and I do not like it, and I don't want that to happen anymore." All three sides of the triangle are there—the "you-issue-me" triangle.

"Joe, what is bothering me is something you do. Since we have been dating, you have increasingly seemed to take me for granted. Let me give you some examples. Last Friday night you had not called all week, and then at 4:00 in the afternoon you called and wanted to know what I wanted to do that night, as if you expected me to be waiting for you. On Monday you left all of your rented ski equipment at my house with a note for me to drop it off at the rental place. You said that it 'had to be there tonight to avoid late fees,' assuming I would just do it. When you do those things, I feel taken for granted. I want you to ask me if you want me to do something, like go out or do a favor, instead of assuming that I will automatically do it."

"Sally, here is why we wanted to talk to you. We are
concerned about your drinking. For a while now, we have
been worried, but lately it has gotten to a point where we
can no longer remain silent if we are truly your friends. We
are concerned for your safety and also for the way that your
drinking is affecting us and our relationship with you. Let me
give you some examples. At Jesse's birthday party you drank
so much you got sick in the bathroom. Before you got sick,
you were loud and disruptive to the point where some people
told us they had decided to leave. As a result, Jesse's birthday
was impacted. In the Christmas committee we all decided
that you would be in charge of dropping the children's gifts
off at the orphanage. When they called us to tell us they had
not gotten them, I called, and you did not answer. I went
over to your house to see if I could get them, thinking you
had forgotten them. When I got there that afternoon, you
were drinking and had forgotten the gifts altogether. Last
Saturday, when we went to dinner, I was totally embarrassed
at the restaurant as you got louder and louder, and everyone
was staring at our table. I could give you other examples, but
those are the things that have led us here today."

"Jared, I want to talk to you about the way you talk to me. I
want you to understand how it hurts me. For example, the
other day when you asked me for the report in the meeting
and I had left it in my office, you said, 'Way to go, Einstein!
Just when we need it.' Or yesterday, when the two of us
and James were together and he asked me about that loan
application, you said, 'She wouldn't know a good rate if it
hit her in the butt.' I don't know what you mean by these
comments, but I want to tell you that I don't like them. They
hurt. I want you to not do that anymore."

"Tom, I want to talk about our sex life. When we have had sex lately, it is not a good experience for me. It feels disconnected. Let me tell you what I mean. You often don't talk to me much in the evening or are sometimes not very nice, and then after we are in bed, you want to make love. Often I am still feeling lonely from the hours we have been together and we haven't talked, even when I have tried. Another example is when you have been critical about dinner or something. We don't talk about it, and I feel far away from you, then you want to have sex. Then I feel *really* far away from you. I want something different. I want us to talk first, so that I can feel as though you are with me and know that we are connected. I want sex to be an experience of closeness, not just something physical."

"Ron, I want to talk to you about how you are using your time here. After you graduated, you moved in to take some time to figure out what you wanted to do, and your mom and I said okay. For a few months now, you haven't gotten a job, and to the best of my observation, you are not making much headway in that department. We have been giving you money as you have needed it, thinking we were helping you to buy time to find out what you want to do. But it seems as if you are not doing that. So I want you to stop spending the days at home or playing basketball and not going on interviews. I want you to submit a deadline of when I can expect you to have a job, so I can feel better about where we are. I feel used. I feel like I am doing my part to help you get started, and you are not doing yours."

In all these examples, the people doing the confronting are clear and direct as to what the problem behavior is. They are not minimizing the problem or beating around the bush.

LISTEN AND SEEK TO UNDERSTAND

After such exchanges, you may get a response that ranges from a total apology and ownership to outright defensiveness and denial. This is an important part of the dialogue. It is good to seek a response, to ask the other person for their perspective on what you have said. Here's how the people in our scenarios might ask for a response:

"What do you think about what I have said, Joe? What is your perspective on it?"

"Sally, I am wondering how you see what I have said and also your view on your drinking."

"Jared, what do you think about how you talk to me?"

"Tom, what do you think about how I feel?"

"Ron, how do you see what you have been doing? I am interested in the way you are viewing it."

The idea here is that a confrontation is not a one-sided conversation. It is a dialogue, and it is important to let the person know that you want to hear their response. We hope you will hear the person exhibiting understanding and ownership or else a good explanation of the behavior that helps you to see it differently. But the other person may become defensive or attempt to get you off track. If this happens, you need to do something that helps you stay centered and on track. The following formula might be helpful.

SPEAK TO THE FEELINGS, THEN RETURN TO THE ISSUE

Sometimes people get really lost in their confrontation because the other person throws them off course.

Remember this formula for response: *Empathize with the other person's feelings or position, and return to your issue. Empathize and return.*

Here is how the confronter can use this formula in our scenarios:

> **Joe:** "What are you talking about? I show you a lot of attention. How can you say I take you for granted? What about all the time we spend together?"
>
> **You:** "I understand that you feel like you show enough respect to me through other ways. I appreciate that. What I am saying is that when you do the things that I just told you about, those are a problem for me. That is what I want you to understand."

Empathize and connect with what the person says, and then *stay clear again on the issue that you want to confront. Do not drift.*

> **Jared:** "What? I can't believe you took what I said like that. You joke around with people more than anyone here. That's hypocritical of you to say that to me."
>
> **You:** "I understand that this is hard for you to see. I am glad you see it as joking and are not trying to be hurtful. What I am telling you, though, and don't want you to miss, is how it affects me. I don't want to be talked to like that."
>
> **Ron:** "That's not true. I have been looking hard for jobs. It's tough out there, and, with the recession, it's hard to find something. No one is hiring. I can't believe you are on my case about this. You have already made it in life, and you have forgotten how hard it is to start. Everything seems so easy to you."

You: "I understand that you are going through a tough
time in life. I do. But let me be clear about what
I want so we don't miss it. I want no more days
spent playing sports while I am paying, and I want
a written plan."

Don't get sidetracked or hooked into an argument. Just empathize with the other person's response, and get back to your point.
Stay centered.

REQUEST SPECIFIC CHANGE

Many times a confrontation begins well, but the person doing the
confronting does not have a specific enough request to bring the
conversation to a fruitful outcome. Instead, feelings only are aired.
Although communicating feelings can be important, solving problems is, too. Figure out ahead of time what changes you want to
request. Ron's dad is a good example of making a specific request
for change. He asked Ron to spend no more days playing instead of
job searching and to give him a specific written plan.

Joe's girlfriend is another good example. She said she wanted
him to ask her in advance if he wanted something. If he wanted to
go out, she wanted him not to assume she would go out with him at
the last minute. If he wanted her to do a favor, she wanted him to
ask ahead of time and not just assume she would do it.

If Sally's friends continued, they might ask for a commitment
from her to go to an Alcoholics Anonymous meeting and get a
sponsor or go into treatment. Or they could just ask that she agree
not to drink anymore in their presence. (This is a requirement she
would probably not be able to keep, but it is specific enough to lead
to further ones such as the requirement for treatment.)

Jared's co-worker could ask that he not make those kinds of comments to her or about her and agree to be open to her letting him
know when he had stepped over the line in his kidding, and then
agree to respect that.

Tom's wife could ask that he check with her whether or not she felt connected before he makes a sexual advance.

Sometimes you may need to ask a person not only to stop a specific behavior, but also to deal with the larger picture. The request for Sally to go to treatment is an example. For another, the wife of a sex addict may ask her husband not only to stop looking at pornography, but also to attend a sexual addiction group, see a pastor or counselor, or take some other action that shows he is committed to dealing with the problem. This step is usually used after repeated requests for a change in behavior. If Ron does not get a job, his dad may ask him to attend a resume coaching class or a job fair or something else to address the problem if he is going to continue to allow him to live there. By making more extensive requests like these, one gets closer to the end goal of stopping the problem's effects on others.

Again, there are no "right" requests. Each situation is different, and at times you may not even have a request for change. But if you are serious about wanting a problem solved, be specific about what you want so the other person can know what to do and both of you will be able to tell whether or not it has been done.

IF LIMITS APPLY, COMMUNICATE THEM

Often, in these kinds of confrontations, things have gotten to the point where limits are needed. If denial or defensiveness in the above scenarios could not be worked through, then it may be time for limits. Limits come in many forms, but a few are very important and most common.

The first is that you are not going to allow yourself to participate in the behavior anymore. The limit is on yourself.

"Joe, I won't allow myself to go out when I feel taken for
granted. So if you call at the last minute, I won't go. Or if you
leave things for me to do without asking ahead of time, I will
not do them."

"Sally, we want you to no longer drink in our presence, and we want you to get some help. If you do drink, we will leave the party and won't be seeing you again until you do something about your problem."

"Jared, if this continues, I will leave the situation and not talk to you until you acknowledge the problem and apologize. I can't stop you, but I don't have to participate."

"Tom, if you don't try to see where I am or listen when I try to tell you, I won't participate in sex when I feel hurt or alone."

"Ron, if you do continue to play on the days when you are supposed to be searching for a job, or if I don't get a written plan for job seeking by Saturday, I won't be giving you money any more or offering my house."

Another limit involves consequences that go further than setting limits with what you will participate in.

"Joe, if you don't see this and stop doing it, we will have to take a break from each other so I can think about what I want to do next."

"Sally, if we see you drive after you have been drinking, we will call the police."

"Jared, if you continue to do this, I will go to human resources and file a grievance."

"Tom, if we can't get on the same page here, I will talk about it only with a counselor."

"Ron, if you don't stick to your deadline, you are out."

It is sad when a relationship comes to the point where setting limits and consequences are needed. But sometimes, as we wrote in *Boundaries*, this is the only time a relationship begins to change. If it does not change, at least the hurt and destruction is limited either for you, for the other person (like Sally and Ron), or for others.

MAKE A PLAN FOR AFTER THE CONVERSATION

If necessary, make a plan for what will happen after the conversation. This is needed particularly if there has been a continuing pattern and you question the person's willingness or ability to change the behavior. Many times, the person being confronted will give a very sincere, or sincere-sounding, apology and the confrontation ends, but the behavior reappears soon thereafter. Obviously, it takes time to change, but sometimes the other person exhibits a pattern of non-change as opposed to an imperfect path of true change. So it is wise to be prepared for noncompliance.

One of the best ways to do this is to pose a question.

> "I appreciate your apology and your concern for this. I'm glad you are committing to doing it differently. I look forward to that. But what do you think we should do if you do it again? What do you suggest I do at that point?"

The options can range from "Remind me," which is totally legitimate and helpful for someone on the path of true change, to consequences with someone who is not.

> "How about if I let you know if I notice it again. Will you be open to hearing that?

> "Thanks for saying you will do it. I hope that happens. But I have to tell you that if it doesn't happen, I will follow through on leaving the house until you can get back in control of your anger."

In very difficult situations such as addictions, infidelity, or physical abuse, the person being confronted should be required to commit to a process that addresses the cause of the problem. Then, if she drops out of the process, other consequences apply.

The best scenarios are the ones where both agree to a plan. "Let me know if I make you feel that way again" is a great response to a confrontation. So create a plan and ask for buy-in on it.

"I appreciate that you want this to change. How do you feel about our having a plan of what to do if it occurs again? I would suggest _____."

As you plan to have a difficult conversation with someone, remember this principle: There is a future, and you do well to know ahead of time what you are going to do with it. Many options are available. If the problem is a one-time occurrence and you are with a "wise person" who sees the problem and commits to solving it, a plan is probably not necessary. Unless she needs some help seeing where she is wrong again, she will follow through on her own. With others, you would do well to have a preset plan for the future.

Remember also, as we saw in chapter 14, that forgiveness for the past does not mandate trust in the future. The confrontation itself might structure what has to occur for the other person to get back into the "trusted" category. One of the biggest problems we see is people hearing a "sorry" and letting an unchanged person back into a position of power over their heart. With serious breaches of trust, be more careful.

> **You:** "Thanks for your apology. I forgive you. But we have to talk about what has to change before I can make myself vulnerable to you again. I want to see you committed to recovery for a while and engaged in the program. And then, in X amount of time, we can look at getting back together day to day. Until then, we will only be talking in the counselor's office."
>
> **Other person:** "But, but, but...."
>
> **You:** "I understand that this is difficult for you and that the waiting will be hard [empathy]. I need to do this to make sure things are changing [restate your position].

LOOK FOR BUY-IN

Trust and reconciliation after a confrontation result from the other person's taking ownership of her problem and its effects on you. (See the next chapter for dealing with defensive responses.) But remember, if the other person does not take ownership of the problem, the past will repeat itself.

When the other person blames you, excuses herself, or minimizes the problem, empathize with her view of the problem, but return to your position.

> "I understand that you feel justified in what you did. No matter why you did it, it is not okay. I want to know that you can see that, so I can know it is not going to happen again."

BE PATIENT—BUT NOT ALWAYS

How long has it taken you to get to your level of maturity? Are there still some areas in which you fail? Aren't you glad that God and others are giving you time to get it right? I think we all are.

However, sometimes we are not so patient with others. We sometimes expect instant change or no slip-ups. We don't give each other time to change. What should you do? How many times should you forgive? Jesus had an answer to that question: "If your brother sins, rebuke him, and if he repents, forgive him. If he sins against you seven times in a day, and seven times comes back to you and says, 'I repent,' forgive him" (Luke 17:3–4).

This is a lot of patience. The key here, though, is that word *repent*. Repentance means *more* than someone saying, "Sorry." It means he truly has had a change of mind about his behavior and shows it by changing direction. He turns around and does things differently. His turnaround may have missteps in it, but you can usually see whether he has changed or not. If he is really sticking to the plan and fails and then repents and gets back into the plan, be patient. If repentance has no change of direction, you are back to setting limits.

You can be patient with some things while they are being resolved without giving the other person freedom to hurt you. Patience does not mean that you let down all limits or guards. Some things, such as physical or drug abuse, are too hurtful and dangerous to be around to just forgive and forget. Forgive and remember to be careful while you are being patient. With less serious things, if the pattern is being addressed, forgive and forget. This is part of life: to fail each other and go forward.

USE FORCE, IF NECESSARY

I will always remember the day one of my clients turned around. He was a sex addict with several failures that had really hurt his wife and were destroying his soul. There had been multiple confrontations and multiple "I'm sorry's." But each time, he would stop going to his group and fall back into a problem. On this particular day, he came in after being "caught" by his wife.

"What happened?" I asked.

"If she would meet my needs better, this wouldn't happen," he replied. "All she does is nag, and she has to have things perfect. She can't see the good things I do. I feel like I can't win, so I end up acting out. I feel like she drives me to it."

I looked at him and said, "Just shut up. I do not want to hear it. I have heard this before from you, and I have worked you through it, and you have understood that blaming your wife for your behavior is not going to fly. I have given you more patience than you have deserved on many occasions, and I'm done. I'm sick of the lying, deception, and blaming, and I want you to listen to yourself. You sound like a washed-out alcoholic who is one step away from his face on the pavement and no life left. I am going to tell you the truth—I am scared for your life. You are very close to losing it. I'm frightened for you.

"You can take this as if it came right from God [which I believed it did!]—you are one step away from ruin, and if you don't get back into your group and work your program, you are going to lose everything. You have spit on patience, forgiveness, and understanding long enough. Get with it or I'm done!" I surprised myself as I listened to the severity of my words. It was a strong warning, with no wiggle room.

He looked at me, and as the ears go back on a dog when it submits, he submitted to my warning. I got through to him. His willfulness was broken. And he turned around. Sometimes soft rebuke or correction does wonders, as we have said. I had spent a lot of time giving this man grace, understanding, encouragement, and support. I had given him a lot of education about the process of recovery and the importance of staying in his groups. I had warned him, with a lot of softness and acceptance, over time. But at other times a "sharper" approach is needed (Titus 1:13)—as I made clear that day. Words have to get more serious and carry greater weight and warning.

STAY IN CONTROL OF YOURSELF

A fool shows his annoyance at once,
  but a prudent man overlooks an insult (Prov. 12:16).

If you are the one doing the confronting and you have prepared as we suggest, then you have the self-control to evaluate and speak to another's behavior. But we all know that being prepared does not turn you into a robot that has no feelings or reactions.

Difficult people often have a strategy to get you upset and out of control. Just as a toddler infuriates his parent until he is in control of the out-of-control parent, so difficult people can arouse your emotions until they are in control of you. In fact, people with behavior problems and toddlers have many developmental similarities. The key is to not regress into a toddler yourself!

Stay in charge of the only person you can control: yourself. Do not get hooked into saying something you will regret; if you feel that happening, take a breath or a timeout before you say anything. There is nothing wrong with saying, "I am going to just be quiet here for a moment," or, "I need a moment to gather my thoughts." It is better to be silent than to say something you might regret. At certain times you would do well to use these two proverbs as a guide:

> A gentle answer turns away wrath,
>   but a harsh word stirs up anger.
> The tongue of the wise commends knowledge,
>   but the mouth of the fool gushes folly (Prov. 15:1–2).

Stay in control, and stick to your agenda. This is your meeting—you called it!

ASK, "HOW CAN I DO THIS?"

Sometimes, if a person is reacting to your feedback in a way that is shutting down the process, stop for a moment and ask a question.

"Joe, is there a way I can give you some feedback about your behavior that is not offensive to you?"

"Jim, are you open to feedback? If so, then tell me how to do it in a way that shows me you can listen and show your openness."

"Susie, how can I give you some feedback without it feeling like I'm saying you are 'bad' or that I 'don't care about you'?"

"Sarah, how can I let you know how I'm feeling without your getting angry at me for telling you?"

At times the other person does not even know she is being defensive, so asking this kind of question gives her a chance to observe her defensiveness and get it under control. She has to ask herself at that point, "Am I really the kind of person who can't receive feedback?" That thought can sober any of us up pretty quickly at times.

GET TO THE REAL ISSUE

In every situation, you are dealing with two factors: the problem and the other person's ability to deal with it. The greater the other person's ability to hear what you are saying and deal with the problem, the more smoothly the conversation will go. But if the other person is not willing to listen, you may have to get away from the problem you wanted to solve and go to the greater problem — the inability to solve problems or the inability to hear feedback.

At times you might have to stop confronting a particular problem after you see that the other person is not going to hear you. Then you should take a different focus. Confront the problem of not hearing instead of the original problem. It would sound something like this:

> "Joe, I want to talk about our ability to solve problems. It seems that when I bring things up that are bothering me, you get mad at me and do not listen. I get nowhere, and I go away disheartened. I don't know how to bring things up to you so you will hear me and not get mad at me. I want to discuss that."

If you are driving a car and it veers into the other lane, you have a problem that you may be able to fix by turning the steering wheel and guiding the car back to your own lane. If the steering wheel does not work, however, you have a different problem to address. You will need to stop the car as soon and as safely as possible, then examine the steering mechanism. It is the same with relationships. If the steering wheel (feedback and correction) is not working, pull off the road to address that problem before you address the other ones. You may have to call in a third party if the person cannot hear it from you.

CLARIFY TO MAKE SURE THEY UNDERSTAND AND YOU HAVE AGREEMENT

Sometimes, at the end of a confrontation, it is helpful to ask the person to say back to you what he has heard. This way you can clear up any confusion as well as draw out any lingering feelings that might interfere with resolution. Then you can both go away with the same understanding of what the issue was.

> **You:** "Joe, please tell me what you heard me say. I want to make sure we are on the same page."

If what he says sounds like what you want to be heard, you can go forward. At other times you might need to clarify.

> **You:** "No, Joe. I did not say that I was 'sick of you' at all. What I said was that I love you and that I want this behavior to change."

When you know what the other person heard or feels, you can address it and make sure that he is hearing what you are saying. Also, it often reinforces the commitment to change if he hears himself say it.

> **Joe:** "You are hurt by _____ and you want me to never do that again. I hear you."

DON'T GO IT ALONE

In the chapter on getting ready for the conversation, we talk about the "confrontation sandwich," in which we advise you to get support from a trusted counselor or support group before and after the difficult conversation. But you don't have to do the confrontation alone, either. In fact, in some cases it is unwise to do so. Jesus tells us that if previous confrontations by one person have been unsuccessful, take one or two others along, and if that does not work, take even more (Matt. 18:16). This is what an "intervention" is—several people coming together to help put an end to a pattern of behavior. If you do an intervention, get the help of an objective person who knows how to run one (see chapter 16).

At other times you may want someone present for support or to be a witness to what happens. This is often done in business situations with employee discipline. If an employee is not hearing what is being said, another manager is called in to witness the meeting and sign off on it. Sometimes you may need someone to help do the work of the confrontation itself. The person you are confronting may be too difficult for you to handle alone. Again, here is the way Jesus put it:

> "If your brother sins against you, go and show him his fault, just between the two of you. If he listens to you, you have won your brother over. But if he will not listen, take one or two others along, so that 'every matter may be established by the testimony of two or three witnesses.' If he refuses to listen to them, tell it to the church; and if he refuses to listen even to the church, treat him as you would a pagan or a tax collector.
>
> "I tell you the truth, whatever you bind on earth will be bound in heaven, and whatever you loose on earth will be loosed in heaven" (Matt. 18:15–18).

Progressively "turn up the heat" if someone is difficult. But bringing someone along does more than turn up the heat; it adds strength to you as the confronter, aiding your ability to get the job done. Notice that Matthew 18:19 talks about the power of two people agreeing on something: What they ask for will be done. You may need the strength of others for a variety of reasons, one of which is that you feel too vulnerable to do it alone. If you are too vulnerable and the person being confronted is very adept at arguing, you might get off course and hurt even worse. If you need help, don't go it alone.

Telling someone else that they are out of line is a tough assignment. It has the greatest possibility for miracle cures and turnarounds and also for disappointment. That is why we do not take it lightly. But we want to encourage you as you think about having that difficult conversation. After writing *Boundaries*, we heard of many, many seemingly hopeless situations that have been turned around through good confrontation. It is our prayer that you will find the same results. Yet, even if you don't, "you will have saved yourself" (Ezek. 3:19).

We are excited about the possibility of good confrontation turning your tough situations around. And we hope it goes smoothly. But as we mentioned, there is always a possibility of counterattack when you try to confront. Unfortunately, even when you are being as gracious as possible, a person can still retaliate. The next chapter will show you what to do when you run into counterattack and other problems.

18

Dealing with Blame, Counterattack, and Other Problems

Jennifer and I (John) were discussing her marriage to Roger. Like all couples, they had had their struggles, but they had been married awhile and they loved each other. When I asked her what she thought his biggest limitation was, she said, "Ownership of his part in our problems."

"What do you mean?" I asked.

"He doesn't do well when I bring up an issue. Whatever is wrong, he either puts it back on me, blames others, or just acts like it's not that big a deal."

"That sounds hard. Why did you pick ownership as his number one problem?"

Jennifer thought a minute. "Well, I think that if he didn't have that problem, we could deal with most of the other things. I mean, we're both pretty decent people. We could both see what we are doing and change. But in our marriage, the problems we have today are the same ones we've had for years. I'm afraid that as long as Roger doesn't see his part in things, they will never change."

"What if Roger never sees his part?"

"If you are asking me if I would leave, no, I wouldn't. I do love him—and us together. But I'm scared that I will have to settle for a lot less love and happiness than I would like."

I had to agree with Jennifer. As a psychologist, I concluded long ago that a couple with big problems but also the ability to listen, own one's part in the problem, and change has a better chance of success than a couple with smaller problems and less ability to own them. When one person in a relationship resists looking at, taking responsibility for, and changing his actions, it is like damming up a river. The relationship moves sluggishly, choked by the inability to process issues and move on in love. Relationships between two people who can hear and use feedback sail along much more easily: "A rebuke impresses a man of discernment more than a hundred lashes a fool" (Prov. 17:10).

THE FEEDBACK-RESISTANCE PROBLEM

Speaking the truth in love may be uncomfortable for us, but it is one of God's primary means of solving problems, bringing people closer in relationships, and growing us up. Confrontation, as we have taught in this book, was designed to be our friend, not our adversary. In an ideal world, all the people in your primary relationships would invite you to give them feedback and helpful correction, as would you.

The reality is sadly very different. Since the Fall, we have had problems accepting the truth about ourselves: "The man said, 'The woman you put here with me—she gave me some fruit from the tree, and I ate it'" (Gen. 3:12). Things have not changed a great deal since Adam first blamed Eve.

When it comes to accepting the truth about ourselves, things have not changed much since Adam first blamed Eve.

Many people avoid confrontation at all costs. It can make them feel unloved, bad, defeated, ashamed, or offended. Sometimes they feel persecuted by feedback, as if they were the victim and the other person were the perpetrator when, in reality, their behavior victimizes others. So they make it hard for those in their lives to tell them the truth in any context: marriage, dating, family, work, or friendships.

The irony is obvious: People who resist feedback negate the very thing that might give them hope, improve their lives, or even save their relationships. (For a fuller treatment of this problem, see *Hiding from Love*.)

What follows are the major ways people resist confrontation. The more aware of these you are, the better prepared you will be to deal with them.

Shooting the Messenger

When a person attacks you for bringing up a problem, he is "shooting the messenger." The trigger is not so much that he doesn't like the problem, but he sees you as the problem for mentioning it. He is unable or unwilling to look at the issue at hand because it may make him face something. He is often also upset with you because your bringing up the truth has disturbed his sense of well-being, a sense that often has no relationship to reality.

For example, a man may open the credit card statement and, with no anger, comments, or opinions, simply say, "We overspent our limit this month." His wife might explode, saying, "There you go again! You're always coming down on me!" In reality, he was not coming down on her. He was bringing a reality to her that she did not want to look at. Her sense of peace and calm was disturbed by the truth, and she blames him for it.

Rationalization

People may create reasons for their behavior that satisfy themselves but are inaccurate and reduce their responsibility. People who rationalize will not deny the problem exists; however, they will devise reasons that ultimately make no sense except to them.

Suppose your boyfriend is a fun, charming fellow, but he is late to everything—dinner, movies, sports events, and church. When you say, "You're forty-five minutes late again," he responds, "Well, these things don't start right on time anyway," or, "I thought I had the time right. Are you sure?" Often, over time, you will find that the person rotates through the same excuses and, when you try to pin him down, will sometimes come up with several rationalizations. What seldom happens, however, is that he says, "I'm sorry. This was nobody's fault but mine."

Minimization

People who minimize will admit an issue but speak of it as less serious than it is. They often will not see how bothersome or hurtful their behavior is to others, because in their minds it is no big deal.

You may ask the co-worker in the next cubicle, for example, to lower her voice when she is on the phone. If she minimizes, she might say, "I'm not talking that loud; it's not that bad," when you wanted to hear, "Oh, sorry! I'll try to keep my voice down. Let me know if it happens again."

Blame

When a person blames, he finds an external source that, in his mind, caused the problem. As in rationalization, he doesn't deny the problem; he just regards someone else as responsible. While rationalization emphasizes the reason, blame focuses on the source. As Adam blamed Eve, who then blamed the serpent, this is an ancient and often-used approach to deflect responsibility.

When you tell your teenager her grades are unacceptable, for example, she immediately complains about how hard her teachers are and how unfair you are. When you are not prepared for blame, you may be caught off balance and mysteriously find yourself defending yourself instead of dealing with her problem.

Denial

Some people deny a problem even exists. This is serious resistance, because when the person being confronted denies the problem, it is impossible to find a common meeting ground of terms and perceptions from which to solve the problem.

CHAPTER 18: DEALING WITH BLAME AND OTHER PROBLEMS

Sometimes denial is part of an entire family's approach to dealing with problems. You may be the only person in your family, for example, who realizes that Dad is an alcoholic. Mom and your siblings might say, "That's not true. He's just a normal social drinker." Typically, people in denial are not good processors. They do not explore problems and issues; they have little curiosity about them. They state their denial and change the subject.

Projection

When people disallow that they are responsible for a problem but then see their problem in others, they are projecting. People who project are unable to tolerate a bad thing within them; however, since it exists, they find another person on which to place it.

Jesus referred to this process of projecting when he taught,

"Why do you look at the speck of sawdust in your brother's eye and pay no attention to the plank in your own eye? How can you say to your brother, 'Let me take the speck out of your eye,' when all the time there is a plank in your own eye? You hypocrite, first take the plank out of your own eye, and then you will see clearly to remove the speck from your brother's eye" (Matt. 7:3–5).

Sometimes people try to control the person in whom they have placed their badness, in order to keep the badness away from them. This is technically called "projective identification." Simply put, however, projection involves seeing one's problem in another.

In a group I was leading, I confronted a woman for being indirect and dishonest in her dealings with the group. She had always prided herself on being a good person, and it was intolerable for her to see herself as I did. Even I was surprised, however, when she lit into me, saying, "No, you're the one who is indirect and dishonest!"

A Multi-Tasking Resister

People who resist confrontation sometimes stay away from owning a problem by using more than one of the above approaches in a single conversation. It can be very confusing, and sometimes their intention is to confuse you.

Take, for example, the critical person who puts you down and hurts your feelings time after time. When you bring this matter up, his answer may be something like, "There you go again, jumping all over me [attack]. It's not even that bad; I'm just kidding most of the time [minimization]. But it wouldn't happen if you didn't provoke me [blame]." The combination of ways of resistance distracts you from directly confronting what is going on.

DEALING WITH RESISTANCE

If you have a resistant person in your life, the number one stance you will need to adopt to learn how to deal with her is this: *Stop being surprised that she does not welcome the truth.* Nothing can happen until you accept the reality that, for whatever reason, she avoids confrontation. Many people who want to confront someone adopt a "false hope" stance; they simply hope that one day the other person will hunger for feedback. While one purpose of this book is to help make that happen, simply hoping against hope is not enough. So take the steps below to increase the chances that in time she will see the truth as something that heals her and brings her life.

Show Grace and Love

When you are preparing to confront a resistant person, remember that he also needs relationship, safety, and grace. He may resist due to hurt or past experiences that made truth dangerous or unsafe for him. *Grace and love are not everything a person needs; however, they are the most important elements he needs.* In addition, *without grace and love, it is unlikely that anything redemptive will happen in your conversation.*

Come to the talk being "for" him, knowing that you also are in need of love and grace: "Above all, love each other deeply, because love covers over a multitude of sins" (1 Peter 4:8). This doesn't mean to avoid truth. Grace is not the absence of truth. Rather, it allows truth to be accepted and digested more easily.

It is easy to forget this, especially when you have tried many times to address problems and have been frustrated or hurt by a person's avoidance. You may be tempted to start off with something like "I am fed up with trying with you. I doubt that this talk will even help; the others sure haven't. But I will try this one more time to get through to you. I will not be surprised if you throw this back in my face, like you have a million other times." If you are feeling this way, you may need to receive some grace yourself from others to process your own emotions about the difficulty of the situation.

> *Without grace and love, it is unlikely that anything redemptive will happen in your conversation.*

Say, for example, that you want to confront your roommate about not picking up after herself in the apartment, but she tends to divert the conversation away from her problem. A good way to start with grace and love might be to say, "I'd like to talk about keeping the apartment neat. I have a problem with how you leave dishes and clothes all around, and I'd like to find a solution to this problem. At the same time, I want you to know that I'm not trying to put you down. I really value our friendship, and I like being with you. In fact, I am bringing this up because the problem is getting in the way of our relationship. I want to be closer, not farther from you."

There is, of course, no guarantee that your roommate will respond openly, even though you have done your best to lay a foundation at the very beginning that attempts to reach out to her. The next step is for her to either receive that attempt or refuse it. Even if she refuses it, you have done a good thing by beginning with grace and love.

Don't React to Reactions

When the person you are confronting reacts in one of the ways we have mentioned, you will be sorely tempted to respond in kind: anger to anger, blame to blame. This is the most natural thing in the world. When we are attacked, we protect ourselves, and sometimes we attack back. At the same time, the most natural thing in the world may not be the best, most helpful, or most mature thing to do: "Do not repay anyone evil for evil" (Rom. 12:17). This is why you need to be in control of how you respond to an attack. If you are not, the talk can quickly degenerate into an argument or alienation.

Suppose, for example, you tell your wife that you need for her to be less distant and more interested in your life. She may say, "You're the one who is distant. You don't care about what I think or feel; it's always about you. Why don't you ever talk to me about how I am doing?"

You might be tempted to say, "Listen to yourself. You just proved my point. I couldn't even bring up how I feel without you throwing it back at me. Can't you for once just listen to my side without blaming it all on me?"

Even if these statements are true, they are not helpful.

Give up the right to pay back in kind. Remember that there needs to be at least one adult present in the room for a problem to be solved. You may have to have a "tight rein" on your tongue (James 1:26) and speak from your maturity rather than from your hurt or anger.

You could respond to your wife this way: "I'm really sorry you feel that way. I don't want you to think I'm not interested in what is going on with you. I want to pursue this with you, because maybe you can show me when I discount your feelings so I can avoid that. But for now, I'd like to continue with solving the problem of my not feeling I have your emotional interest."

There is no lecturing or power play in this response. It is a straightforward approach of hearing the reaction, dealing with it, and returning to the matter at hand. You can often get through reactions by patiently turning the other cheek and pursuing the problem.

This example also illustrates another important point about reactions: Do not make the counterattack or defensiveness the issue at first. You may not need to do that, because your love and balance will get through so you can resolve the issue. Often, when a person finds that you didn't react to her reaction, she drops it and gets to the problem. Try to overlook the resistance: "A man's wisdom gives him patience; it is to his glory to overlook an offense" (Prov. 19:11).

It is sometimes easier to point out rationalization or to blame someone than to overlook it for the moment. However, in winning that point, the person may feel you are lying in wait to prove her wrong, and you risk losing the true goal of solving the problem and reconciling. Don't be shortsighted; keep the main goal in mind.

Let us show you next what to do when overlooking does not work.

Make the Defensiveness the Issue

If you have made several attempts to listen and overlook someone's minimization or projection, yet the other person persists, you may need to address his attitude directly. This becomes necessary when it is obvious that the resistance will continue to get in the way. If you ignore it, the person may either dig in his heels for an indefinite period of time or even escalate emotionally, making things worse.

Often the person is not even aware that he is being defensive or blaming. He is caught up in protecting himself. Bringing the topic up can help him see what he is doing, take responsibility for it, and give it up. So it can be helpful to get off the subject to talk about why you can't talk about the subject. Here are two approaches:

Approach #1: "I need to point out something. I'm noticing that as I try to get us talking about your temper, you keep getting angry and blaming everything on me. I've tried to get past that several times now, and I'm feeling discouraged that I can't get to the problem I wanted to solve with you, nor can I connect with you, either. I don't want to make you mad, but I do want to talk about your temper itself in a way that we can both feel closer. Is there some way I can talk so that you can hear what I'm saying without blaming me? For instance, if you want me to know how I bother you, too, maybe we can do that first, if that means we can get back to my issue with you."

Approach #2: "Do you notice that we can't talk about your temper without your getting mad at me and starting to blame me? I don't know if you are aware of this, and I wanted to check that out with you before we go any further. Maybe we can drop the temper thing for now and talk about how you are feeling about this conversation, to see if we are on the same page. We can return to my question after that."

Avoid playing counselor. It can sound patronizing: "Seems like you are reacting to my confrontation. Maybe it's fear of hurt or some anger from your past. Do you want to talk about it?" This forces the person to push away from you merely to save face.

Listen and Contain

In the last section we suggested that you sometimes invite the defensive person to tell you the problem she has with you. Besides helping you take responsibility for any part you play, it can also help her be less resistant to your confrontation. When a person feels her perspective is heard and understood without evaluation or judgment, she often becomes less reactive.

This may also require that you not only listen to her viewpoint, but also hear her negative emotions, such as anger at you or disappointment in you. When you can be with her and her emotions without reacting yourself, you help her bear them and process them. Helping a person deal with her emotions by being there, hearing them, and not reacting is called *containment*. A mother who soothes and calms her unhappy infant, who is experiencing emotions so large and primitive that he cannot bear them on his own, is containing. The mother acts as a container for her infant's feelings so that he can learn over time how to feel what he feels without panicking or becoming overwhelmed. (For more on the containing functions of mothering, please refer to *Our Mothers, Ourselves*.)

Bear in mind that listening and containing do not mean agreeing. You may have a very different viewpoint from the other person. She may have legitimate or illegitimate grievances against you. Your task is simply to help her be heard on an emotional level.

When people do not contain, the conversation's process may be hampered, as the other person feels negated or discounted. For example:

"My fault? How can any of this be my fault?"

"I know you feel that I provoke this in you, but that's just your feelings and your opinion."

"No, I don't understand your side in this. It makes no sense."

"Your anger at me is irrational and unjustified."

A better approach is to be emotionally present without editorializing:

"Tell me why you feel it's my fault. What does it look like I do to you?"

"That must make it hard to feel connected to me when it appears to you that I provoke you. What are some situations in which this comes up?"

"It's hard for me to understand how you think I do this. Can you tell me more about it?"

"I feel sad that you become so angry at me. That doesn't help us feel attached. That has got to be difficult for you."

Listening and containing require us temporarily to shed our own point of view and self-interest to connect with the other person's heart. It is the ability to identify with another's pain and experience, similar to the way Jesus lowered himself to help us: He "made himself nothing, taking the very nature of a servant, being made in human likeness" (Phil. 2:7).

Containing does not mean, however, that you should allow yourself to be emotionally injured by the person. Evaluate whether her anger or negativity toward you is uncomfortable or harmful to you. Sometimes, if you are in a fragile season of life or if the person has wielded great power over you, you may need to limit the amount of containment you can tolerate until your situation has changed.

Look at Your Contribution

When you confront a defensive person about a problem, one thing he will try to do is to find another source for the issue. This often means that he will attack you. However, even if he is trying to avoid responsibility, do not discount what you are hearing because it is coming from an attacking person. Rather, listen and reflect on what you are hearing to see whether it is true. If you are making a problem worse, you will want to know that.

Further, *even if you are not being blamed, take the initiative to search out whether you are provoking the problem.* Do not wait to be confronted; rather, be a self-scrutinizing and self-correcting person: "I said, 'I will watch my ways and keep my tongue from sin'" (Ps. 39:1). Make this process a part of the boundary conversation with the other person. It can go a long way toward helping resolve defensiveness.

We tend to deflect in response to another's deflection, and that can be a mistake. For example, you might wrongly do any of the following:

- Disqualify his remarks because of his behavior: "With what you have done, you don't have the right to criticize me."
- Hide behind the moral imbalance: "I am the good guy in this. I couldn't have done what you say."
- Use her defensiveness to negate: "You're only saying that because you don't want to look at yourself."

These statements lessen the chance that the person will see what he is doing, and they give him more opportunity to focus on you as the problem. Here are some ways to help move things in the right direction:

If you agree: "You know, I think you are right that I nag you about your not getting around to doing things. I'm sure that doesn't make things easier for you. So I am really willing to take a look at that with you and change it. But for now, I need to get back to the problem we began with."

If you don't agree: "It may be true that I nag you. I'm not sure about it, and I want to think about it. If it is true, I really want to talk to you more about it and change things. But for now, I need to get back to the problem."

These examples demonstrate how you can table your part until later, but this is not a hard and fast rule. It may be that you could deal with your own contributions right then, as long as there is time and willingness and as long as you are assured that the other person will get back on topic with you when it is done:

"Tell me how I nag you, so I can identify it when it happens. I am really sorry about this, because I don't want to do that to you, and I don't want to make our problems worse."

Finally, be honest and not manipulative. Looking at yourself is fundamentally not a strategy to solve a conflict, but an attitude to take toward your own soul, growth, and responsibility. Use what you are hearing to find weaknesses within you that you need to repent of, change, and work through.

Speak of the Effect on You

Though the person's attacks and blame protect her from confrontation, they often have another result: They negatively affect you — the person doing the confronting. It is difficult to try to reach out, to not be defensive, and to confront a problem while the other person is being hostile toward you. It cuts off relationship, and it hurts. Tell the person about the effect of her resistance on you. It could help her access that part of her that cares for you and doesn't want to see you get hurt.

When you do this, however, avoid the mistake of making her responsible for your emotional stability and well-being. That indicates a dependency of such a depth that it may be a problem.

A not-so-good response: "When I tried to talk to you about our problem and you came at me like it was all my fault, it totally crushed me. I got depressed and I couldn't go to work."

If this is true, make sure you are finding a supportive and experienced growth context in which you can safely work out the dependency issue.

A better response: "When I tried to talk to you about our problem and you came at me like it was all my fault, I was really hurt. I didn't expect that response, and I felt sad and unloved by you.

> When I feel like I can't talk to you about problems
> without being attacked by you, I can't feel close to
> you, and I go away from you inside."

Confront Defensiveness from an Adult Position

Having been kind, nonreacting, humble, and containing, you may still find that the other person continues to evade looking at himself. To go further at this point, you may need to deal firmly with that attitude. Take an adult stance, not that of a parent or a child.

On the one hand, you may be tempted to respond parentally when you hear the immature blaming of the person. You might find yourself saying things like this:

> "You should be ashamed of yourself for the way you rationalize
> your part in the situation."

> "I expected much better from you. How can you act like none
> of this is your fault?"

> "Just stop denying the truth right now."

These approaches will only force the defensive person to push you away even more to ward off the guilt and attack he feels.

On the other hand, you may feel so intimidated by the other person that you can't even think straight. Especially if you have ascribed a lot of power to the other person, you may have a tendency to regress to a childlike emotional state. If this happens to you, you might say things like this:

> "I'm sorry, please stop being so mad. You're right, this is my
> fault. I'll drop it, just don't be angry or upset."

The fear of experiencing the anger and blame of the other person causes you to lose your truth and objectivity about the situation.

In the adult role, neither child nor parent reigns. This way, you are still making your points, standing firm, and yet not attacking or condemning:

"When you blame me for your Internet porn, it hurts my feelings, but more than that, it's just not true. I want to work on this with you, and I want the problem to be solved, but it is not okay to make me responsible for what you are doing. I will not continue our relationship the way it is until you are open to looking at your part."

"I didn't bring up the problem so I could judge you or put you down. Neither you nor I am perfect, and that's okay with me. It doesn't help us reconnect for you to keep attacking me as the critical judge here. Can you try to hear what I'm saying without seeing me as the parent? I don't want to be in that role with you. At the same time, I can't ignore your attitude, because it prevents us from solving anything."

"When you are so angry about my bringing up the problem, it makes it tough for both of us, and it prevents us getting closer and solving the issue. Your anger is unpleasant, but it will not make me stop working on this issue. I want us to find ways that you can look at these issues and feel safe, without having to go out of control."

Admit Helplessness

When you confront a person who is invested in a power struggle with you, you may have to let her know that she can win the control game. This kind of person will refuse to see your side at all costs, will insist on your seeing things her way, or will want you to see that you can't push her around.

Let her win. For one thing, she is right: You cannot make her see your side, you do need to look at her side, and you can't control her. So don't fight reality; that's the way things are. While you have many choices for yourself, you are helpless to control her. In fact, the Holy Spirit gives us the ability to control ourselves (Gal. 5:23), but never the ability to control another person.

Further, when you stay in the power game, you can actually influence the other person to feel more threatened, become more competitive, or escalate the conflict. Often, what was a mild issue can become an ugly screaming match if both people get caught up in a power struggle.

When you admit you are helpless to go any further, you are being vulnerable with the other person. This shifts the playing field from power to relationship. This can help her see your openness and make it safe for her to look at things, too.

Here is an example of the wrong way:

> **You:** "I want you to look at how your negativity affects me and our relationship."
>
> **Other:** "You're just overreacting."
>
> **You:** "No, I'm not. You really bring me down, the kids down, everyone."
>
> **Other:** "You just need to see things so positive that you don't live in reality."
>
> **You:** "No way. I try to look at both sides. You never try."

This conversation could go on forever. She is entrenched in her blame, and you are still trying to interest someone who is not interested. Here is a better way:

> **You:** "I want you to look at how your negativity affects me and our relationship."
>
> **Other:** "You're just overreacting."
>
> **You:** "I know you think that, but I'd like to explain what I see and feel."
>
> **Other:** "Doesn't matter! It's your reactions, not my negativity that is the problem.
>
> **You:** "If you are telling me that you aren't interested in understanding my side of the problem, then I accept that. I am helpless to convince or change

you. I guess I'm stuck then. I don't know what
to do."

This is not the end of the talk, but holds open the possibility
that she will be more emotionally responsive to your vulnerability
rather than avoiding what she perceives as your attempts to control
her. Next, we move beyond admitting helplessness to doing those
things with which we have some choice.

Being Right versus Doing the Right Thing

People sometimes tend to approach a confrontation as if it were
a debate. In a debate, individuals take opposing sides and present their arguments, with the intent of someone being wrong and
someone being right. In personal confrontations, however, and
especially with a resistant person, this can work against your desire
to solve the problem at hand. Keep in mind that, above all, you
want the person to do something redemptive about the issue of
concern. Make sure your own emotional investment is more that
the person will see the truth and less that you have won the argument: "If it is possible, as far as it depends on you, live at peace with
everyone" (Rom. 12:18).

When you confront, you are likely trying to make your point in
the face of defensiveness or denial. Many times you need to tell the
truth about a person's behavior to break through his denial systems.
However, disagreeing on the truth is different from trying to prove
that you are right and the other person is wrong. The latter focus
might well convey to the other person that you are more invested
in winning the debate than you are in nurturing your relationship
with him. Often you will find that you are going too far when the
person is either so upset that he can no longer understand your
point, or so disconnected from you that it does not matter. At that
point you may need to regroup.

Here is an example of someone invested in being right:

> **You:** "You are drinking too much. I know it, and I have experiences with you that prove it."
>
> **Other:** "I'm not drinking too much."
>
> **You:** "Yes, you are. I can give you a lot of examples."
>
> **Other:** "No, I'm not."
>
> **You:** "Yes, you are. Listen to what I am saying!"
>
> **Other:** "It doesn't matter what you say—you're wrong."
>
> **You:** "No, I'm not. You're wrong."

This conversation quickly deteriorates to a point of disconnection and uselessness. If a person is defensive and shows no interest in the truth as you see it, move on to what you want to tell him without insisting he agree with you:

> **You:** "I think you are drinking too much. I have experiences with you that prove it."
>
> **Other:** "I'm not drinking too much."
>
> **You:** "Are you open to hearing what I have to say about your drinking?"
>
> **Other:** "It doesn't matter what you say. You're wrong, I don't have a drinking problem."
>
> **You:** "If you don't want to hear my side of it, I won't try to convince you. I can't do that if you don't want to hear, and I don't want to force you to do anything. It makes me sad, however, because whatever I do next about the problem, I do without your involvement, and I really wanted us to deal with this as a team."

In this scenario you have illustrated that you care about the person and simply want to solve the problem. This demonstrates an attempt to keep the peace, and you have not gotten stuck on trying to show the person that he is in the wrong. This is the best way to increase the chances the person will respond well.

Persist and Give It Time

When the person you are trying to confront blames, rationalizes, or attacks, she has probably spent a long time avoiding the discomfort of feedback and creating ways to divert it. This means you will probably not have one conversation with her, but several over time. This can be discouraging for you, but time and persistence can pay off.

Even in the face of his people's resistance, God continued to repeat his appeal for them to be obedient: "From the time I brought your forefathers up from Egypt until today, I warned them again and again, saying, 'Obey me'" (Jer. 11:7). God does not insist on us getting it together immediately, because he knows how broken we are.

Persistence and time allow confrontation to do its work. The safety and grace you give can help melt a hard heart. The truth you speak can cause enlightenment. The feedback you provide can give perspective on how the other person's actions affect those she loves.

Some people's defensiveness is a thin layer over fear, need, and vulnerability. They tend to need less time and effort to receive your confrontation. Other people have little or no interest in deeper connections, or they have built up a grandiose idea of themselves that doesn't allow them to receive feedback. In these situations, while more time and persistence are needed, they are also likely to need consequences and limits along with the conversation (see the next section).

Persistence and time allow confrontation to do its work.

The wrong approach in this area would be to say, "You are still attacking me for bringing up the problem. That is unacceptable. I don't want to have to hear you come after me for telling you the truth again." In this instance there has not been enough discussion or time spent dealing with the issue to warrant this style.

It would be better to say instead, "It is really difficult to bring up to you any problem that affects our relationship when you attack me for talking about it. Then we are even farther apart, and I don't want that. This is the first time I have brought this up, and it may be new or surprising for you. I need to pursue it, though, because I think it is very important for our relationship. If you don't want to talk about it now, when is a good time in the near future?"

Then, in subsequent conversations, you can say, "I need to bring up again your attacks on me for talking about problems. The last time we talked, I thought we had made some headway, but it's still happening a lot. I don't want to drop this subject; it is very important for the health and future of our relationship." With a balanced, caring, yet firm approach, resistant people are more prone to connect with you over time.

Have Consequences Ready If Needed

Sometimes, no matter how hard and how long you try, a person will persist in deflecting, blaming, and avoiding. This attitude will prevent any growth or change from occurring. A person who will not recognize or own an issue is not able to address and resolve it. Because of that, you may need to realize when it is time to end the feedback and set appropriate consequences.

There is a time to give up trying to correct someone with your words. As Solomon wrote, "Do not rebuke a mocker or he will hate you; rebuke a wise man and he will love you" (Prov. 9:8). To someone who is deeply invested in always being right, or in others always being wrong, your words, being perceived as mistreatment, can further incite him to anger and resentment.

In these situations you may need to let the person know that you are not giving up on him. However, you are giving up on your attempts to confront him, at least until things change. At this point you may want to tell him you are no longer interested in debating with him about whether he thinks he is doing what you say he is. You are sure, as you have scrupulously checked out the facts with others, with God, and with your own heart. So, whether or not he blames, minimizes, attacks, or projects, it's irrelevant. You will now deal with the problem as you see best, without his cooperation.

This takes you to the limit of a boundary conversation. That is, words have accomplished as much as they can. The other person's attitude toward the problem requires that you move to consequences and actions. It will be important to warn the person of the consequences, however, so that he can still decide to change. If this becomes necessary, be sure that whatever you say, you say with grace and truth.

Think through what particular problem you are setting a boundary with. Sometimes it is a behavior that does not go away, such as irresponsibility, control, or withdrawal. Sometimes it is a defensive attitude, such as rationalization, denial, or blame, that prevents any processing of problems. Determine what changes you are requesting based on where the most serious relationship-breaking problem lies.

Avoid using control as you talk about consequences:

"You don't take responsibility for the problems you cause in our relationship. Instead, you deny your part and make excuses. So I'm telling you that you had better start owning things."

This is not a boundary; it is an attempt to control someone. Instead, allow freedom while being very clear on the consequences:

"You don't take responsibility for the problems you cause in our relationship. Instead, you deny your part and make excuses. I can't see that anything I have said has made any difference in how you see the situation. So I need for you to know that I cannot go on with things the way they are. If you won't deal with this by at least owning your tendency to let things go and blame me for them, I will start taking steps on my own. I will be joining a support group and talking to our pastor about how to handle this. I will also be changing how I relate to you in this marriage. This may mean that I won't be as open and available to you as I have been. I want to solve this with you, but if you have no interest in looking at it with me, I won't belabor the point. But I want to be clear that until you change, things will not be the same in our relationship, our closeness, and the things you value in our connection."

Finally, always provide a path back if, down the line, the person repents:

"If you decide to change, I will be happy to look at stopping these consequences, at least the ones that are safe and appropriate to stop. Let me know if you do change your mind."

It is not easy to be both firm and caring when you are confronting someone who is attacking you. However, you may be the first person who ever truly gave that person the right amounts of grace and truth he needs in order to be aware of, own, and repent of his problem.

It is no small matter to approach someone with a confrontation. To do things well, you will need to think through how you want it to go. Part 4, "Getting Yourself Ready to Have the Conversation," is designed to help you with this preparation.

PART IV

GETTING YOURSELF READY *to* HAVE *the* CONVERSATION

19

Why You Need
to Be Ready

How did it go?" I (Henry) asked Sandy, my client. "Terrible!" she replied. "In fact, I don't really want to talk about it because it went so poorly. I'm embarrassed." I could tell from her body language and expression that this was true.

Sandy was talking about the confrontation she had had with her boyfriend, Rollie. After struggling with the relationship for about six months, she had finally decided to tell him that although she thought they had a lot of good things going, some of his behavior patterns hurt her and he had ignored her when she had told him about them.

Rollie was often inconsiderate with time. Sometimes he would pick her up for a date an hour late, without calling first. Other times, he would not plan anything until the last minute and then expect her to go with him. Also, he often seemed to put his interests way above concern for the relationship. In addition, he put a lot of pressure on her to go past where she felt comfortable in their physical relationship.

In the few times we had met, Sandy had talked about how stressful this relationship was. It was clear to her that she needed to have a serious talk with Rollie and set some limits. Before, when she had talked with Rollie about his hurtful patterns of behavior, he had not listened. This time she had planned to tell him she wanted them to take some time off from each other while he thought about the things that distressed her. Then they could get back together and talk to see if he was ready to take her concerns seriously.

"What does 'not very well' mean?" I asked. "You mean he didn't take it well? What happened? Did he get upset or explode or something?"

"No, nothing like that," she said. "Nothing like that at all. He was really nice, his most charming self. He was the person I had liked from the beginning."

"So what went wrong? Sounds like he wasn't too hard to deal with after all. How did the breakup go? Did you tell him?"

"Yes, I did," she said. "I told him all the things I had been thinking and that I needed some time apart."

"So far so good," I said. "So why did you say it went 'terrible'? Sounds like you were doing fine. Good start. How did it end?"

"I slept with him," she said sheepishly, like a very ashamed little girl. I could tell that the shame was not only about having sex with Rollie. It was also about her lack of ability to take a stand in the conversation. She knew she had caved in and *failed herself.*

"Oh...," I said, not really knowing what else to say. I certainly did not want to make her feel guiltier. It was clear that she was feeling guilty enough. I felt sorrow for her more than anything. I could tell that she was captured by some weakness, entrapped in something hurtful to her, yet she was unable to end it, as Galatians 6:1 describes. "That's pretty tough" was all I said.

> *She went into the conversation to end that pattern, but instead had burrowed deeper into it. What went wrong?*

Think about the 180-degree turn Sandy had made. She had gone into this conversation planning to confront a distressing issue and set some limits with Rollie. She had planned to protect herself by saying "no more" to him; instead, she had betrayed herself. She had given herself away and had allowed herself to be used in a way that was just more of the same. Rollie was treating her not like a person he cherished, but like an object of gratification. She went into the conversation to end that pattern, but instead had burrowed deeper into it. What went wrong?

The Need to Be Ready

In short, Sandy had not been ready. She had gone into the confrontation with the best of intentions, but she was unprepared to deal with Rollie's best weapon: his charming ability to get her off her agenda and onto his. Her agenda was to take a look at the reasons she was unhappy, to put an end to the pain. His agenda was to use his charm to have her think that things would be different and then have his way in the end. He won.

In many ways Sandy was not prepared to deal with Rollie's weapons. It would take much counseling for her to conquer the vulnerabilities that caused her failure. She had a great need to be loved. She did not have relationships in her life that would support her and build up her strength to resist a man like Rollie. She saw Rollie in a very distorted way: When he was romantic and charming, she was unable to feel and remember his hurtful parts. And she had very little experience in taking a stand on the things important to her. She was too interested in finding love to find what she truly needed.

Yet, even though Sandy had much to work on, I knew something else. She did not have to arrive at a full state of maturity to deal with the likes of Rollie. I had seen it too many times. If someone has only a little understanding of what is happening, a few skills, a little coaching, and a little support, it is amazing what she can do, even before she "has it all together."

The good news is that we went to work, and things did turn out very differently. Sandy prepared herself and had the conversation with Rollie; today she is married to a wonderful man, and they have two great kids. I shudder at the thought that she might have ended up with Rollie. What a workout that would have been! If not for growth in the ability to "have that conversation she had been avoiding," she well might have.

Let's explore some of the ways you can prepare for your difficult conversations so that no 180s happen to you.

Too Many Chinks in Your Armor

Maybe you can't identify with Sandy's failure. You can't see yourself going to break up with someone and ending up sleeping with him. But chances are, no matter who you are, you *can* identify with having some vulnerabilities that keep you from confronting as well as you would like. Maybe you can identify with one or more of the following:

- You beat around the bush too much and are not as direct as you want to be.
- You become too angry and argumentative instead of remaining calm and clear.
- You feel sorry for the other person and lighten up too much.
- You're too anxious.
- You break down and are overwhelmed with the pain of it all.
- You know exactly what limits you intend to set, and you give in to more than you wanted.
- You allow yourself to get sidetracked into arguments or having to justify what you think or want.
- You fear the consequences of the confrontation (rejection, disapproval, conflict) so much that it gets in the way of your dealing with the problem.
- You have some other personal vulnerability that gets in the way.

Most people have made at least one attempt to have the conversation they have been avoiding, but something proves to be too much to overcome. So they don't know what to do. They become stuck or, worse, get discouraged about ever making things better.

This doesn't have to happen. We have seen many people learn the skills needed to overcome their difficulty with having boundary conversations. It happens every day. But you need to prepare yourself for confronting issues in a way that will make you as ready as possible and will give the interaction a better chance of being redemptive to the other person and to the relationship itself. Let's look at the first thing you need to do to prepare to face issues with another person.

Getting the Log Out

As we touched on earlier, Jesus says that we need to remove the plank from our own eye first, then we can see clearly to remove the speck from someone else's eye (Matt. 7:3). This verse contains much wisdom for the art of preparing to confront well.

First, notice that Jesus says to remove the plank from our own eye "first." In other words, we need to work on ourselves before we are ready to have a confrontation. We may need to change some things about ourselves before we are ready. So the concept of "first" is extremely important, as Sandy discovered.

Second, notice that Jesus says "plank" versus "speck." A plank is obviously much bigger. One obvious way to interpret this is that when we have a big issue to face about ourselves, we are in no shape to confront someone else about something.

Third, Jesus says that when we face ourselves first, we see clearly. In our clinical experience, we have found this to be one of the most profound things about people's confrontations with each other. The ones who do not own their own "stuff" have great difficulty in seeing whom they are dealing with on the other side of the table. Their tendency to distort based on their own blind spots can go in many directions. Sometimes people do not see how destructive the other person is and do not take a hard enough stand. They don't see and deal with their own codependency. At other times they might make a villain of the other person, seeing them in a much more negative light than is accurate. As a result, the confrontation neither goes well nor leads to resolution and a better relationship.

So we hope we have convinced you of the need to look at yourself first before you confront. In the next chapter we will look at some of the common things you will need to prepare for before you are ready to have a good boundary conversation.

20

How to Get Ready

I'm so mad at him," Terri said. "He's so inconsiderate of my time and what I have to do. He always assumes I can do favors for him. And then the way he talks to me sometimes feels demeaning. I'm sick of it!"

"What does he say when you tell him how you feel? And why don't you say no to the favors he asks when you don't want to do them?" I (Henry) asked.

She hemmed and hawed a little, then admitted, "I haven't said anything to him about it."

"Well, then, I don't think you have a lot to be mad about. After all, he might not even know you think his requests are excessive. He just sees you as a giving person and probably even thinks you take pleasure in helping. You can't be mad at someone if you're agreeing to what he asks. That's your problem, not his.

"The demeaning part is different. No one should talk to another like that, and I'm sure that it does not feel good to you. So you do owe it to yourself and to him to tell him how what he says feels to you. Again, he might not even know.

"But here's my biggest concern: Because you've waited so long and you've been passive with him, you've built up a lot of resentment. I can see it in your face. You had better deal with your resentment first and see how your own passivity has contributed to that, so you won't be so mad at him. Then you can talk to him directly and, I hope, solve the problem."

She looked at me with an expression on her face of having gotten caught doing something sneaky or wrong. She knew what I said was true. Once she admitted this, she could work on her part of the problem.

Owning your own failure to confront is one of eight steps you can take to prepare yourself to have that difficult conversation you've been avoiding. We will discuss all eight and then provide five specific strategies you can use to take the fear out of your confrontations.

1. Own Your Own Failure to Confront and Stop Playing the Victim

The principle behind this first step is this: *To the extent you allow someone to do something you resent, you are part of the problem.*

As the Bible tells us, "Do not hate your brother in your heart. Rebuke your neighbor frankly so you will not share in his guilt" (Lev. 19:17).

The word *rebuke* here is not necessarily an adversarial word. It can mean to "reason together" or to "correct." This verse directly ties our resentment to our failure to talk to someone about something. In addition, if we avoid confrontation, we share guilt in the problem. We are enabling the problem. To the extent that we are not talking to someone, we are part of the problem and have very little right to be as angry as we sometimes get.

As soon as we own the fact that our anger results from our not talking to someone, the confrontation goes much better. We don't blame the other person, and we approach him from a much less angry position and a much more "problem solving" stance. In addition, we see the conversation as helpful to the other person, as we are making him aware of a possible blind spot. The conversation becomes an effort of love while

> *To the extent you allow someone to do something you resent, you are part of the problem.*

at the same time ridding us of our resentment so that we can love
the person more freely and have a better relationship with him.

The big kicker of taking responsibility is this: If you recognize that the problem is your own passivity and you no longer see
yourself as a "victim," you are less likely to leave the conversation
without dealing with the problem. If you avoid dealing with it, you
know you've just signed up for more misery, and it's your own fault.
That will get you going!

2. Own Your Motives

There are many reasons to confront someone—some good, others
not so good. The majority of the time we probably have a mixture
of motives, or at least a mixture of feelings that motivate us to confront. We saw in Terri how resentment can get in the way of how
we see someone.

We live out our true motives one way or another. They show up
on our face, in our choice of words, in the amount of emotion we
take into a confrontation, and sometimes even in the way we con-
struct or design the outcome of the confrontation. If you want to
punish someone, for example, your conversation with that person
and its resulting plan for the future would look much different than
if you desire to help the person and the relationship.

Our first piece of advice in owning your motives is, don't be so
hard on yourself. We all have reactions, feelings, and not-so-loving
responses to other people at times, especially when we have been
hurt. As Solomon said, "Do not pay attention to every word people
say, or you may hear your servant cursing you—for you know in
your heart that many times you yourself have cursed others" (Eccl.
7:21–22). In other words, having negative and unloving feelings
is human. So be open to that, confess these feelings to God and
someone else (1 John 1:9; James 5:16), ask God to help you with
them, and go on.

Once you are in a "grace-giving state" toward yourself, take a
good look at your motives. Turn from the bad ones and deal with

them, then go forward with the good ones. Remember, the bad ones
are those that do not help you, the other person, the relationship,
or anyone else; they just bring about more bad things. Here are
some examples of bad motives:

- The desire to punish and get revenge
- The desire to make someone feel "bad," such as toxic shame
  and guilt
- The desire to get back at someone for things you have not
  dealt with
- The desire for a sick alliance with a third party against the
  other person
- The desire to feel power when you have been powerless and
  to make the other person feel powerless
- The desire to control when you have been controlled by the
  other person, thus reversing the roles
- The desire to dump your pain and hurt
- The desire to use the other person as a target for other
  similar wrongs you have suffered

Here are some examples of good motives:

- To stop a bad thing happening to you and end the hurt
- To bring to light your and the other person's contributions to
  a problem so you can both move forward
- To restore closeness
- To achieve greater intimacy
- To restore a breach in a relationship
- To correct something wrong in a relationship
- To help the other person see something he or she would do
  well to see
- To help the other person grow
- To stop a destructive cycle, pattern, or behavior in someone's
  life
- To protect others from the other person's behavior

- To problem-solve when you are at an impasse or see a destructive pattern
- To bring to light a change in the relationship
- To voice your desires or expectations
- To confess your wrongs and make amends for something the other person legitimately has against you

Therefore, remember that your motives will probably come to light in the end. As the King James renders Proverbs 4:23, "Keep thy heart with all diligence; for out of it are the *issues* of life." If you don't do a good job of looking into your heart at your motives, you will create other issues in your life with which you will have to deal. These issues will come back to haunt you, for what we sow, we reap. Sow good motives in a confrontation, and you will reap good fruit in the end.

3. Own Your Fears

Sandy feared losing Rollie. She was so afraid of being alone that she could not say no to him. Blinding herself to the problems, she would take any chance of staying with him. She was controlled by fear.

Have you thought about what you are afraid of in confronting another person? If you haven't, your fears will probably interfere, and you won't get the outcome you desire. Here are some common fears:

- Fear of rejection
- Fear of disapproval
- Fear of retaliation
- Fear of loss
- Fear of the other person's anger
- Fear of hurting the other person
- Fear of requiring another person to take responsibility
- Fear of depriving someone
- Fear of conflict

- Fear of being mean
- Fear of being seen as the "bad guy"
- Fear of not knowing how to confront
- Fear of a lack of closure in a relationship or conflict
- Fear of one's own imperfection and the feeling of "What business do I have confronting? I'm not perfect either."
- Fear of being "out-maneuvered"
- Fear of being overpowered or hurt

Fear does many things to our performance. Being too afraid can affect our ability to think quickly, speak out, take a stand, and do other things as well. Be aware of your fears and deal with them. Knowing what they are and being aware will help you see your fears when they arise, observe them, and not give in to them. You can stop using them as "cues" to back down. Much fear operates in this way, as a cue to stop. People do not even know they're afraid until they automatically back off. Knowing what you fear and how you tend to back off may be the step of awareness that helps you make better choices.

Later in this chapter we present some strategies for dealing with your fear. If your fears prove too big for you to deal with by observing them and making a different choice, get some help. Talk to a trusted friend or see a counselor.

4. Own the Other Person's Legitimate Complaints about You

Since we dealt with this matter in detail in chapter 10, we will simply mention here that you need to own your part of a problem before you have a difficult conversation. If you look at yourself and your contributions to the problem in the relationship *before* the conversation, you will be much better prepared when the other person brings them up. You will not be caught off guard, feel defensive or guilty, react, try to explain them away, feel too "bad," or blame your contributions on the other person's behavior.

Also, if you have dealt with your part in the problem, you are in a better position to bring it up to the other person to illustrate all of the good things that can result from a good apology. Some people wrongly say they have no responsibility to go to another person with their failures. They say, "Well, if he has an issue with me, he should come and tell me. That's his problem." But that's not altogether true.

It is true that the other person should come and tell you, but it is not true that it is only "his problem." If someone has something against you, it is your problem, too. You are required to go to him first, to be proactive, and to do anything you can to make it right. Jesus said, "Therefore, if you are offering your gift at the altar and there remember that your brother has something against you, leave your gift there in front of the altar. First go and be reconciled to your brother; then come and offer your gift" (Matt. 5:23–24).

Being proactive is good not only for the relationship, but also for you. It puts you in a position of being pure in heart before God and others and of doing all you can from your side to make things right (Rom. 12:18). It is *always* to your advantage to be as clean and pure as possible in every situation. It will affect not only that relationship, but also the rest of your life, often in ways you may never know.

5. Own Your Distortions of Who the Other Person Is

A woman came to see me once for help in her marriage. She described her husband as so "powerful" and "intimidating" she just could not find it in herself to talk to him about things bothering her.

"Why don't you just talk to him about these things?" I asked.

"Oh, I just couldn't do that," she would reply. "He's too strong. He's so intimidating. I just don't know what to do."

After seeing I wasn't getting anywhere by suggesting she talk to her husband, I asked her if her husband would come in to see me. She said she would tell him I would like to talk to him.

I had no idea what I was in for.

On the day of her next appointment, I went into the waiting room to find the woman sitting there with a small, frail-looking man. He stood and said, in one of the least intimidating, squirrelly little voices I had ever heard, "Hi, Dr. Cloud. It is so nice to meet you!" I remember describing him later as "mousy." He came across as just a whisper of a person.

I could see immediately that his wife and I had some work to do. I had to help her see where her distorted view of her husband as powerful and intimidating came from. After much work in counseling, we discovered that as a result of growing up with a powerful, intimidating, "unconfrontable" father, this woman saw all men she needed in the same way. She had never worked through her tendency to distort.

We all have such "transferences," or tendencies to see people in light of past experiences. We distort authority figures, men, women, romantic ties, people's neediness, and their imperfections.

I worked as a consultant in a church split several years ago in which resolution was impossible because of the leaders' distortions of each other. They had villainized each other's faults to such a degree that they could not see any good in the other at all. I don't know exactly what ghosts they were bringing into the room, but they certainly were not the people they were accusing.

In dating relationships, a woman will sometimes so idealize her boyfriend that she cannot even see the problems that need confronting. She idealizes him to the extent that she does not confront ongoing problems, and then there is a big blowup later. Or the "idealized" one loses interest because he has so much power in the relationship. Whenever someone is too idealized, the power imbalance is destructive to the connection; it will ultimately break down.

In some organizations, followers sometimes so idealize their leaders that they do not deal with ongoing issues and problems with them, then later they hate the leaders when they fail. The proverbial "other shoe" drops, and we find that the idealization covered up much anger and many problems. In the same way, we see others as "all bad" at times, and far from idealizing them, we have difficulty seeing their good points. In this situation, a confrontation becomes a lynching. The distortion arouses destructive rage, which is directed at the person who is "all bad" in the confronter's eyes. (This happens in many romantic breakups, too.)

In corporate consulting, I have heard many leaders and bosses say they wish that their people would give them more negative and direct feedback about themselves and what problems they see. But because of their distortions of the leader, they keep quiet.

Another very common scenario is one in which someone who has been enabling another person is afraid to set limits because she fears it will destroy the person who is so "weak." Obviously, when someone is in a vulnerable position, confrontation is not a good idea. If it could put the person "over the edge," or if he truly would not be able to take care of himself, to cut him off would be cruel. But in many situations, a family is enabling someone to stay sick and dependent because they see him as too weak and unable. It is often time to clear up that distortion and see him as a fat little bird who needs to be pushed out of the nest so that he can learn to fly.

The point is this: Obtain a realistic view of the person you are talking to, and be aware of your tendencies to do the following:

- Idealize and romanticize
- See as "all good" or "all bad"
- See as overly powerful
- See as overly needy or fragile
- See as a parental authority figure

As you become aware of your distortions, look also at the behaviors and choices these distortions lead you to make, and use that awareness to make the changes you need to make.

6. Seek Understanding of the Other Person

Many times we look at a problem without trying to understand what causes the other person's struggles and defensiveness. We just know that we don't like what she does, and we become angry and upset.

Certainly those emotions are understandable, but it often helps before a confrontation to take a look at why the other person might be acting the way she is. Has she been hurt in the past? Has she ever had anyone model for her what a good relationship looks like? Is she carrying a lot of pain? Have the ways you have responded in the past been part of the problem?

Take a good look at the person, and as the old saying goes, "Walk a mile in his shoes." It may help you to approach the confrontation with more understanding, empathy, and compassion. This does not mean that you avoid dealing with things directly, but it does mean that when you do it, you might do it with a different attitude. Some of your anger and feelings of being persecuted might subside when you realize that most of the time, people are not trying to hurt other people intentionally, but just do it as a result of their own problems.

7. Deal with Your Emotions Somewhere Else

"I just lost it," Jeri said. "I went in to talk to my sister about what's been going on in the family, and as soon as she criticized me, I broke down. All of the hurt I had felt for so long spilled out onto the floor. I was a mess, and I couldn't go on. I told her I would have to talk to her another time, and I left. It was too much."

Can you identify with Jeri? Have you ever gone into a conversation with so much hurt or anger inside that when someone touched the hurt place, it all came out? Your hurt feelings affected your ability to stay centered, focused, and goal oriented.

I remember a meeting several years ago in which I was going to clear up some things with a group of people with whom I had been working on a project. One member of the group was not doing his job, but had criticized all of us who were working so hard doing our work and his. I knew exactly what the problem was and what solution I wanted. It all seemed so simple.

As soon as we started the meeting, however, this person not only criticized how everyone else had handled the project, but also stated that he wasn't getting out of the project what he thought he deserved. When I brought up how he had not participated in the work, he became angry and made even stronger assertions to the contrary.

That was enough to set me off, and all of what I had been feeling got in the way of my being able to deal effectively with the problem. I was so angry and sick of it all, I said, "Fine! I'm done!" and walked out.

I had never done that before and, thankfully, have never done it since. But I learned a lesson: Deal with your emotions *before* having a difficult conversation. Not only will you do better in the conversation, but you will also not be destructive to others in the process. (Actually, I learned two lessons that day. I had forgotten my car was in the shop and I needed a ride home from one of the people in the meeting. After walking out like that, I could not go back in and ask someone for a ride, so I ended up walking all the way home. Needless to say, it gave me some time to think about my actions. Deal with your emotions, and don't blow up without a way to get home!)

As a counselor, I have seen many people who have been told that as part of their healing they need to "confront" their parents or their abusers for childhood exploitation. Yet, to do so means only that they will get injured all over again. This kind of confrontation usually does not lead to healing.

I believe in reconciling relationships and in talking things over when that would help estranged parties come back together. But these talks are not the place to have wounds healed. Be as healed as possible and as strong as possible before going into a difficult conversation. Find your healing somewhere apart from the ones who hurt you, then take your strong, healed self into the conversation to reconcile the relationship.

In situations where you are still actively hurt or angry, go somewhere else to get support and work through those emotions. Then you will be better equipped to deal with the conversation, because you won't be as hurt or angry and you will have a better perspective and more insight. Also, you will be better able to respond than if you reacted out of untamed emotions.

8. Seek Healing

Seek healing for all of the weaknesses that play into your inability to confront—from fears to distortions. Often, talking to a friend or reading a book will give you insight, awareness, or new skills and strategies to overcome these weaknesses. At other times, more is needed.

If, for example, you have such a need for love and approval that you feel empty and devastated when you are not getting it from someone, you probably need some structured healing such as that found in counseling, a support group, or a recovery group. The same would be true if you have debilitating fears, abandonment or abuse issues, a history of addictions or relationships with addicts, or patterns of finding yourself in bad relationships. These things can be greatly helped by people who have experience in dealing with them, and we would encourage you to find such help.

Seek healing first so you can focus on the issue with the other person's behavior. Neither the focus nor the agenda is about your healing. Otherwise, besides not getting what you need at that moment for healing, you will lose focus and might even become further hurt. Resolution is unlikely. So, become as strong and as well as you can get. It will help both in confronting relationship issues and in all of life.

SPECIFIC STRATEGIES FOR PREPARING

Besides "getting the plank out," other preparation may be needed before you go into a difficult, "facing things" conversation. Here are some strategies we have found more than helpful for people; for some, they have made all the difference between success and failure.

1. Get Plugged In

Because some confrontations are difficult and because you might have fears and needs for love and acceptance that can make you vulnerable, plug into your support base before you confront. Have in place a team with whom you have reviewed things, faced your weaknesses, cried, and practiced so that you know you have support on your side. The Bible says that sometimes we are weak and need help (1 Thess. 5:14), but even when we are not, we are human, so things go better when we have someone on our team. Think of it as Solomon said,

> Two are better than one,
>> because they have a good return for their work:
> If one falls down,
>> his friend can help him up.
> But pity the man who falls
>> and has no one to help him up!
> Also, if two lie down together, they will keep warm.
>> But how can one keep warm alone?
> Though one may be overpowered,
>> two can defend themselves.
> A cord of three strands is not quickly broken (Eccl. 4:9–12).

So get on a good team first, before you play the game. For example, find out if your church provides healthy small groups that would be a good fit.

2. Script What You Want to Say

For many people, confrontations are so scary, the other person is so difficult, or there has been so much history, that they find great help in writing down beforehand what they want to say. Reading what you want to say helps on so many fronts. If you are interrupted by negation or defensiveness, for example, you can say, "Wait until I'm finished. Then I will listen." And you won't have lost your train of thought or gotten confused or sidetracked on a rabbit trail. Or, if you do let the other person talk, you can go right back to where you were and not miss a beat.

In addition, this strategy gives you a lot of time to think about what you want to say. You can get it right. You can have others review it and see how it sounds. They can check out your tendency to minimize, overstate the issue, blame, or not take a hard-enough stand. Your weaknesses can be worked through beforehand.

It also helps you avoid the interference of emotion with your thinking in the moment. You will be writing it at a time when you are centered and clear, and if you tend to become upset, you won't lose your ability to think about what you want to say and later, after the conversation, say to yourself, *Why didn't I just say . . . ?*

Another option is to draw up a list of things you want to bring up without writing them out word for word. The list serves the same purpose, but is less detailed. Do what is helpful to you.

3. Practice and Role-Play

You might find it helpful to practice the conversation with someone on your team. Let her play the difficult person, and you be yourself and say what you want to say. Have her play all the possible scenarios you fear, such as defensiveness, excuses, blame, or outbursts. Then practice how you will respond to them. We will role-play some things for you in the next section of the book, but doing it yourself in real life will be really helpful.

You may find it helpful to play the role of the person you will be confronting and have your friend be you. Then you can see some other options for responding as your friend plays your part.

You might be surprised at how well you do in difficult situations if you have practiced being assertive and holding your ground beforehand. Like anything else, "practice makes perfect."

4. Get Expectations into Proper Perspective

What can you realistically expect from the conversation you are going to have? Sometimes you can expect wonderful things to happen, depending on who the other person is. Miracles happen. But sometimes people enter into boundary conversations with very unrealistic expectations. We have heard people complain, "I tried boundaries, and 'they' don't work."

"What do you mean?" we ask.

"Well, I set boundaries on my husband, and he just got mad and did what he wanted anyway."

"Well," we say, "if you consider that boundaries are not something you set *on* someone else and that he is free to do whatever he chooses, then you wouldn't think boundaries didn't 'work.' Boundaries are something you set *with* yourself, such as what you will allow yourself to participate in, or what consequences you will enforce if others make certain choices. So, if you see boundaries as having to do with your choices, then if they don't 'work,' it is because you didn't do them. Setting boundaries is not a way of controlling another person."

> You can expect to be in control of what you do, but what another person does is totally up to him.

So what can you realistically expect from the conversation you are going to have? *You can expect to be in control of what you do, but what another person does is totally up to him.*

Boundaries and limits can, however, *greatly influence others.* We have seen amazing turnarounds when one person sets boundaries

CHAPTER 20: HOW TO GET READY   203

with another. You can hope for a turnabout, but there are no guarantees. Yet you can expect to end the problem from your side.

People often get hurt when they desire to be understood and loved by people in denial. It may happen, but many times it doesn't. It is good to want and desire favorable relational outcomes, but to expect or demand them is not wise, nor should it be the sole reason for confronting someone.

We do not want to cover everything with a wet blanket. After all, this whole book is about hope and turning relationships around. And many, many times that will happen. But some people are deeply in denial and defensiveness, and they don't respond favorably to situations designed to work with the truth. Other people respond wonderfully, and still others respond at various points in between. So there is a range of possibilities, depending on whom you are dealing with. Recall the proverbs we quoted earlier, which show the differences in how wise people and mockers respond to confrontation (Prov. 9:7, 9).

There are many possible outcomes, but we can tell you this: As a general rule, dealing proactively with situations offers the best chance of resolving them. Avoidance rarely fixes anything. Keep hope alive, yet stay in reality.

5. Set Up a Confrontation Sandwich

When you face a difficult confrontation, set up a "confrontation sandwich." The difficult conversation is the middle of the sandwich, and your supportive allies are the pieces of bread on either side of the conversation.

Talk to your supportive people right before you go in. Tell them you want to connect, get courage, review your goals, know that you are loved, and know that you will have their support when the confrontation is over. Whatever it is that you need is what you work out with them in that phone call or visit. Then have the conversation. As soon as it is over, you repeat the support call or visit to debrief, get put back together if needed, celebrate, get support, get validation, or just know that someone understands. The conversation may go very well, but whatever happens, it is helpful to know someone will be there when it's over.

This may sound like a lot of preparation, but in a sense, it really isn't. It is just good practice for all of life, whether or not you are planning a difficult conversation with someone. We would all do well to take ownership of our faults, work through the things that cause us to distort our view of people and situations, deal with our fears and problems, and seek healing. So don't see this chapter as burdensome, but as proposing a good way to live. If you are doing these things day to day, when a boundary conversation comes along, you will already be prepared.

PART V

HAVING *the* DIFFICULT CONVERSATION *with* PEOPLE *in* YOUR LIFE

21

With Your Spouse

When my wife, Barbi, and I (John) were first married, we had conflicts about conflict. Our boundary conversations were about how bad our boundary conversations were. They weren't a lot of fun. I would approach Barbi to talk to her about a problem, and it wouldn't go well. One of us would misunderstand, we would pull away from each other, and the problem wouldn't get solved.

I felt bad for her. "That's so sad," I said, "because I never stop loving you. Is there anything I can do to make this better for you?"

She thought a minute and said, "Maybe if you let me know you love me before you confront me, that might help."

I thought that was a good idea, so I agreed. The next time I wanted to have a talk with her about a problem, I walked in the room and said something like, "Honey, I just want to let you know I really care about you and I hope you feel safe with me." Then when I brought up the problem, things went better for her and for us.

This method of having successful boundary conversations went on for a while. One day, however, something changed. I needed to bring up an issue, so I began with, "Honey, I just want you to know...."

"Stop!" Barbi said. "It's okay. I know you love me; just get to the problem."

We had a good laugh about it. Over time, she had begun feeling safe enough not to need reassurance before each conversation. She realized that I love her even in the midst of confrontation, and she was ready to go straight to solving whatever problem needed to be solved.

CONFRONTATION IN MARRIAGE

Confrontation should be a part of any marriage, good or bad. The closeness of the marital relationship makes confrontation essential.

When God created marriage, he gave us one of his best gifts. He provided a permanent and safe connection for a man and a woman to experience love, joy, meaning, and purpose together: "For this reason a man will leave his father and mother and be united to his wife, and they will become one flesh" (Gen. 2:24).

> *The closeness of the marital relationship makes confrontation essential.*

God designed marriage to be a whole-person connection. This means that, more than in any other human relationship, every part of you ideally is to connect and cleave to every part of your spouse. The love you share should be complete as you intertwine your lives and emotions around each other. Ultimately, in marriage spouses give up a lot of "you" and "I" freedoms in order to create a "we." Though there are still separate individuals with two distinct souls, there is now a new, third thing called the marriage bond. This mystery of being both "you and I" and "we" is impossible to explain completely. Paul uses this mystery of the marital relationship to illustrate God's relationship to us, his people. He quotes Genesis 2:24 and then says, "This is a profound mystery—but I am talking about Christ and the church" (Eph. 5:32).

Every Good Marriage Has Confrontation

Because marriage is such a wonderful type of relationship, confrontation within the marital relationship is very important. You are a central delivery system for grace and truth in your spouse's life, and vice versa. You have a responsibility to both care for and confront one another. You are an agent for change and growth in each other. Love does not blind either of you to the other's problems; in fact, love demands that you pay attention to them so that you can help resolve them.

> *Love does not blind either of you to the other's problems; it demands that you pay attention to them so as to help resolve them.*

Who is better qualified to understand and speak to someone about a problem than the person who is living life right next to him? You are intimately involved with him. You see the real person, imperfections and all. His ways and actions affect you; you are not dispassionate about him. More than anyone, a spouse should be able to see what her partner's true problems are.

This idea, however, is foreign to some people. They have the notion that their spouse's job is to make them happy. Then when they are not happy, they think their spouse is not doing what he should be doing.

In reality, nothing could be further from the truth. *Marriage is not about making each other happy; it is about growing and helping one's spouse to grow.* Good marriages are a large part of how the body of Christ "grows and builds itself up in love" (Eph. 4:16). Happiness can and does come to a good marriage. Happiness, however, is a byproduct of growth and life. It is not the goal. (For more on this topic, see *Boundaries in Marriage*.)

The "Problem" of Intimacy

The irony is that *the very closeness of marriage partners makes confrontation more difficult.* When two people pass through the idealizing honeymoon season and dive into knowing each other in day-to-day life, they see the problems, weaknesses, immaturities, sins, and eccentricities of the other person. And often, because of this awareness, a spouse will dismiss her mate's feedback and truth about her. It is as if she is saying, "Since I know you aren't perfect either, you have no credibility to confront me."

It is true that we are less credible if we do not do what we say. The person who is not looking at himself but is pointing out things to his spouse can expect very little openness. At the same time, no one should have to "have it all together" in order to be able to tell her spouse that his behavior or attitude is a problem. As the old preacher used to say, "God used an ass to speak to Balaam, so you better listen to your friends" (see Num. 22). We all need to be open to reality, no matter what its source.

PRACTICAL STEPS TO FOLLOW

Be aware that your spouse may have a built-in resistance to a boundary conversation. Here are some things to remember in having a healthy confrontation with your mate.

Be the Best Spouse Possible

Though you can't be perfect, you do owe it to your mate to be the best "fit" that you can be. Sacrifice your comfort to his legitimate and appropriate needs and wants. Get into the growth process and learn to love and care about his life. Repent of and change whatever habits and patterns are bad for you, him, and the relationship. He is more likely to be open to hearing the truth from someone who is growing, involved, fun, and fully living life. People who are involved in the life of God stand a better chance of influencing their spouses than those who are standing on the sidelines of life.

Appeal to the Relationship Itself

Marriage is fundamentally about relationship, and it rests on the attachment and covenant of the husband and wife. Though your obvious problems may revolve around responsibilities, money, and tasks, do not stop there. Talk with your spouse about the relationship itself. This is where the marriage lives.

When you bring up the problem, for example, let your spouse know that you are doing so because it affects you, her, and "us." Here's what this conversation might look like:

> **You:** "I am not telling you this because I want to fix or change you. I want more closeness and good times with you, but this problem is like a boulder between us; I can't get around it to get back to you. I want to get it out of the way so I can get back to us. The problem causes me to miss you."

> **Your spouse:** "You're not being loving with me."

> **You:** "I'm sorry it feels that way, and I want you to know I love you. But I need to get back to the problem, because it really affects our relationship."

Use Your History and Credibility

In marriage you have, in a way, earned the right to be heard. Without sounding superior, let your husband know that you have been around him and with him long enough to see the patterns you are concerned about. For example, say something like this:

> **You:** "I am not basing this on one event. I have seen it happen many times over the past few months. I live with you, so it's pretty clear what's going on."

In addition, use your "spousal equity" to bring up the effects of your mate's behavior on you. Your lives are intertwined, so what he is doing most likely has a large effect on you. Make that part of the conversation. Go over the emotional, relational, and practical results of the problem.

> **You:** "Your involvement in Internet pornography is bringing disaster to us. It has totally distanced me from you; I can't feel at all close to you or safe with you. It may ruin the marriage if you do not

do something about it. And it is dangerous to you, our kids, and maybe even your job and livelihood. I want you to stop and get help now."

Persist

If the problem you want to talk about has been going on for a while, chances are you will not get immediate results the first time you bring it up. Your spouse may be set in her ways. This is even more likely if your previous attempts at confrontation were poorly done.

If the problem is serious enough to hurt you, your spouse, and the relationship, it needs to be addressed more than once.

Your spouse may ignore you or react, hoping you will drop it. As a result, it is easy to fall prey to thinking, *I brought it up, and it didn't work, so that's just the way it is.*

However, a bad outcome is not cause for dropping the issue. If the problem is serious enough to hurt you, your spouse, and the relationship, it needs to be addressed more than once. Often the spouse doesn't understand how strongly her mate feels until he goes to the trouble to bring it up again. When I read through the Old Testament, I am always struck by how many times God brings up a problem to his people. He doesn't drop it the first time: "I spoke to you again and again, but you did not listen" (Jer. 7:13).

Let your spouse know how strongly you feel about solving the problem by saying something like this:

> **You:** "I know you aren't comfortable with this topic. I'm not either. But it's important enough to me that I will keep addressing it with you until it's resolved one way or another. Is there another time we can talk, or another way we can talk about it that will be easier for you?"

Your spouse: "I don't want to talk. It's not my problem."

> **You:** "I know this is uncomfortable for you, but I have
> to insist that we talk sometime soon. What works
> for you?"

Learn to Persist If You Feel Unable to Persist

You may find that persisting is difficult for you. On our radio show we hear many callers say, "I've tried everything and nothing works." When we get down to specifics, we will find that "everything" often means that she tried to talk about the problem a time or two, then gave up when her spouse didn't respond well.

Often, this has to do with a person's dread of conflict. She is not used to it, and she fears the possible repercussions. She had to work up a lot of courage even to bring up the problem. So when the spouse ignores it or gets defensive, she is almost relieved to let it go. The despair and resignation are a little more tolerable than the anxiety.

If this is your situation, get outside help on confrontation. Use friends, a support group, or a mentor to help you work through your fears of telling your spouse the truth. Once you become more comfortable with the language of honesty, you will be more able to persist. Persistence pays off.

Realize That Your Spouse Needs Something from You

Sometimes a spouse has problems confronting because he feels powerless and helpless. He is afraid his words will have no effect: *She won't listen, I can't control her, I don't matter to her, why should she listen?*

This is often a misconception. The reality is that often the out-of-control person is more likely to be very dependent on the spouse. This is because the spouse is often unknowingly enabling, rescuing and protecting the out-of-control mate from the consequence of her ways. She needs her spouse's responsibility, structure, acceptance, and other strengths since without those things she would most likely be in a lot of pain due to her behavior. The enabler is the strong one, though it doesn't look like it from the outside.

Use this reality in your confrontation. If your mate is not responsive to you on the problem, say something like this:

> **You:** "I don't think you are taking this seriously, and it's a serious matter. I really want you to change in this area. I have appealed to our relationship and to the possible hurt you are going to cause. But if this is not enough, I will need to start removing things in our relationship that you want and value. I don't want to, but if that is what it takes for you to take responsibility for your problem, I'm willing to."
>
> **Your spouse:** "Go ahead, you're destroying us."
>
> **You:** "I'm sorry you feel I'm doing that. It must be difficult to feel that way. But I want you to know that I am clear about what will happen next. Are you sure you won't reconsider?"

Be prepared to follow up, and use friends for support and feedback. It may come to that. However hard this may seem, we have seen many, many marriages transform and heal because a spouse was willing to set and keep a limit by removing something his spouse needed.

Be "Satisfiable"

If your spouse agrees to deal with the problem, be thankful and content that this particular goal has been reached. Let him know that if he stops doing something bad, or begins to do something good, you will not need to press for another boundary conversation on this topic.

Your spouse needs to know that you are "satisfiable." Otherwise, you run the risk of his becoming discouraged and giving up altogether. Some individuals can be insatiable. When their spouse changes, a deep well of demand and desire is unearthed. You will often hear statements such as "I know you are taking the trash out now, but what about the clothes on the floor?" or "Even if you are more open to having sex, you don't seem really excited enough about it." Curb this part of your personality and, in your own growth context, work out the unhappiness you feel and be truly grateful for what you have.

SPECIFIC PROBLEMS RELATED TO MARRIAGE

Because it is a unique relationship, marriage has its own problems that need to be addressed. Here are the main ones, with suggestions on how to deal with each.

Conflict Style

It is helpful for husbands and wives to learn *how* to communicate about problems (as I learned!). Problems are part of any marriage, and having a good conflict-resolution language can be very important. However, when you find you can't talk about problems without things escalating or someone disconnecting, you need a boundary conversation about this issue itself. Otherwise, any other topic is doomed to failure.

Bring up the lack of a good conflict style by saying something like this:

> **You:** "I want to solve issues between us, and I think you do too. But every time we disagree, things get too heated and nothing good happens. In fact, I really don't want to talk about any problems between us until we solve this one; it's pointless. So can we sit down and talk together about why we can't resolve problems? Maybe we can change some things to make it easier."

Finances

Money is an emotionally laden issue in marriage. Finances are very important in life, and when couples disagree about money, they often have very strong feelings about the problem.

Many spouses ignore financial discussions because they feel uncomfortable. However, if you have a fiscally irresponsible spouse, do not beat around the bush. Your future, your children's future, and your stewardship to the Lord may be in jeopardy. Say something like this:

> **You:** "I want our financial dealings to be the way we want our marriage to be: honest and responsible, and determined by our agreed-upon values as a team. I don't think this is happening. I don't feel like my input or feelings are taken into consideration, and I'm terrified that you're putting us in danger. This issue will not go away. I want us to go see a financial counselor this week before things go too far."

Sex

What was designed by God to be a beautiful expression and symbol of his love and intimacy for us can often be an area of great unhappiness in marriage. Sex is important, and if it is not happening, or if it is happening in ways that are not life-producing for both spouses, you must address it. This might include problems such as one spouse's lack of sexual interest, one spouse's insistence on sex without having emotional intimacy, and any extramarital sexuality, from pornography to an affair.

When having a boundary conversation about a sexual problem, remember that sex outside of the context of relationship has little meaning. Understand and bring up the issue as a relationship issue, because it probably is.

> **You:** "I want a better sexual relationship with you, but it is difficult, because I have to take most of the

initiative. I think sometimes that if I didn't bring
it up, you'd be happy never being sexual with me.
It makes me feel lonely and undesirable. And I
wonder if it's how you feel about me in general,
not just sexually. I want you in my life, and I want
you to want me, both in bed and emotionally. I'd
like to talk about why this is so, and what we can
do about it."

Parenting

When a couple has children, their personal differences are often
reflected in their parenting styles. For example, the more controlled
and structured spouse is more rules-oriented with the kids, while the
more relational one is more fun and less likely to discipline. While
both parents bring their own contributions to parenting, if they are
too far apart, they run the risk of rais-
ing children who develop two incompatible views of reality in their heads.
On the one hand, the child views life
as performance-based, but does not feel
loved; on the other hand, she views life
as all love and fun, but is not required
to achieve anything.

*If the parents'
contributions to parenting
are too far apart,
they run the risk
of raising children who
develop two incompatible
views of reality.*

As best you can, talk about how the
two of you can defer to each other for
the sake of the child so that she has a
world of both love and limits. Do not
avoid a boundary conversation in order to keep the peace. Your
child has no voice; you are her only real advocate. Say something
like this:

> **You:** "I am concerned that Kelly is going to have
> problems from your lack of structure with her. I
> know you love her, but when you don't correct her
> or hold her to consequences we have agreed on,
> she learns some bad things about responsibility

and life. I want us to get on the same page with her, and stay on the same page. This is really important for her and to me."

In-Laws

In-laws were designed to be a blessing to a marriage. Their maturity and wisdom can have much to offer. Yet the in-law problem can be severe. They can interfere with the marriage, get between the couple, or bring the couple into their problems.

In most cases, the root of the problem is that one of the spouses has not yet been able to truly "leave and cleave." That is, he has not emotionally left home, and he is still unduly enmeshed with his parents. He may look to them for affirmation that he doesn't get from his wife, or he may be in constant conflict with his parents because they don't give him the respect he craves.

If you have an in-law problem in your marriage, be sure to address it. It is best to do so in a way that gets you out of the loop and helps your spouse (who may be overinvolved with his parents) learn how to lovingly detach from them and connect to you. Say something like this:

> You: "Whenever your mom disagrees with me, it seems as though you take her side. I don't mind it if that's your opinion. But I think it is more that you feel protective of her. This is hard for me. I am your wife, and you are number one in my life. But I feel like I am number two in your life after her. I want you to become aware of this so that we can work on it together."

Good confrontations can play a large part in creating good marriages. Work on making your talks a normal and necessary part of your relationship with your spouse.

22

With Someone
You're Dating

One afternoon I (Henry) was teaching a small group on confrontation in relationships, and a woman raised her hand with a comment: "I don't really know what to do with my boyfriend. I know I have to confront some things, but I don't know if I'm being too rigid, or expecting too much, or even how to do it."

"Well, let's see," I said. "What's happening?"

"He's not really committed to our relationship, though he says he is. I don't feel as though I have all of him. He doesn't seem to be fully in the relationship to the depth I want him to be."

"What makes you say that?"

"Well, he was married before, and he has difficulty letting go of his ex-wife. He says he doesn't, but although they divorced more than three years ago, he was sleeping with her up until the time we met. And now, since we've been dating, he still sees her occasionally, 'just as old friends,' he says. But it makes me feel insecure about the relationship."

"I can't imagine why."

"Well," she countered, seemingly embarrassed by my sarcasm. "It isn't as bad as it sounds. He's very nice to me, and I like him a lot—except for the ex-wife thing and his not being totally committed to me."

"Would you just listen to that last sentence?" I asked. "'I like him a lot—except for the ex-wife thing and his not being totally committed to me.' Do you hear anything strange about that?"

"I know. It sounds stupid. I know I ought to take a stand and confront it, but I don't know how."

"Why don't you just tell him what you just told me? Tell him that you don't like the ex-wife thing and his not being totally into the relationship. Why won't that work?"

"I just like him so much, and I don't want to lose him."

"You like him?"

"Yes, a lot—well, except for those things."

"But those things *are* him," I said. "If you are going to be with him, *then you are going to be with those things until they are confronted and he stops doing them.* You act as if there is a 'him' that does not include those things. Right now, that 'him' does not exist. So the 'him' you like is not the 'him' you have."

She looked at me and said, "I think I know what I need to do."

Whether she ever did confront her boyfriend, I don't know. But I do know that she experienced one of the most important things I see singles facing. She was dating a man with behavioral patterns that if not confronted could lead to heartache. I could look down the timeline and know that if she did not deal with this well now, the future did not look bright.

I hope she took the needed steps. And who knows? If she confronted well, maybe things would turn around, and her boyfriend could get his life together and become the man she wanted and thought he was in the beginning. It could have a dreamboat ending. But here is the point: *If you don't confront, you will never know.*

In dating, confrontation achieves more than just making sure your dates and times together go well. It means you deal with issues that if resolved could lead to a happy future, and if ignored will lead to disaster. In this chapter we look at some of the issues worth having boundary conversations about.

You Are Establishing Patterns

By its very nature, dating is a time of "checking someone out." I don't mean this crassly, but dating is a relationship that has an end point: One either makes a long-term commitment or parts ways. So in a sense, each person is in both a buying and a selling mode. They are checking out whether they want to make a commitment to this person, and if they do, they also want to come across as someone the other person wants. It is an exciting time of relationship, curiosity, risk, and fun.

But often something goes wrong. For fear of "not being chosen," one person in the dating relationship does not confront, or "face," things that emerge. He fears disapproval, rejection, conflict, or other disruptions in the path of "winning the object of his desire." So he lets things go unaddressed. Sometimes he allows small things to pass; at other times he does not bring up large things. Many times the person being hurt or disappointed hopes that once the relationship is more "solid," or they are married, these things will change or at least he can address them then.

> *The less one addresses problems in a dating relationship, the less likely these problems will be easy to deal with in marriage.*

Nothing could be further from the truth. In fact, the *less* one addresses problems in a dating relationship, the *less likely* these problems will be easy to deal with in marriage, for a couple of reasons. First, the date who is unaware or unconcerned about how she treats her partner is being taught that her behavior is okay. Her partner is enabling her to be that way. Then, when he finally can't take it anymore, sometimes even after they marry, he confronts the behavior, and she cries foul. She feels as if her mate has changed. All of a sudden she finds herself getting confronted, and she doesn't take it well. Often it turns into a major crisis.

Second—and this is the real danger—a person who can go for a long time being disrespectful or hurtful to another will also not be the kind of person who is likely to take later confrontation well and to make the necessary changes easily. She may have become very comfortable with a pattern of not worrying about the feelings of the one she is with. At that point, usually only very strong limits turn her around.

Therefore, if you are in a dating relationship where you do not confront issues as they arise, you set yourself up for heartache later. You train someone how to have a relationship with you. You teach her what is acceptable to you. Then, later, when you finally grow tired of her behavior and want to deal with it, it will be a much rockier road than if you had dealt with it earlier. You also run the risk of ending up with a person who will not deal with things then, either. It is too late.

So, confronting things in dating is extremely important. As we say in our book *Boundaries in Dating*, "nip it in the bud." Then you will know very early if things are going to change and if you are with a person who is even capable of making changes.

Over and over we ask married people who are struggling with a selfish or irresponsible spouse, "Didn't you see this before you married him [or her]?" And they say something like "Yes, sort of. But I was so in love, I just ignored it" or "My gut was telling me something was wrong, but I never dealt with it."

Deal with it.

You Find Out Much by Confrontation

Earlier we talked about the different kinds of reactions you can get from someone you confront. Think about the following two possibilities in terms of the person you are dating: "Do not rebuke a mocker or he will hate you; rebuke a wise man and he will love you" (Prov 9:8).

One of the most important things you can figure out in dating is how the person responds to your bringing up issues. A wise person is grateful for information that will help the relationship or help him to be a better person. A mocker will get angry and defensive when confronted. In other words, how he responds to confrontation helps you diagnose what kind of person he is.

Few things are more important to a good dating relationship or marriage than a couple's ability to resolve conflict. Test it out in dating; see how the other person faces issues you bring up. This will give you a major clue into the future quality of relationship you will have with this person.

> **You:** "I want to talk to you about the party tonight. I wanted to be there with you, but throughout the night, I felt ignored. You talked to everyone else and pretty much left me on my own all night. At times I felt embarrassed as my friends kept asking me where you were."

Not-so-good response:

> **The other person:** "Oh, come on! Get serious! That's what parties are about, to talk to everyone. You don't appreciate anything I do. You're always on my case, and I don't feel like I can even go to a party without your finding something to gripe about."

More promising:

> **The other person:** "Really? Gosh, I didn't know you felt that way. I'm sorry it was like that for you. I was just enjoying everyone, and I guess I wasn't thinking about how it was feeling to you." (Or some response in which the other person acknowledges the ability to see your feelings and at least show concern.)

You can tell a lot about someone by his response. You don't have to look for perfection, but at least require that the person have the ability to see and care about how you feel, even if he does not agree or understand.

Begin with Values and Stand on Them

A woman called us on the radio and described her boyfriend, Tom, as pushing her for sex when she did not want to have it and also as being lax about their spiritual life. She was always the one who suggested they have spiritual times together.

"I don't know what to do," she said.

"If you did not know Tom and were not attached to him, what kind of man would you tell me you were looking for?" I asked her.

"Well, I would be looking for someone who respects me for who I am, who shares my worldview, who has the same values as I do, and who attends church with me."

"I think you've just answered your own question," I replied. "You've lost touch with what you value and what you want. You used to think about what you wanted in a partner, but then something happened. You got attached to *this man*, and now because of your attachment, you feel like you want *him*, and you've lost touch with what you want that is not him. You've lost your focus.

"I suggest you get back in touch with your values and make *them* the standard, not your attachment to him. Say to him, 'I want someone who has the same spiritual values I do and takes the same stand for them that I have. I do not want to have to always be in charge of implementing those by myself. That is who I am looking for. Tom, I hope you turn out to be the man I'm describing, but right now you are not that man. And I'm going to look for those qualities and not settle for less. When you are that man, then let me know."

What you tolerate is what you will get.

Do not nag a person about issue after issue. Take a stand on what is important to you, and then let that stand select for you. Let that be the gate people have to get through to make it to your heart. If you get confused because you are attached to a person, and if you lose touch with what you want because you feel like you want a particular person who is *not what you truly want*, you are in trouble. I repeat: Take a stand for what is important to you, and let those values do the selection, not your attachment or attraction:

- "I will only get serious with people of my same values."
- "I will only get serious with someone who is honest."
- "I will only get serious with someone who is respectful."
- "I will only get serious with someone who is faithful."

What you tolerate is what you will get. It is up to you what you value, and if you take a stand on your values, you will more likely find someone who values what you do.

The "Where Is This Going?" Talk

At some point in a dating relationship, you will reach the "land of the unknown," where one person feels his or her heart getting involved and is unclear where the other person is. This is one of the scary times of dating, when someone feels himself or herself becoming vulnerable and does not want to go there alone.

This fear is unavoidable, at least for a time. You can't reasonably expect both of you simultaneously to "know" you want to go further. Attraction happens along a timeline, and the moment of epiphany is rarely exactly the same for both parties. So most of the time, someone will find himself feeling as if he is hanging in midair. That is the nature of the game.

But this does not mean you should hang in midair forever. One person might be perfectly willing to let a dating relationship be casual for a long time, while the other person is falling deeper and deeper in love. If you feel as though this is happening to you, it could be the time to speak up. Find out where things are going. Again, timing is important, as you don't want to pressure someone, but there comes a point when it is good to know.

The main point here is that we do not want you to be used. Many noncommittal types are perfectly willing and able to use you for as long as you allow yourself to be used. If you sense an unequal investment in the relationship, remember a few things.

First, it is helpful to clarify the relationship. No matter what side
of things you are on, it is good to clarify so that you will have your
integrity and your heart in check:

"Mary, I enjoy spending time with you and really have come
to enjoy your companionship. Sometimes I wonder, though,
where you are in our relationship. I see us as just friends, and
I just want to make sure we are on the same page. I don't
want anyone to get hurt. Where are you on that?"

"Mary, I enjoy spending time with you and really have come
to enjoy your companionship. Sometimes I wonder, though,
where you are in our relationship. I see us as friends, getting
to know each other, and enjoying that. At the same time,
it seems as though there is the possibility there could be
more, and I want to continue to spend time together to find
that out. I'm not ready for more right now, though, but I
wanted you to know what I'm thinking. I would like to keep
spending time together as friends and see where it goes. How
is that for you?"

"Mary, I enjoy spending time with you, and I've really come
to enjoy your companionship. Sometimes I wonder, though,
where our relationship is going. I really like you and find
myself getting pretty attached. I would like us to move to the
next step, and I think I'm feeling like more than friends. But
I don't want to go there alone. Where do you think you are
heading with me?"

Each of these statements clarifies where you are and where you
want to go and, at the same time, finds out where the other person
is. Don't think that by bringing in a bunch of rules and structure,
we are throwing cold water on the natural process of getting to
know someone, dating, and falling in love. Far from it. Too many
rules can kill the process. But some structure is needed. There is a
place for knowing where you are headed and knowing where the

other person is as well. When you find that place in your heart and experience, take the appropriate action to clarify things. You might save yourself or the other person a lot of heartache. Do not enable someone to use you if he is not headed the same place you are.

The "Fish or Cut Bait" Talk

With longer dating relationships, a point comes when you have to say either the person will commit or you will get on down the road. How long is that? It depends on what you want.

If you want to get married and the person you are dating is fine with dating forever and is not moving any closer to tying the knot, take responsibility for how long you are willing to wait. This is your choice. A general rule on when to have the talk is the point at which you see that "just more time," without anything different happening, is not going to change anything. Then it's time to talk. "Something different happening" would be counseling or some other new experience to help the person get past where she is stuck.

Waiting for someone may be necessary. But if you have waited and waited and it looks as if your waiting could go on forever, you might want to require that something different take place, or you may want to set a deadline. (See "Kiss False Hope Goodbye" in *Boundaries in Dating*.)

The "Let's Face Our Differences" Talk

Sometimes there are personal differences you should address and not continue to ignore, such as differences in tastes, philosophies, faith, sexual and physical limits, values, and long-term plans. Often these differences are not faced because one person fears losing the relationship or having conflict. But these issues are like the behavior problems we talked about earlier. If you do not face them now, you develop a pattern of acting as though they are okay with you.

If you have physical and sexual boundaries the other person does not share, you cannot ignore those until you get into a situation where it is too late. Let those be known up front. Be clear about what your values are. Then you will find out if the other person shares them or shows resistance. Past that, if you are clear about your values and then he pushes you, be very strong. Someone who does not respect your physical and moral boundaries is not likely to respect other ones you set later, either, especially where they call for self-denial. This is a good test to see what the future looks like in other areas as well. (Again, see *Boundaries in Dating* regarding physical boundaries.)

Talk about other life direction-setting issues such as these: Do you both want children? Where do you want to live? Where do you want to go to church? What other faith practices do you want to share? These differences must be addressed clearly. Make sure that before you go too far, you are talking about your differences and you know where the other person stands.

> **Suzanne:** "Tom, I want to talk to you. Last night I felt as though you were pushing me past where I want to go physically. I thought I was pretty clear about my limits in that area. But it did not seem as though you were respecting those. I felt pressured."
>
> **Tom:** "I wasn't pressuring you. I just really want to be with you. I want us to express ourselves to each other in that way. I am really attracted to you, and I want to be with you."
>
> **Suzanne:** "I understand that. But I want to talk about our differences there and know that you can accept my values and respect them. I do not want every date to be a time of worry for me about whether or not I'm going to have to fight you on it. I want to know that you know me and respect me. And that you accept my boundaries. Also, I want to know about your views. I think we are way apart here, and I need to know more about what this means for us."

> **Tom:** "You don't have to make such a big deal out of it. I wasn't meaning anything by it other than I really want you and am drawn to you. It's a compliment. Don't take it as something bad."

> **Suzanne:** "Tom, I want to know that you are getting this. It's a big deal to me. I want to know that you know that. So I will make a big deal out of it until I know we are on the same page. If not, I can't be with you until we are. It *is* a big deal. Can you hear that?"

You would have a similar conversation for the other life direction-setting issues. Those can be spaced-out, more fluid conversations that unfold as you become more serious, but they have to be faced if you are thinking about a long-term, committed relationship. Life-changing issues are just that—life changing. If you do not get on the same page, someone is in trouble.

The Breakup

"Breaking up is hard to do," or so the song says. In reality, for some people it is almost impossible. They hem and haw, procrastinate, or do it and quickly get back together over and over again so often that you can't really call it a breakup at all. It is more like the break between quarters in a basketball game. It's just a time-out.

If you have decided to break off a dating relationship, be clear and decisive. You do not have to fight or even be adversarial. But don't leave the other person with mixed messages. Many people go into the breakup conversation and leave it muddled—"Maybe

Don't leave a little wiggle room for the reason that you are afraid of hurting the person or you can't stand the hurt yourself.

we can see each other after a while, and then who knows?"—or something else that is not clear. If you want to leave it there, that's fine, but *don't leave it there if that's not your plan.* Don't leave it there as a defense against saying the hard thing. *Don't leave a little wiggle room for the reason that you are afraid of hurting the person or you can't stand the hurt yourself.*

Be clear. State what you want and don't want. And if your date maneuvers, use this formula: Empathize and stick to your agenda.

> **Steve:** "But why do we have to break it off completely? Let's just see each other now and then. Then we might figure out what is wrong. Let's do that."

> **Julie:** "Steve, I understand this is painful and not your first choice. But I've made up my mind that this is what I want. I don't think we should see each other at all, even as friends. At least until we are way over and done with dating. That is what I want."

If you want something else and are willing to live with the consequences, fine. If you do take the other person's suggestion and get off your agenda, you'd better have a good reason or you are merely putting off what you have already seen as inevitable. If you want to change your mind, *don't do it during your conversation.* Go away, talk it out, and wait for a cooling-off period. Say something like this to buy yourself time:

> **You:** "I don't know if I could even be friends right now. But I don't want to answer right now. I do not feel ready to make that decision at the moment. I will call you in a few weeks after I have had some time to think more about it."

People get into trouble in the breakup when they change their plan on the spur of the moment and not as a result of using their brains with friends or their support systems. They may change their plans impulsively when they are alone that first weekend or the night after the breakup. They become too lonely, and the other person calls. He is nice and seductive, or charming, or promising, and all of a sudden, she invites him over for a visit. It turns into more than a friendly visit, and then you are right back to where you started.

Do not make decisions to modify a breakup impulsively or because of how you are feeling. Remember, there are reasons you chose to break up. If those reasons have not changed, what are you doing? If your reasons were wrong and you go back, fine. But use your head and your support systems to help determine that.

> *If you want to change your mind, don't do it during your conversation. Go away, talk it out, and wait for a cooling-off period.*

Be Direct, Be Clear

Dating can be one of the most enjoyable times of life. It is a time of getting to know others and finding out what you want, what you need, what you don't want, and lots more. But if you don't have the boundary conversations you need to find that out, you will have wasted one of the most important times of life. Worse than that, you might make a big mistake. We don't want you to do that.

Have the conversation that makes clear whatever it is you need to face. Make sure that it ends with whatever structure is needed for the relationship or the problem you're confronting. No matter what happens, you win. If she comes around to your values and needs, you have made a much better future for yourself. If not, you will be much better off knowing that now instead of later, when the stakes are much higher and the pain much greater. Go for it.

23

With Your Child

I (John) am a small-group leader for a group of both elementary boys and junior high boys in my church. Kid's Church ended one morning, and I was leaving the room, when Brett, one of the boys, started running across the room to chase a Ping-Pong ball and almost collided with a couple of people. Without thinking, I quickly said in a loud voice to get his attention, "Hey, Brett, slow it down!" He reduced his speed. Then I looked around and saw his mom a few feet away from me. Not knowing her well, my first thought was, *Well, my career as a volunteer is over now. I'll be reported for being mean to kids.* Instead, she caught my eye and said, "Thanks."

I thought to myself how fortunate Brett is to have a mom who supports her child's being corrected. And I thought further about how important parents are in teaching their kids about receiving face-to-face boundaries. Parents, more than schoolteachers, Sunday-school teachers, or neighbors, are the key to influencing their children to make truth their friend and ally.

KIDS AND BOUNDARIES

If you are a parent, you have received a divine gift: "Children are a gift of the LORD" (Ps. 127:3 NASB). With the gift comes a great responsibility that begins at birth and continues until your child leaves home. You are to help her develop good and mature character. We define "character" as *the sum of your child's abilities to meet the demands of life.* (In our book *Raising Great Kids* we discuss the six needed character abilities.) Life has all sorts of requirements, from getting and maintaining good relationships to having self-control to developing a spiritual life. As a parent, you invest in providing those needed skills and abilities.

Boundary talks are a very important part of child rearing. They are one of the main ways kids learn the rules of life, such as right and wrong, obedience to authorities, being able to curb their impulses, learning to stay on task, and delaying gratification in favor of future goals.

Kids need the structure that comes from a parent who has good and loving boundaries. Over and over again, the Bible teaches parents to correct their children with "the talk" of correction and instruction. Sometimes the talk is also followed up by consequences and limits for the child as part of the discipline process:

- "A wise son accepts his father's discipline, but a scoffer does not listen to rebuke" (Prov. 13:1 NASB).
- "Discipline your son while there is hope, and do not desire his death" (Prov. 19:18 NASB).
- "Correct your son, and he will give you comfort; he will also delight your soul" (Prov. 29:17 NASB).
- "Fathers, do not provoke your children to anger; but bring them up in the discipline and instruction of the Lord (Eph. 6:4 NASB).

Boundary conversations with your child are most useful as they become *internalized*, that is, taken in emotionally and cognitively. When the internalization process works, the work of the parent becomes part of the makeup of the child. What was external is now internal. Over time, the child becomes a self-monitoring, self-correcting person in contrast to someone who needs constant supervision and correction from others. When the day comes that your child is faced with an invitation to take drugs, have sex outside of marriage, or cheat, you will not be around to help; however, the internalized conversations you have had over the years will be inside her and part of her and, if all goes well, will help her do the right thing.

All parents need to come to terms with this reality: One day your child will be on her own in the world. It is sad but true that your child is on the way out as you read these words. This is the goal of parenting. The parent-child relationship is unique: It is the only God-designed relationship whose goal is separation, not connection. Your child's leaving sometimes hurts so much because your heart investment in her wants her to stay, but God has designed her to use that very same investment to leave and find the way of God for herself.

How your child has internalized grace and truth from you will make a big difference in how she handles relationships, responsibilities, stress, temptations, and failure. So be sure to make boundary talks a normal part of your child's life.

Over time, the child becomes a self-monitoring, self-correcting person in contrast to someone who needs constant supervision and correction.

Boundary conversations both put good things into your child's character and help her experience the world as it really is. In the real world, friends and dates will confront her. Bosses will correct her. Police officers may pull her over for speeding. On the one hand, the child whose parents have set limits and consequences to help her adapt to a world with boundaries is readier for life. On the other hand, the child whose parents have avoided confronting her often has great difficulty when she encounters the real world. Not being used to that world, she may react, rebel, or withdraw from it.

Moms and dads are often hesitant or afraid to confront their child. Some do not want their child to be unhappy. Others are easily worn down by their child's persistence. Still others are afraid their child is too fragile, and her self-image might suffer. While you need to be concerned about how your child experiences your boundary conversations, this does not mean you should not confront. You may need to get support in how to confront well.

PRACTICAL GUIDELINES

Here are some suggestions for having face-to-face confrontations with your child.

Take the Initiative

Address a problem with your child right away. The longer you wait, the greater the chances he will have trouble making the important association between his actions and your talk. His behavior diminishes in importance to him as time moves on.

One night I took a bunch of kids home from an event in our van. They started getting very loud and physical. One even jumped out of his seat. I immediately pulled the van off the road and said, "Everybody, stop it, NOW." Then we talked about the danger of what they had done. The immediacy of the confrontation helped them understand how serious their actions were. They had endangered everyone's safety.

Don't wait for your child to become aware of his actions on his own, at least at first. This is your responsibility. If the boundary conversation process goes right, in time he will catch himself without you. My own kids are so used to that process that now when I see them doing something wrong, they will sometimes say, "I caught myself before you said anything, so it's okay." And even though it still might not always be okay, that does score a few points.

So, instead of waiting, you might say something like this:

> **You:** "Jen, I need to talk to you about your attitude lately."
>
> **Jen:** "I'm busy."
>
> **You:** "I want you to finish what you were doing, but no, this really can't wait. Let's go to the den to talk."

Keep up the initiative firmly but gently. If you think it's important enough that you need to talk right away, say so. At the same time, don't take the initiative when you are upset or likely to overreact. Make sure you are stable enough to intervene calmly. Remember that there needs to be at least one adult in the situation, and it should be you.

Stay Connected

Be sure to reach out emotionally to your child when you correct her. Children have difficulty feeling loved while they experience truth. This is a developmental milestone for them, and good parents help them reach that goal. Even when you must be very direct, do not pull away emotionally. As Josh McDowell says, "Rules without relationship equals rebellion." You might say something like this:

"Your attitude toward the family is very disrespectful. This is a problem, and we are going to have to deal with it. At the same time, I want to make sure you know I am on your side, and I am for you and for the family."

Hear your child out and stay connected with her feelings, as in this example:

> **You:** "I understand that you don't think I am being fair with you and that you are upset and angry, too."
>
> **Child:** "Well, you won't let me see my friends."
>
> **You:** "You're right. I'm drawing the line with these three kids. I know you really like them and want to be with them."
>
> **Child:** "There's nothing wrong with hanging with them, and you're being so unfair."
>
> **You:** "You're very mad at me. I understand that, and I'm sorry you feel this way. I want to talk to you about my decision, so that at least you will know why I am making it."

Provide the Four Essential Elements

Any good disciplining conversation with your child contains four essential elements: love, truth, freedom, and reality. *Love* allows the child to feel enough grace to tolerate the truth without feeling hated and bad. *Truth* provides the rules and requirements for his desired behavior so that he is aware of your expectations, what to do and what to not do. *Freedom* involves letting the child make a choice to respond to your requests (except in areas of safety, danger, and situations he is not ready for) so that he learns to "own" his decisions. *Reality* is the consequence or result of what happens to the child if he uses his freedom to defy or ignore your rules.

Your child needs to hear about all of these:

> "Kerry, I care about you, but your grades are unacceptable. They are too low for your abilities. You can choose to start studying, and I will be glad to help you. Or you can choose not to; I won't make you study. But if you decide not to pull your grades up, I will restrict you from the phone and from weekends with your friends until your grades improve."

Go Further Than Talking

With grownups, often the conversation is all you need. You make the person aware of the problem and state your desires and requests, and the problem is on the way to being resolved. Children are different. Because they are still forming a connection between words and experiences, they may need you to go further than a talk or a warning.

As we have mentioned, be prepared to establish consequences appropriate to the situation. Many parents assume they have done their job when they have had the talk. However, help your child to understand that the talk has actions behind it.

Contain and Empathize

Confrontation may cause your child to feel as though you don't care. Nothing you do will be able to convince her otherwise for now. This is not a time to try to prove your love with facts. It is a time to contain her protest, anger, and emotional distance from you and to empathize with her misery. If your child insists that you don't care about her, say something like this:

> "I really do love you, but it looks like I can't convince you of that right now. I'm sorry you feel so disconnected from me. It must be hard to feel that. At any rate, I want to come back to the problem with your grades."

This is hard for a parent to do. We tend to think our child will be swayed by logic and clarity. While this is true sometimes, don't make that your agenda, especially when your child is full of strong emotions. Great healing and connecting power rests in being empathetic over and over and over again:

> "I know, it's really sad you can't play with your friends today. I know you miss them, and that's really tough."

You are not being patronizing. Rather, you are helping the child metabolize, or digest, the limit in a context of grace and support. At the same time, resist the temptation to "remind" your child of why she is being deprived right now: "Yes, if you had just treated Sharon better, you would be playing with her right now." If you say something like that, your child will experience you as punitive rather than caring. The limit itself is enough for her to bear. Let the limit do its job.

Admit and Change When You Are Wrong

If your child is right about your part in the problem, don't be defensive. Judge yourself with the same rules you want him to live by. This doesn't mean stopping the conversation, but it might mean allowing a detour so that your child understands he has a parent who truly lives what she says:

> **You:** "You're right, I was too angry with you right then. I was wrong about that, and I'm sorry. I'll try not to do it again. But let's get back to the problem we started with."
>
> **Your child:** "But you were really mean...."
>
> **You:** "I'm sorry I yelled at you, but let's get back to the problem we're talking about."

If the child persists, empathize and agree again and keep returning to the problem at hand.

Remember Your Child's Age and Maturity Level

Gear your boundary talk to the appropriate developmental level of your child. Children go through many emotional, relational, and intellectual developmental changes. Try not to communicate on either too low or too high a level for your child to understand.

Also, don't assume that your child's chronological age and her emotional age are the same. Some kids are very mature, and some are very immature. Some teens, for example, are basically three years old on the inside. They need to be addressed with that in mind. Get to know where your child is on the continuum so that you can convey your boundary conversation to her in a way she will be able to grasp.

You may say to a toddler, "Don't hit your little sister, or I will put you in time-out." A teen may require something different: "You may not be aware of it, but it's starting to seem like the family needs to revolve around your needs and your schedule. I want you to know that's how we feel, and I want you to try to pay more attention to what everyone else is into."

Avoid Guilt Messages

When you confront your child, stay away from guilt messages. Guilt never helped anyone learn how to experience truth and grace; it brings the anger and condemnation that comes from the Law alone: "Law brings wrath" (Rom. 4:15). The wrath gets directed either toward you or at the child.

Your child's conscience, which receives the guilt message, is still in a formative stage. Sometimes it tells him he has been bad when he has not, and sometimes the converse is true. When you give him guilt messages, such as "You are killing your father and me with your drinking," he often takes in the statement in a brutally self-condemning way. This can lead to debilitating self-hatred, a harsh system of morality, or even a total rejection of your entire value system in order to stay away from the pain of guilt. Stay direct, and keep guilt away by saying something like this:

> "Dad and I are really worried about your drinking. It affects you and all of us. We will not allow this to continue, and we are going to do something about it quickly."

Normalize Protest and Anger

When you correct your child, you take a stand against her immaturity, self-centeredness, lack of self-control, and impulsivity. You draw a line against those aspects of her character that need to grow up. This is a central aspect of all good parenting. You say no to the part of your child that thinks she is God and wants to be treated as such.

Your child will find this stance unpleasant. You stand in between her and what she wants when she wants it. She will often protest, get angry, or say she hates you for confronting her. That's part of her job: to test the limit, find that it holds, give up, and accept that life is sometimes bigger than she is. This is how children mature.

So don't be caught off guard, surprised, or disappointed by your child's resistance to your confrontation. Realize that things are going as they should. If your child resists, say something like this:

> "I know you are really angry at me right now. I understand it's hard to lose your privileges. But no, I'm not changing my mind."

Be Prepared for Manipulation

When your child is confronted, he may do everything in his power to avoid blame, responsibility, or consequences. He might try to deflect you, blame it on you, or say you are not fair. Have your answer worked out ahead of time:

> "Lee, I know you think I was mean and unfair when I said I want you to do your chores better. I explained why I think that, and I think I've explained enough. I don't want to get into a fight with you that will just make things worse. I'm ending the conversation for now; maybe we can talk again later when you cool down."

This is much better for your child than insisting he accept and like what you say.

Allow Some Withdrawal, but Not Forever

When you confront, your child may pull away from you emotionally in anger or disappointment. Some parents have difficulty tolerating that distance. They want to feel close to their child. This can be a real problem, because the child needs some freedom to pull away from you and not like you for a while. Then, once she has emotionally resigned herself to the limit, she can return to the connection. Don't chase her down; let her come back by herself.

At the same time, if the withdrawal does not diminish, but stays the same for a long period of time, don't ignore it. Your child may be losing her connection with you or even getting depressed. Seek her out and insist on a talk that can help you reconnect at some level. Say something like this:

> "I understand that you are mad at me for what happened. But mad is different than staying withdrawn permanently. It's not good for us to be this disconnected. I need to find out what you're feeling so we can work something out."

Your child needs the loving and balanced truth you have for her. She may not ask for it, but as you make it part of your family life, her future will reap good fruit for her. (For further information on this topic, see our book *Boundaries with Kids*.)

24

With Your Parent

A woman in her fifties came up to me (John) at a conference and said, "I have a problem with my mother. She calls me all the time, sometimes more than once a day, and it's very inconvenient for me."

"What would you like to be different?" I asked.

"I would like to talk to her two or three times a week."

"That sounds as though you would still be giving her a generous amount of talk time. Have you told her this?"

She looked shocked. "No, no! I couldn't tell her that this is a problem."

"Why?"

"She would be upset."

"Maybe, maybe not. If something is very important to you, it might be worth it to bring it up in a kind way."

The woman gave me a strange look and repeated, "But it might upset her."

"Perhaps. Sometimes people get upset when they work out problems, but it isn't the end of the world."

By this time, however, I became aware that this woman was trapped in her past. I could see the scared little girl in her eyes, as she said once more, "But she might get upset."

"I understand that the prospect of upsetting your mom sounds very frightening to you. So at this point, if I were you, I probably wouldn't bring it up to her until I dealt with my anxiety first. Talk to some wise people about why confronting your mom is so scary for you, work through that, and then approach her about the problem."

I felt sad for this woman, knowing that, in the space of a couple of minutes at a conference, I could do no more to help her. She had hit a wall inside of her, where the rule was this: *At all costs, don't upset Mom.*

WHEN THE TABLES ARE TURNED

Confronting a parent or guardian or whoever reared us is probably the most complex of all face-to-face boundaries. You are now an adult, but you have a long history of being her child. You have been under her care, authority, training, and nurturing. You have been corrected and confronted about your life and behavior. Her primary job was to help you grow. Your primary job was to grow.

Then, in your adulthood, the tables are turned. The one who was corrected is now doing the correcting. The one who confronted is now being confronted. Even when the process works well, it can seem weird. When it goes bad, it can be disastrous.

Having healthy boundary conversations with parents can be helpful, producing growth and building relationship. When the Bible speaks about the value of speaking the truth in love to each other (Eph. 4:15), it includes your parents. They need confrontation the way anyone else does. And who is better qualified than an adult child who understands them, knows them, and loves them? However, for the process to go well, you need to understand the uniqueness of your relationship with your parents. Here we will present some perspectives on the parent-child relationship, then offer some practical suggestions for confronting a parent.

THE PARENT-CHILD RELATIONSHIP

Love and Honor Your Parents

First, make sure you love and honor your parents. They need your love, and the Bible singles them out as deserving of honor: "'Honor your father and mother'—which is the first commandment with a promise—'that it may go well with you and that you may enjoy long life on the earth'" (Eph. 6:2–3).

All confrontations require love so that the person you confront can metabolize the truth without feeling hated, bad, or defensive. When we honor our parents, we respect their previous role in our lives. We do not pretend that our parents were perfect, nor do we thank them for something that was not good or right. Even so, loving and honoring may be difficult if your parent was unloving, controlling, abusive, or absent, or if he did something that injured you deeply. In these situations you may feel that your parent does not deserve love and honor. It doesn't seem fair.

All confrontations require love so that the person you confront can metabolize the truth without feeling hated, bad, or defensive.

In reality, it is not fair that the person you needed for survival, love, and guidance didn't provide for you or even wounded you. But God understands your hurt; in fact, he acts as one who will provide what you did not receive: "Though my father and mother forsake me, the LORD will receive me" (Ps. 27:10).

Yet, every adult child must come to a point in her life when she gives up the demand for justice and lives in grace. She accepts God's solution of forgiveness and acceptance—the one he showed us in the "unfair" death of his Son—so that we can live in relationship. As we live in grace, we are to extend it to others, especially our parents: "Be kind and compassionate to one another, forgiving each other, just as in Christ God forgave you" (Eph. 4:32). If you cannot

love and honor your parents, get into God's healing process: Find a
trusted friend, a support group, or a counselor to help you deal with
the wounds your parents caused. This will help you come to love
and honor them.

Do Not Obey Your Parents

Loving and honoring do not equal obeying. God placed you with
your parents for a season of time to help you grow into a mature
adult. At some point this season ends, and your relationship with
your mom and dad changes from child-to-parent to adult-to-adult.
The roles change from dependency and authority to mutuality.
While you are to respect and care for your parents, you are no longer
under their protection and tutelage. Children are to obey parents,
while adult children are to love and honor them. Therefore, sometimes you will need to confront parents, disobeying their desire for
you to agree with them or go along with a bad situation.

People often have difficulty confronting parents because, like
the woman in the opening story, they still feel like a little child
with them. Emotionally they have not left home, so they do not
feel free to be separate, truthful, and honest with them. There is
too much to lose.

I don't know anything about the woman at the conference, but
I suspect that she still needed something from her mom she never
received—nor was she likely to receive it, barring some big changes.
She may never have received love, validation, affirmation, freedom,
or respect. If this sounds like you, it might be very helpful to work
on these issues in a small-group setting or with a counselor in order
to free yourself up from the past so that you can be an adult in
the present. (Our book *Our Mothers, Ourselves: How Understanding Your Mother's Influence Can Set You on a Path to a Better Life* is
a good resource. It identifies issues caused by a mother, shows how
to deal with them, and shows how to reconcile with your mother.)

One concrete example of moving out of obedience and depen-
dence on parents happens when you decide that you will not spend

some traditional holiday time with your parents. This can often be a cause for a confrontational talk:

You: "Mom, I wanted to let you know as soon as I could that I've made plans to go to the mountains with some friends this Christmas. I know this will be the first Christmas I won't be with you and Dad, so I wanted to talk to you about it."

Mom: "What are you talking about? You always spend Christmas with us. Your father will be so hurt."

You: "I'm so sorry you feel that way. I would never want to hurt you. But this year I have a really good group of friends from my singles group at church that I want to spend the holidays with. It's not about not caring about you; it's about wanting to be involved with these people at a deeper level."

Mom: "Can't you do that at another time? I mean, it will ruin our holiday."

You: "I hope it doesn't ruin things for you. That's why I'm telling you this several months in advance, so you can make sure you have time to make any other arrangements you need to so your holiday will be good."

Mom: "Don't you care about how we feel?"

You: "Yes, Mom, I care very much. And I do like spending time with you. If you think that I don't care, then maybe we can talk at some other point about your feelings, because I would like to reassure you that I care. But the point of this phone call was simply to give you a heads up so that we can plan and adjust for this change."

In addition, don't forget that your parent may need for you to be a change agent in her life. You may be one of the few people in her circle who is aware of her hurtful behavior or attitude. So, just as her job was to correct you in years past, your job (without the parental authority role) may be to correct her in the present. I know of many situations in which an adult child's confrontation of a parent was life changing for both.

Confront from Concern, Not Dependency

Before you confront, however, look at your motives. The highest and best motive, of course, is love: "The goal of this command is love, which comes from a pure heart and a good conscience and a sincere faith" (1 Tim. 1:5). Confront because you want to help solve a problem getting in the way of your parent's love, growth, or relationship with you and others.

Sometimes the motive waters are muddied because we still have needs from the past that get in the way. We have mentioned how the inability to leave home may prevent confrontation. Here the adult child may confront for the wrong reasons.

For example, a woman may want to talk with her father about the loving, warm relationship she never had with him. The right motive for the talk might be that she wants to forgive him and reconcile with him. The wrong motive might be that she wants him to give her the warmth she missed as a child. The problem here, of course, is that time has moved on. She needs to get those intimacy needs met, not by her dad, but by God's other resources, such as a healthy support group. Her dad can't "reparent" her.

Another problem motive is when the adult child has a desire to punish or get revenge. That is, to be able to feel connected and whole, he wants his parent to experience what he himself went through. While bad parenting can cause very deep hurts, revenge is not in our hands, but the Lord's (Rom. 12:19). Deal with those feelings elsewhere, and confront not out of revenge as a hurt child, but out of love as an adult.

Don't Idealize the Confrontation

Sometimes a person will think that when she finally confronts Mom's drinking or Dad's control, she will be free of the past and be able to move on. She sees this as the emotional key that unlocks her life.

While a good confrontation with parents has great value, it is not the key to freedom. *The key to freedom is spiritual and emotional growth:* "It is for freedom that Christ has set us free" (Gal. 5:1). When you go through the steps of healing, recovery, and growth, you receive the good you did not get, and you are repaired from the bad you did get. In fact, *often a confrontation is not the way to healing, but the result of healing.* When you have worked through the leaving-home issues, you are better able to validate what you have done by having a successful adult talk with a parent.

> *Often a confrontation is not the way to healing, but the result of healing.*

In fact, often when people resolve their childhood issues, they feel less of a need to confront their parents. Things that weighed heavy on them do not bother them as much. The focus of the confrontation changes from things that affected them as children to things more destructive for the parent now. For example, a slightly complaining mother may not bother an adult child much as he moves past his dependency on her, but her addiction to prescription pills might be the impetus for a serious talk, because it harms her.

Distinguish Between Hurt and Harm

Ultimately, you may have to distinguish between hurting and harming your parent. You might cause your parent discomfort in the conversation, which hurts, or you might say something unkind or unloving, which harms. The truth you want to communicate may be painful for your parent (hurt him), but it will not injure him (harm him). Some adult children perceive their parents as fragile and brittle, and they do not confront needed problems because they fear any hurt will injure them. Give parents time and space to evaluate their reactions, and see if they are being hurt or harmed. If they are angry or somewhat pouty, that is one thing. But if they seem more deeply affected—for example, withdrawing from the relationship due to pain, rather than in a manipulative "Look what you did to me" way—that is another thing. Consult with others who know your parent to see whether your parent is genuinely unable to digest feedback without injury or is merely reacting.

PRACTICAL SUGGESTIONS FOR CONFRONTING A PARENT

Convey Your Love and Honor

When you decide to have a conversation with your parent, make sure you are explicit about being "for" her in your conversation. If you have never confronted her before, she may not be prepared for this role reversal. She may feel persecuted, betrayed, or unloved by you. Try something like this:

> **You:** "I want to talk about a problem that concerns me and gets in the way of our relationship. You mean a lot to me, and I want you to know I really love and honor you for being my parent."
>
> **Parent:** "No, you don't. If you did, you wouldn't say these things."
>
> **You:** "I'm sorry you feel that way. It must be horrible to feel I don't care, but I really do."

You may need to return to the love and honor time and again during the conversation, especially if your parent can't hold onto the grace you offer. Just stop making your point and go back to the reassurance, as you would with a frightened child.

Know Your Parent

Context is very important in parental confrontations. Is he generally a person who welcomes feedback? Or is he resistant or defensive when something is brought to his attention? You might want to address resistance or defensiveness as issues in and of themselves, especially if your parent has a history of problems in this area. Try something like this:

> "When I have brought up the issue of my feeling criticized a
> lot by you, it hasn't seemed to go well. I think you may feel
> that I'm misunderstanding or attacking you, and I don't want
> you to feel that way. Is that how it is for you?"

Sometimes this approach will help a parent work through his perceptions and make it safe and normal to discuss problems.

Take into consideration his life situation, also. If he is dealing with serious health problems, a job or marriage loss, or aging issues, you may want to be sure those are stabilized before bringing up a problem. This is part of honoring a parent as he becomes older and more burdened with the cares of age.

Evaluate the Resistance

If you encounter resistance or defensiveness, figure out if your parent resists everyone or only you. Some parents can accept feedback from others, but they have not yet made the transition to seeing their child as one who can give them feedback. You may need to address that with them.

> You: "Dad, it seems to me that when I talked to you
> about how you sometimes disrespect Mom, you
> become really angry and upset with me."
>
> Dad: "You had no right to talk to me that way."
>
> You: "I'm sorry it affects you badly, and I want to resolve
> this with you. But I also noticed that at the party,

> your friend, Hal, said something to you about it,
> and you listened to him."

Dad: "Hal made sense."

You: "I'm sure he did, but he said essentially the same
thing I did. I'm wondering if it is more difficult to
hear things from me, as your daughter, than it is to
hear it from others. Can we talk about what that
might be like for you? Is it difficult to have me
bring up this problem with you? I don't want you
to feel that I don't respect you. At the same time,
I want for us to treat each other as adults. In fact,
I do want to hear how you feel about me, as we
talk."

Make your approach as humble, equal, and mutual as you can.

Be Direct

Recently a woman asked me, "How can I get my dad to open up and
be more involved in my life?"

"Well, have you asked him to?" I responded.

"Sure! I told him that it would be nice if he asked me how my life
was going, but he still didn't do anything."

"Well, let's not say that you asked him anything. Call it a suggestion, or maybe a mention of a good idea. But there was no direct
request. If he didn't respond, you probably need to ratchet it up a bit
to something like, 'Dad, you rarely ask me about myself; I seem to
be the only one asking you about your life. I would like you to ask
me how my work, kids, and activities
are doing.'"

Make your conversation
more about the
relationship and less
about your needs.

It is easy to be indirect with parents, given all the emotional com-
plexities involved. Sometimes a person will even think, *She is my mom.*
She should know I need this without

my being blunt about it. But if what you have said is not getting through, you have to be direct and clear, though not mean.

Apply what we said earlier about concern and dependency, and make your requests from your adult stance, not from a child position. The basic difference here is to *make it more about the relationship and less about your needs.* Here are some examples of both:

> **Child:** "I want you to be there for me."
>
> **Adult:** "I want to be able to communicate openly with you."
>
> **Child:** "I need for you to respect me so that I can feel respected."
>
> **Adult:** "I want you to treat me with respect so that it doesn't get in the way of our relationship."
>
> **Child:** "I want you to be able to hear me when I say no, because I feel bad about myself when you don't."
>
> **Adult:** "I want you to be able to accept our different opinions so that we can have healthy conversations."
>
> **Child:** "I want you to stop drinking so that I can have the mom I never had."
>
> **Adult:** "I want you to stop drinking, because none of us can connect with you, and it hurts us and you, too."

Decide Whether a Conversation Is Worth It

After having done all of the things in this chapter and this book, you may discover over time that confronting your parent is just not worth the cost. Barring life-threatening or very serious issues, you may need to let some things go and accept things the way they are.

You don't need to leave the relationship or do anything radical. However, you may need to grieve the relationship you would like to have with your parents and connect with them in whatever way you can. Find the ceiling of what your parents are willing to look at, and love the rest. Again, this is moving from dependency to love.

Your mom or dad may never be part of your emotional support system. However, you can also find much satisfaction and enjoyment in finding ways to safely connect with your parents, and also to "make some return to [your] parents; for this is acceptable in the sight of God" (1 Tim. 5:4 NASB).

Helping Both Mom and Yourself

Let's return to the scenario of the woman with a mother who called incessantly. Here is how a conversation might go concerning this situation:

> **You:** "Mom, I need to talk to you about our phone calls. I like to stay in touch with you, but it is becoming difficult to keep up with the calls."
>
> **Mom:** "So you don't want to talk to me anymore?"
>
> **You:** "No, I'm not saying that at all. What I am saying is that I can't do several calls a day anymore. My life is too busy, and the frequency keeps me from really missing you enough to look forward to the calls."
>
> **Mom:** "You don't look forward to hearing from me?"
>
> **You:** "In a way, yes. I find that if we talk two to three times a week, I do want to hear from you. But more than that, and there hasn't been enough time to actually not have you around me."
>
> **Mom:** "This is really upsetting."
>
> **You:** "I am so sorry it is upsetting you, and I want to talk to you about that, because I would hate for you to think I don't love you. At the same time, can we

> try limiting the calls to a few times a week and
> then see how it was for each of us in a few weeks?"

As much as possible, bring truth and grace to the relationship with your parents. What a blessing to be a redemptive force for their lives, even in their later years!

25

With Adult Children

What is an adult child, anyway? Sounds like an oxymoron, doesn't it? But we all know what it means. An adult child is one of your offspring who is all grown up. And, by and large, if that were true, you probably would not need to read this chapter. If all the people you brought into the world, or adopted, were "all grown up" in more than the chronological sense, you might not need to have any difficult conversations. You would coexist as friends and adults, share things with each other, help each other out, and enjoy God's multigenerational plan.

For many people, that is what happens. They enjoy their children as adults and find those years some of the most fulfilling they have ever had. Many people have told us that those are the best years of parenthood, especially if there are grandchildren.

You no longer have the responsibility of "parenting" your adult children. You don't have to be the source of things they need, guardians who protect them from the dangers of immaturity and the world, or managers who oversee them to make sure they are getting everything done responsibly. You've done your job, and you get to enjoy the benefits. As Paul says, the "day" set by the father has come when your children are no longer "under" you and you no longer have to guard and manage them. They now are answerable to God (Gal. 4:2). You can be the "sugar parent" to the grandkids without having all the hard work! In addition, your child also has a

256

responsibility to take care of you as you grow older, to make a return to you for all you did in taking care of her (1 Tim. 5:4).

This is the plan. Your child was supposed to "leave and cleave," and now you are on easy street, right? Well, we hope so. But this is not always the way it works in some families. Many things interfere with this ideal scenario, and parents find themselves still acting in the role of parent to an adult offspring. The adult offspring has remained an adult "child." Her parents are still serving as a source of things she needs, as a guardian, as a manager. For whatever reason, she has not totally grown up and taken those roles over for herself.

Circumstances may put the two of you in this role. Divorce, illness, economic factors, and previous bad choices may have prevented your child's total transition into adulthood. Sometimes no one person is at fault. Bad things have happened, and you find yourself in the strange position of still overseeing or helping an adult make life work.

> *Many things interfere with this ideal scenario, and parents find themselves still acting in the role of parent to an adult offspring.*

In addition, you may have difficulty making the shift from parent to adult friend. Your offspring can live her own life, but you have trouble letting go, or getting out of the role of telling her how to live or what you think she "should" do.

These factors can affect how you have those difficult conversations with your adult child. In this chapter we look at how to talk to an adult child.

Deciding How Long Is "Long Enough"

If you have a child who is well into adulthood, yet still does not take responsibility for his life, how long do you think your trying to "make" that happen is going to take? When will that finally work? If the pattern of your helping has gone on for a long time and has not helped, there is little chance that "more of the same" is going to change anything in the future. What usually does help is to change the role you play. Get out of the role of being your child's source, guardian, and manager. It is time for him to become these things for himself. So how do you do that?

Establish boundaries that require him to do his part instead of your doing it for him. If you give help, provide it on the condition that he does his part. In other words, if you provide money or support, he has to hold up his end of things, such as continue in school or actively search for work. And if he doesn't, set consequences. (For more on how that works, see our book *Boundaries*.)

To do this requires some planning and talking. You may need some wise counsel on how to do this if you have not been able to do it thus far. See a good counselor to help you figure out what your stance is going to be. At times, issues, such as addictions, or other potential significant consequences of "cutting someone off" can complicate things. Your adult child, for example, might end up not knowing where he will live or how he will pay the bills. Think these things out very carefully. The principle is still that you move adult children toward independence in whatever way you can and to the extent that it is not dangerous. Let consequences help accomplish that.

To do this also requires some difficult conversations. Many of the principles we talked about in part 2, "The Essentials of a Good Conversation," apply here. Review them. The technique of talking to an adult child is not that different, except that you have a history of your son or daughter not taking advice, if they are in the kind of position we have described. So say things that utilize those "Essential" principles. There will be little or no differences here. You might find especially applicable the parts on affirming the relationship, being an agent of change, and avoiding "shoulds." As you begin, reaffirm the relationship and your desire for the best for your adult child and for your relationship with him. Then, be specific and clear about what the issues and your expectations are.

If you have a conversation regarding boundaries, be clear about the new structure of your relationship and what the consequences will be. Remember Ron's dad in chapter 17? Ron was dragging his feet in finding a job. His dad was clear about his expectations and about the consequences should Ron choose not to create a written plan for finding work. So if your son or daughter is not being responsible with their finances, employment, parenting, addictions or psychological problems, behavior and treatment toward you, here is an example of how you can be very clear:

> "Nick, I love you, I hope you know that. And as you know, I have been doing some things to help you out for a while. But I want something different for the future. I want you to take over those parts of your life I've been doing for you. This is best for both of us. So, as of two months from now, you have a couple of options. You can begin to pay rent here or get your own place. I do not want to pay your way any longer.

> "Also, I know you have been having some problems, but you have not gone to get any kind of help. I'm open to suggestions of how I can continue to help you get back on your feet, but only if you see a psychologist or counselor to get some help. It's your choice. If you want me to participate, you have to get a plan and stick to it."

Notice that you use no "shoulds" here. You give Nick choices and clear expectations, with very clear consequences of what you will choose to do or not do. For example, Nick is free to not see a counselor; you do not dictate that he do that. But you do say that you will only participate if he does. You are controlling not him, but yourself. You only provide help to people who are diligent while they are receiving it. He is free to do whatever he wants.

Likewise, Nick does not have to continue to stay with you. He can live wherever he desires. But if he chooses your house, you will require that he pay rent. He is free to do what he wants, and you are free to do what you want with your own home.

Review the earlier chapters to see what emphases fit your grown child the best. Remember that if this has gone on for a while, you will probably need some help to plan your conversation, especially if potential bad outcomes are involved, like drugs or mental illness or depression. Consult someone who has dealt with this. We see many parents try to make their adult children healthy; they try to be their psychologist or pastor. This rarely helps. You can't be the one who cures them. What you can do—and very effectively—is be a bridge to their getting help outside the family system. That's what is effective most often.

Also, remember that long-standing problems with adult children like Nick require a wind-down process. "As of two months" gives the son or daughter time to get a plan together and do what he or she needs to do. Two is not a magic number—depending on the circumstances, the amount of time could be shorter or longer. But you will probably need some kind of a process.

Facing Less Serious Issues

We have been talking about more serious situations, but you will face rather ordinary ones also. Otherwise responsible young adults will sometimes continue to play the child with you and not take ownership for things they should be providing for themselves. If you think your help is excessive, you would do well to get out from under the role of "source" for the good of both of you.

For example, your daughter may look to you for money to live beyond her income level, which undermines her drive and self-confidence. Or your son and daughter-in-law may lean too much on you to take care of their children, which gets them out of some of the duties of parenting, even if it is only the duty of having to modify their schedule at times or find other baby-sitters. Some adult children want to continue to act like teenagers and just assume that their parents will enable that behavior by taking care of their kids.

These problems are not large enough to be big issues, but they can get out of hand. Your child does not live up to the requirements of adulthood, and you do not enjoy the freedom of having already raised your children. It is not good for either of you.

So watch out for those voices that say, "How can I say no? She's my daughter. A parent is always a parent." This is not true. Your parenting job should end, and you should get an adult in exchange. If you remain a "parent," you will still have a child, even if she is wearing an adult's costume.

Treating Your Child as an Adult

Sometimes there are not really responsibility issues with your child, but there are other issues you would do well to confront. If your child is hurtful to you, or if there are any other kinds of things that you would not want in your relationship, just follow the rules that we outlined earlier.

The problem is that sometimes parents have special rules for their own children, and they do not confront them as they should. They fear rejection, or they continue patterns that have been in the family for years. When your child is an adult, treat him like the other adults you care about in your life.

Take Deb, for example. Deb did not know what to do. Her twenty-two-year-old daughter, Randi, was really getting to her. Randi had just had a child, was unmarried, and lived with her boyfriend. Neither of them seemed to be taking the full rein of parenting seriously, and they would often call on Deb for help when they were in a bind.

Deb was glad to help and would do anything to see her grandchild, Tiffany. The problem was that many times they would call on Deb, and she would change her life around to help them out and see Tiffany. At the last minute, Randi and her boyfriend would change their plans, call Deb, and say, "Never mind. We don't need you now."

Deb would be very disappointed, but as time went on, she was also becoming more and more resentful. She thought to herself, *If this were anyone else, I would just tell them I am done. Call someone else. But it's my daughter and grandchild. It just feels like I can't do that.*

She felt caught between wanting her daughter to treat her with common courtesy, as she would require of anyone else, and feeling as if she should go the extra mile for her own child. *What am I to do?* she wondered.

Facing things with each other in life applies more to family than anywhere else. For the sake of your ongoing, long-term relationship, face problems and solve them. It may be time for all of you to talk and become an honest and loving family for the first time. Much healing could take place if you do.

Learning to Let Go

Your wish to remain a parent may be the real problem. This is a tough one to see and admit. After all, if you changed their diapers and did all those other things, you should get to remain in control as a return for all that hard work! And really, in your heart of hearts, don't you sometimes think that you truly do know what is best for them? Maybe you do. But they will never learn for themselves if you stand in the way by trying to continually oversee them.

So, sometimes the difficult conversations have been more difficult than they need to be because you have been putting a lot of "shoulds" on your adult child or trying to control her life in some way. Get out of the parent role and become a friend. Here are some tips:

Apologize. If you have been playing the parent too much, go to your adult child and have a conversation such as those mentioned in chapter 10, "Apologize for Your Part in the Problem." Tell her you have been too much like a parent and not enough like a friend. Tell her you are sorry for any problems this has caused. Then tell her that you would like to establish a new kind of relationship, and talk about how to do that.

Treat Your Adult Child as an Equal. Stop talking "down" to your child as if he were still ten years old. Assume that he is an equal, and do not maintain the "one-up" position.

Assume Competence. Stop and think before you suggest what she "should" do. Does your comment assume that she is a big person now? Or does it suggest that only Mom or Dad knows how to live?

Respect Separation. "Leaving and cleaving" involves both space and freedom. Watch out for intruding or being hurt when your child is living out his God-given independence as an adult. He has a life now that has many parts that do not include you anymore, and you should have a life also.

Respect Freedom. A free adult makes choices of her own. Certainly you can have opinions about your friends' choices, and you are free to voice them at times. But after you do, your friends are free to do what they want. Remember that your adult child is also free to make her own choices.

Live in Acceptance. Watch for guilt messages in your communications. If you are judging your adult child in guilt or shame or condemning ways, you are still playing the parent. Accept your adult child as God does, and do not judge (Luke 6:37).

Becoming Some of Your Best Friends

We hope you can get a vision from these suggestions of one of the greatest relationships in life: parents and their adult children as friends. It is a beautiful thing to see. And you might be amazed at how much of this has to do with the way you communicate. Through your communication you can show your adult children that you respect their adulthood and that you desire to be their friend and not their perpetual parent. If you do this, you might find that you have one of the best friendships available in all of God's creation.

But as we have said, sometimes that is not completely under your control. You may have a son or daughter who is resisting the adult role in life. If that is the case, hopefully some good conversations can begin to turn that around. And, in addition to those situations, to have good friendships you are going to have to do the maintenance of normal confrontations as well.

Any way you look at it, confrontation is a part of relationships, even with your own grown children. Face into it well, and the fruits will last for you and generations to come.

26

At Work

I (Henry) was consulting for two manufacturing companies that had merged and, as a result, had created a relational nightmare. Structures put into place in the new company called for more accountability and less freedom for some of the managers, and they were not happy. In fact, they had formed an angry coalition.

The addition of a new structure was not the only problem. According to the middle-level managers, the woman who had been put over them and was implementing the new rules was a nightmare. They said she was "mean" and "insensitive." Some threatened to quit if she were not removed; others said they could not work for anyone as domineering and cold-hearted as she was. The situation sounded brutal.

My job as consultant was to straighten out this relational mess and get the team working together. As I listened to the middle-level managers, I did not have a lot of hope. When I interviewed them, they all had the same story: Their supervisor was mean. I braced myself for meeting with her. I was ready to confront her about her relationship skills and the ways she would have to change. It did not look as though it would be easy.

I began by asking the woman to tell me her side of the story. And I got what I expected. She said she was dealing with a bunch of whiners who had been allowed to do nothing and now she had to get them to work, and they did not like it.

"Have you considered how you might be adding to the situation?" I asked.

"What do you mean?" she said, taken aback.

"Well, I understand they have to make some changes. You have been very clear about that. But what I need to know is what you think you might be adding to the problem. Have you considered the way you have been talking to them? Have you tried to understand their perspective?"

"What do I need to understand? They're a bunch of babies who go crying to their mommy. I am not interested in their whining. I just want them to do their jobs."

"That's what I was afraid of," I said.

"What? That I want more from them?"

"No, not at all. In fact, your president wants more from them as well. That's why someone with your skills was brought in. You were seen as someone who could get more done around here. That's not the issue. What I was afraid of — and what you have confirmed — is that you're not interested in how this change feels to them and, more to the point, how you might be making them feel in the process. What I'm seeing is that you're only interested in your reality and not theirs. I think you're going to have to learn to listen to them and try to understand things from their perspective, or you're not going to be able to get the work from them you desire."

"What do you mean? How would I do that?"

"You could start with telling them that you probably don't understand how difficult it is for them to go through this change and that you would like to hear them better. Then I want you to listen and see if you could say back to them what you understand their reality to be. I don't think you know."

"You mean that you want me to say something like, 'It sounds like you feel _____' kind of psychobabble?"

"Yes, something like that. Then I want you to come back and tell me what you learn."

Although she was skeptical, she took my advice. She asked the employees who reported to her how they were feeling, and she reflected those feelings back to them.

What happened was really interesting. In our follow-up meetings, she started to see that she was lousy at the people aspect of getting things done. As she practiced, she began to improve.

Further on in the process, I sat in with her and the others, and as I coached her on how to relate better, something else surfaced. There was a problem employee who, though fairly new to the company, was the ringleader of all the dissent. That person had to be confronted in her resistance to the changes. When she was confronted, she blamed, disagreed, threw tantrums, threatened to sue, and ultimately was let go. After she was gone, the department was an entirely different place.

But here is the key: *The divisiveness of that employee would never have surfaced if the manager had not accepted my confrontation and learned how she had to change.* My confrontation and the change it brought about in her led to the real problem being resolved. Out of that, she learned how to hear the confrontations of the others who gave her feedback on how she worked, and the whole team changed.

Here is the kicker to the story: This woman is now vice president of the company, and everyone there loves her. It would not be an exaggeration to say that her career, and to some degree the financial well-being of the company, were rescued by my confronting her with her problem, her receiving it well, and then her doing the work that needed to be done. Employees in good companies confront each other every day, and we want the same for you in your workplace.

How Confronting on the Job Differs from Confronting Elsewhere

If you are like most people, you spend a lot of your life at work. Work is a place with many possibilities for stress, conflict, risk, and loss.

It is a place where you put in the best of who you are. You are serving, and at times sacrificing, trying to please, and also establishing friendships on the teams with whom you work. So it naturally follows that you can experience some emotionally trying times there.

In addition, you have a job to do. Sometimes, in the course of doing your job, you have to confront other people who are not doing their jobs well. They may be your colleagues or people you manage and supervise or your supervisors and bosses. Much rides on your ability to confront well. It may make a difference not only in how you feel on the job, but also whether your company or department performs well.

As a consultant, I find that the best performers, the best teams, and the best work cultures are those that confront well. They are the ones who "turn their face toward" the issues at work.

Most of the principles we have presented in this book will help you do a better job at talking about things at work. Obviously, though, confronting people in your personal life differs from confronting people on the job. Author-

Lack of confrontation is more of a personal issue than a "work" or "authority" issue.

ity and accountability structures exist at work, and policies govern what goes on there. For example, if you are sexually harassed, there are usually guidelines in place you are to follow. Or, if you have a problem with someone, there is a predetermined authority chain you can appeal to, including a Human Resources department. But at the same time, once you understand those structures and policies, then the manner, style, and principles with which you deal with issues at work are very similar as with issues elsewhere. The problem is more often that people *don't* confront rather than that they can't. They avoid confrontation in their work life as they do in their personal lives.

While I was consulting with one of the biggest companies in North America, the vice president told me something I hear often as a consultant: "I wish my people would come clean with me. I wish they would tell me what they really think. I wish they would be more open and direct. But they are scared to do that."

Surprisingly, a lack of confrontation goes in the other direction as well. A team member under a vice president told me, "We would be so much better off if he would confront what goes on with individuals on this team. He plays the 'nice guy' role too much, and as a result, the team suffers. Everyone talks about it, too. It breeds a lack of morale."

TIPS FOR CONFRONTING AT WORK

People are afraid to confront those over them as well as those under them. " That is why I regard a lack of confrontation as more of a personal issue than a "work" or "authority" issue. What can you do? Here are some helpful tips for confronting people at work.

Find Out What the Reality Is

Find out what the reality is regarding talking about things that come up. Once you find that out, you know better where you stand and have more freedom to proceed. Or, in the harder settings, you at least know what your limits are. Usually, these realities fall into a few categories.

The first one is the formal structure. Find out what policies guide how things are dealt with. Some things, such as sexual harassment, fall outside of the realm of talking to your co-worker; they require a formal procedure. Your human resources department or your supervisor will probably be able to help you there.

Second, there is the less formal structure of how your boss wants you to do it. The good old-fashioned way of finding this out is to ask. Ask your boss or supervisor how she would like you to handle talking to her about issues the two of you encounter.

"Lynn, I want to have the best working relationship we can, and I want to do the best job possible for you. How do you want us to talk about things when an issue arises between us? Do I have the freedom to be really direct and clear about how we are doing together? Do I have to worry that I will be in trouble? How often would you like for us to 'check in' with each other to clean up lingering issues? Or do you have a preference for less structured meeting times and dealing with issues as they come up?"

Those are probably more questions than you want to ask, but you get the idea. Many times, just talking to a boss or supervisor about how the two of you want to work with each other is very helpful. Remember the essentials we talked about in part 2, and stay positive.

Third is the way that it works with co-workers and people on your team. This is similar to the way mentioned above, with a few additional thoughts. Talk to your co-worker about how the two of you should resolve conflict or solve problems. Putting it in the "solving problems" mode is probably less threatening. Have a talk over lunch or at a coffee break about how to do that, *before there is an issue*, if possible. Coming up with the ground rules and expectations beforehand is key. Covenant with each other to keep short accounts and to help each other by giving feedback.

Years ago, I walked into the office, and one of our employees was crying. I asked her what was wrong, and she just shook her head no, as if to say she couldn't talk about it. I pressed, though, as it was clear she was in a lot of distress.

"I just don't know what to do," she said. "_____ keeps asking me to do favors, and I can't get my work and his done, too. I don't know if I can work here anymore."

"What is he doing?"

"He dashes out the door and asks me if I could 'just drop something by at the printer' for him, as he has an important meeting to go to."

"Have you told him you can't?" I asked.

"I say I don't have time, but he just says it won't take long and it would really help him, so I do it. Saying no hasn't helped."

"Well, saying it might not, but *doing* it would. I know _____, and I would suggest a twofold approach. First, why don't you tell him what this feels like to you? Tell him that you want to help, but you have too much of your own work to do and you can't help him out anymore. Then tell him that you think he probably doesn't know how this is affecting you. Tell him that you are so troubled by the trap you feel you are in that you are thinking of quitting. Tell him how hard it is to be under that pressure and that it is affecting your whole outlook on working here."

She did confront him, and the outcome was great. While poor at seeing how his favors were too much to ask, he was good at responding to how others feel. He heard her and was saddened that he had made her work life so difficult for her.

This is a key point, and it flows from what we have been saying in the rest of the book. Often, if you can be clear about a problem's effect on you and if you can help the other person see that this is the reason you are talking about it, you can resolve it. When you express how you are being hurt by something, as opposed to how someone else is "wrong," many co-worker issues go away. Teamwork begins with understanding how we can help make one another's load lighter.

People feel the need to address many different topics. Only you know what your issues are, but here are some common "talks" you might need to have:

- "Please turn down your radio...."
- "I feel like I am pulling more than my share of the weight...."
- "You interrupt me a lot...."
- "I can't find you when I need you...."
- "I need for you to get back to me sooner...."
- "I have to wait long periods of time for you to get things to me we have agreed on...."

Certainly there are many more issues, but what they all have in common is that another person is working in a way that affects you and your work. If you can face your co-worker and use the principles we have discussed in this book with a focus on how it affects you, you will have a greater chance at resolution. Since you are not the boss, instead of evaluating someone's performance, share how you want things to work better between you and the other person so you can work more effectively.

The best teams establish team values together. Not only will Susie talk to Bill over coffee about how they will work together, but so should the whole team. Have a team meeting on the topic "How We Talk about and Solve Problems with Each Other." Volunteer to do a presentation on conflict resolution. Share one of the essentials from this book in each of your weekly meetings. Team building is done in a million different ways, but the point here is that it is good for teams to set ground rules for confrontation. This team strategy and value becomes every bit a part of the plan as the work itself.

> *A good team addresses the process and the way they work together. They have a plan, and they talk about it.*

Remember that work concerns not only the task, but also the process. A good team addresses the process and the way they work together. They have a plan, and they talk about it.

One very good manager I know asked his team, "What would have to happen this year for us to become the best department this company has ever had?" One of the things they came up with was "We would become a team who could talk to each other honestly, be on each other's side, help each other, and solve problems."

So finding out what the rules are and how issues are faced gives you more freedom within which to operate. Be proactive in both finding out what those are and being a part of establishing them as best you can.

If You Supervise, Do It along the Way

One of the toughest things a manager or supervisor has to do is bring up issues about someone's performance. But this can also be one of the best parts about working together. People improve with feedback. Yet, sadly, managers often do not bring things up as they happen, and then they have to confront in a big way later. Many people are fired or are about to be fired, and nothing in the file shows why this action was taken. While in reality they deserve to be fired, the process has not been documented along the way.

This is not that difficult. Do it in progressive stages as we talked about earlier. Coach along the way in the positive ways. When your coaching is heeded, give praise and complete the loop.

> "You know, Jason, we talked last week about the way that you were handling the Wheeler account, and I made some comments on how I thought you could do it better. Well, I want to tell you that you have really improved. The difference is noticeable and good. Thanks for taking my feedback and using it. It makes working with you such a good experience."

A good confrontation has an entire loop to it. Give feedback either way, positive or negative. This reinforces the value of feedback and makes the person more likely to take it from you the next time. Make it a policy of giving appreciation for how people take your feedback.

But sometimes you have to go to the next step. If your feedback is not accepted and put into practice, remind the person that you talked about it. Ask them how you can help them make the changes. Bring it up in an informal "reminder" kind of way. But if that does not do it, make the reminder more focused. Don't do it on the fly, but sit down specifically to address why the change is not happening. Now the issues to be confronted are not only the problem itself, but the problem of noncompliance:

"Joe, we talked about this a few times, and it is not changing. So let's talk about the process here. Is there some way I can help? I'm concerned that if I just bring up the problem again, we won't get anywhere. Therefore I want to find out what keeps you from dealing with the problem I brought up."

Now the confrontation changes a bit, from the issue itself to the failure to deal with the issue. Maybe help or further training is needed. It may not be Joe's fault. Also, at this point, depending on your company's policy, you might want to document the conversation. Talk to your human resources department about the laws and policies regarding employee discipline, but remember, it is progressive and always designed to help. In fact, most of the time you have to be able to show that you tried to help, gave extra training, or did other things; otherwise, you could have bigger problems on your hands.

> A good boss tries to solve the problem along the way by doing confrontations or coaching or training that helps the person to get better.

Attorneys say that the biggest problem with wrongful terminations (if it gets to that) is not the termination itself, but the process involved. If confrontations were good and helpful — and documented — someone's termination should come as no surprise. By then, they would have had meetings, help, and warnings to try to solve the problem.

When noncompliance is involved, you are usually well served to have other managers or supervisors in on some of those more difficult confrontations further down the process. Laws and policies apply to these processes, and this is not the place to talk about those. Talk to your boss, the human resources department, or the legal department for the proper ways to deal with a difficult employee. Remember, however, that a good boss tries to solve the problem along the way by doing confrontations or coaching or training that helps the person to get better, using the principles we have discussed.

Share Your Feelings

I gave an example in chapter 9 about my failure to know how I made people at work feel when I confronted them. When my colleague told me, I talked to others and found out that I was making work harder for people because of the feelings I aroused. Fortunately, we worked it out, and things were better because of it. But what that incident reinforced was the importance of how people feel interpersonally while they work. How we feel really affects how we work. If we are hurting because of something that is happening at work, we don't do as well.

What do you do when someone at work hurts you? I know what I wish people had done with me earlier: Let me know. That is the ideal way for things to happen—for people to talk to each other. And you will never know if you don't try it.

Obviously, some bosses and colleagues are tyrants and not fair. I am not suggesting you do anything that you know won't work or that will get you fired. But if you use the principles we have talked about, sharing how you are feeling in the spirit of doing better work is very helpful.

> "Sam, I want to talk about something that will help me do a better job here. Sometimes when you give me feedback, it is hurtful to me. Not the feedback itself; I want feedback. But the way you give it leaves me feeling as though you are against me or you think I'm an idiot. I want us to be friends and feel as though we are on the same team. So I wanted to talk about that. My hunch is that you would not want that to happen, and if you knew that it does feel that way, you wouldn't want it to be like that. So that's why I bring it up. Can we talk about a different way to talk to each other?"

In the spirit of doing better work and accomplishing goals and tasks, resolve the issues that are making work difficult for you, such as things that are so hurtful you find it hard to do your job, or people's performance and work styles. We hope that you and your co-workers and bosses can work out a way to make sure that your culture and workplace is one that builds people up and helps them do a better job together.

One more hint. When a boss is unaware he is hurting others and others are feeling it as well, you might go to him together and talk about it. Talk about your commitment to him and the team, and share what you are feeling and how you want to work it out. Again, use wisdom. But at times, people can hear it from a few when they can't hear it from one.

Task and Relationship

When you look at leadership research, management theory, and all the things that have ever been studied about how good work environments operate, two areas always emerge: task and relationship. Work has to do with getting a job done (the task) and getting along well with the people who are doing the task (the relationship). We work hard at tasks, and we do that with other people. It's important that the two work together.

Both of these areas depend on good confrontation skills. To get a job done, we have to solve problems and "face" things. To get along well, we have to work out relational issues with each other through facing things as well. So the entire arena of work requires good confrontation skills to work well. Confront well, and you will work better also.

27

With People
in Authority

I (John) was talking to Greg, a friend of mine, about his problems with his boss, Dave. "I can't work with the guy," Greg said. "When I need to talk to him about some problem, he just gets critical and intimidating with me. He's impossible!"

"Tell me what happens," I asked.

Greg told me of a recent encounter in which he had confronted Dave on not moving him into a position Greg had applied for. Greg had wanted to move out of his administrative role into one with more people interaction, such as marketing. When Greg told Dave how disappointed he was that Dave had not supported the move, Dave had responded, "I just don't think you're that strong in marketing. I need you in this position."

"How did you interpret his comments?"

"They were really critical. It was a putdown of my abilities and skills."

"I don't hear him saying that. Here's another way of looking at it. You might be equating disagreement with criticism. So Dave's in a double bind with you: If he disagrees with your confrontation, he's putting you down. But if he agrees to keep you happy, he compromises whatever he's trying to do in his operations."

What I didn't tell Greg right then, but told him later, was that this problem was similar to ones he had encountered with supervisors over the years. Greg's stance toward authority ensured that he would feel put down in almost any talk he had with a superior.

AUTHORITY AND CONFRONTATION

An authority is anyone who has been invested with the power to command or determine. People in authority include bosses and supervisors at work; police officers, judges, the military, and the IRS in government settings; teachers and professors in academic settings; and pastors, spiritual directors, or lay leaders at church. A person in authority has the role and responsibility of leading and directing others for some common purpose. Ideally, this person has reached the position due to competence, experience, and maturity.

Though many people have great difficulty negotiating successful confrontations with authority figures, structure and hierarchy themselves are good and helpful. Authority is a concept created by God, who is the ultimate and final authority. From his position on high, he sets up authority structures: "Everyone must submit himself to the governing authorities, for there is no authority except that which God has established. The authorities that exist have been established by God" (Rom. 13:1).

God allowed institutions and organizations to form so that they might represent him as he delegates to us his desires and commands for our lives. The church is one of these institutions. God wants us to be co-laborers with him in creating a world of love, purpose, and meaning. He doesn't want to do the work all by himself. Authority structures have many benefits: order, clarity of responsibilities, a way for the mistreated to have recourse, and the prospect of a peaceful life (1 Tim. 2:2). Authority also preserves us from danger. Without proper authority, the two alternatives are chaos (no one in charge) or oppression (a despot in charge).

God allowed institutions and organizations to form so that they might represent him as he delegates to us his desires and commands for our lives.

Authority structures operate best when there is a combination of submission and freedom. Someone is in charge of others, but people have choices and parameters in how they carry out tasks. The more competent and responsible the people, the more the manager can back off the details and allow people under her to achieve the goals that have been set.

In addition, people with a healthy view of their authority give those under them the freedom to confront. Those running a church, school, or business understand the value of honest feedback; it provides information that can help them solve problems, improve, and do a better job. Good organizations take the initiative to be confronted, all the way from suggestion boxes to feedback meetings to 360-type evaluations (which assess employee performance by getting feedback from an employee's boss, co-workers, and direct reports, including his own self-evaluation). Feedback varies from task-related issues to relational conflicts.

PROBLEMS IN CONFRONTING AUTHORITY

Problems in confrontation may lie with either the person in authority or the person under authority, and one should be prepared to encounter both.

Resistant Authority

When the person in charge is controlling, defensive, or resistant to feedback, his reaction can range from nonresponsiveness to, in extreme cases, pulling back from a relationship or involvement with you. If you encounter this sort of resistance, first see if your attitude or behavior could be contributing to the problem.

A person who does not do well in confrontation may have his own issues. He may have problems feeling equal with others, so to compensate for that he gravitates toward leadership. Another may not feel competent in his position, so he is afraid to look at any weaknesses or problems. Still another might confuse task issues with personal attacks. If any of these are true of the person you are dealing with, be on your guard as you talk to him:

You: "Fred, over the last few months, when I have brought up a problem to you, it has seemed to me as though you have become angry and resentful toward me. I would like to work out whatever might be causing this."

Fred: "Well, I don't know what you mean by me being angry. I do know that you have displayed a lack of good judgment and business sense several times in the last few months. You made some real bad decisions in the Schroeder account last week, and it cost the firm time and money to fix what you did."

You: "I know, and I hope I have learned from those mistakes. I really want to take a look at those times and change whatever I need to change. But to clarify what I meant, several times you have raised your voice at me, gotten really frustrated, and even called me some names. That is the problem I want to deal with in this meeting."

Fred: "Well, you have provoked those responses."

You: "And I do want to deal with whatever in my work or attitude may be making things difficult for you. I want to be a contributing team member for the department. For the time being, though, I need to ask if you can let me know in more respectful ways when my work bothers you, like using a less angry tone of voice, not being sarcastic, and not calling me names. I would really feel better working for you, and I think my work would be better, too."

Slavery versus Free Will

When the problem lies with the person *under* authority, one needs to own that she freely entered the authority relationship, with the processes and limitations it entails. That is, she is under authority by choice, because her goals and interests fit with the other person's. However, some people have difficulty with being under authority and instead feel controlled, almost like a slave. This was Greg's problem. He felt put down when his confrontations didn't turn out the way he wanted.

This condition is often due to a person's unfinished work in becoming an adult. She is unable to experience life as an adult when she is around an authority figure. She may respond like a rebellious teenager against a parent, defying the boss's every move. She might fear the wrath of the teacher, not wanting to risk disapproval, as a child might do. Or she may take the parental stance, wanting to boss the leader. None of these three positions—adolescent, child, or parent—is an adult stance.

Adults can give and receive truth without disconnecting or feeling threatened. They can stay separate, free, and in charge of their own opinions, even while working within an authority structure. So, if you identify with any one of these three positions, you may want to work through them with a trusted friend, counselor, or support group. (The books *Changes that Heal* and *Hiding from Love* can help you work through these issues.)

HOW TO CONFRONT A PERSON IN AUTHORITY

Here are some guidelines to help you successfully confront someone in authority.

Begin with Relationship

Whether you are at school, at work, or in a group with a leader, people in authority have feelings, and relationships are important to them. Be sure you open up the conversation with an attitude of concern for the relationship you have with that person, as opposed to simply emphasizing the task and role aspects of the position. For example, you might say something like this:

> "Margaret, I am glad you could make time for us to meet. I want you to know that I'm glad you're here [if this is true], and I want things to be good between us. So what I want to go over will, I hope, not only resolve an issue, but also make us more comfortable with each other."

Remember that many people in leadership have been confronted many times. It comes with the territory. Therefore the confrontation may go more smoothly than you fear.

Clarify the Problem

Clarify with the other person that this confrontation is not about the authority structure itself. You are not protesting the fact that you report to or are accountable to someone else. You want to resolve a problem separate from that.

Make this distinction very clear, especially if you have reacted to this person's authority in the past (taking an adolescent, child, or parent position) or if you are dealing with a defensive person. Here's the way a student could confront his professor:

> **Student:** "My problem with the academic load has nothing to do with being answerable to you. I believe in the process, and I'm okay with being part of it. The issue has to do with the fact that I don't think the requirements are realistic."
>
> **Professor:** "It seems as though you aren't fitting well with the program here."
>
> **Student:** "I don't think that's my problem, and I'll be glad to explore what you're thinking at some point. For now, I need to talk about how my workload isn't reasonable and to explore some possible solutions."

Own Your Part

As with any other relationship, make sure not only that you have looked at your own contributions to the problem, but also that you bring them up with the person you are confronting. People in authority often have a good eye for what you might be doing that makes things worse, and your openness may help them open up. Try saying something like this:

> **You:** "I do think you sometimes avoid the hard decisions and leave those to me. I really thought letting Rhonda go last week was your job, not mine, though I did it. Am I doing something here that might be making the situation worse? Am I missing that these sorts of things should be my responsibility?"
>
> **Your boss:** "Yes, you are. Those things are your job."
>
> **You:** "I wasn't aware of that. Would you show me where that job responsibility is written down in my job description, because that's a surprise to me."

Watch Your Tone

Related to the question of how adult you are in authority contexts, be aware of what your tone might convey to the leader. How you say what you say contains a great deal of emotional information. A resentful or defiant tone, for example, may interfere in a confrontation no matter what you say. Check your tone with friends, and ask them how they would feel if they were your supervisor.

Be Specific

The more you can identify specific events, words, and actions, the better your chances of resolving a problem successfully. Though we would not recommend this as a starting point, if you have encountered resistance in your previous attempts, you may want to bring notes with facts that are not open to interpretation. Try something like this:

> "Meredith, remember when I said last Friday that I needed your approval right away to secure the campground for the outing for the junior high kids? You just okayed it yesterday, but now the site isn't available anymore. This happened last month, too."

Confront Patterns, Not Events

Make sure that you are having the talk about something that is a clear pattern, not an event that has not happened before (unless it is a dangerous, illegal, or immoral act). People in leadership and authority positions are often under a great deal of pressure themselves, and they need to be given the grace to make mistakes. If, however, you see a repeating set of actions that show a trend, you may need to confront the pattern.

Couch your approach in terms of the pattern:

> **You:** "Bill, I really have gained a lot from your preaching and teaching over the years. That's why I do so much volunteer work here at the church. I believe in what you are doing, and I am on the team. However, over the past few months I have noticed at board meetings that you dismiss opinions that differ from yours. It's happened over the parking lot issue, the missions funding, and the curriculum question Andy raised. Can we talk about what goes on and what we can do to fix this?"
>
> **Bill:** "You have no idea of the pressure I have been under."
>
> **You:** "I am sure I don't. In fact, at some point I would like to talk with you about some ways to lessen your burden, as that might be contributing to

the problem I see. For now, however, it does seem that it is difficult for you to attend to differing opinions. I would like to talk about ways to make this better."

Bill: "I do listen to others."

You: "Yes, you do, but what I have seen, and what others have also experienced, is that there are enough instances in which you don't so as to cause me concern."

Bill: "I don't think you understand."

You: "Perhaps not, but, Bill, honestly, what I am talking about is happening right now between us. It is as if I can't even tell you my view on this without you negating it. Would you mind me presenting what I have seen, and then letting me give some possible solutions that might help?

Tie It In to Goals

Though many confrontations have a relational aspect to them, make a clear association between resolving the problem and achieving the goals and agenda of your supervisor. She has her own passions, mission, and goals for being in the position she's in. Use the confrontation to show her that helping you helps her. Try something like this:

"The way you correct my work is difficult for me. It feels as though I'm bugging you or as though you are putting me down. I really want your input, but it's hard to hear it amid your attitude. And then I get so worried about it that my productivity goes way down. I spend more time dealing with this than I do bringing in new clients. Could we talk about some ways you can give me feedback that will help me get you the bottom line you are looking for?"

Suggest Alternatives rather than Schedule Showdowns

Sometimes people want to prove the authority figure wrong. Their confrontation takes on a crusade overtone and becomes a matter of righting an injustice. This often happens when a person has been unhappy for a while and has not said anything about it until he is extremely upset. While a major showdown might prove necessary, involving several people on a serious level after a long sequence of events, it is not the best starting point in a confrontation.

Looking at the issue as a problem to be solved may gain you a warmer reception. Position yourself as an ally and take responsibility for coming up with alternatives to make things better:

> "How about if I email you with a summary of progress notes at the end of every day? Would that give you the information you need instead of your calling and dropping by my desk so much? It might save both of us time."

Use the Existing Structure

People in authority settings, be they church, school, government, or work, are most likely surrounded by a structure. There may be processes in place that can help in serious situations. For example, the person in authority may have someone she reports to, or there may be a governing board in the church, or your organization may have a human resources department.

Appeal to the governing structure only if you have exhausted every other avenue. You want peace between the two of you (Rom. 12:18), but if the problem is serious enough and you have done everything else you can, use those structures. You might need to say something like this:

> "I've brought up the issue of your extreme favoritism toward your cousin several times before, and nothing has happened. And I've brought other people in on it to give you a perspective other than my own. I wanted it to stop here, but I'm sorry, it seems you haven't changed anything.

I have documented all our conversations and what has or hasn't happened next, and I will be talking to your superior tomorrow about it. I would like for you to be there, too, so we can keep this out in the open."

When to Give Up

Finally, you may need to accept that the person in authority won't change. You may be dealing with a person who is unworkable in some area, and confrontation may not help. At some point you may need to evaluate if you need to leave the relationship or setting because of the problem (especially with danger, illegality, or immorality). Or you may conclude that although you don't like what is going on, the advantages and good things make it worthwhile to stay.

Either way, make sure you are freely choosing and owning your choice. If you stay, it still can be wise to tell the person:

"I wanted to let you know that I realize we disagree on this. For now, it doesn't look as if things will change. But I still like working here, and I will accept what is and do my best to work well anyway. But would it be okay with you if we kept the issue open and discussed it from time to time?"

Keep as many opportunities open as possible. People often have a change of heart over time.

The basic point is, don't be afraid to confront a person in authority. You may be helping yourself, him, and the entire setting you find yourself in. Remember that God is your final authority, and he will be there to help you be gracious, honest, and strong: "Do everything in love" (1 Cor. 16:14).

Speaking the Truth
in Love

We hope that by now you have captured the vision for how having face-to-face boundary talks can make a huge difference in your life. There are many good reasons to develop the ability to talk openly and honestly with other people; for starters, your life can be better, others may hear needed feedback, and your relationship with someone can improve. We have seen individuals, couples, families, churches, and businesses become transformed by incorporating ongoing healthy confrontation into their relationships.

So many times the key to people's success in this area has been that they have developed the capacity *to maintain a loving stance and yet to keep returning to the point at hand.* They empathize and then focus back on the problem, again and again. Learning this rhythm can help bring about many things you want to see in your relationships. For example, a resistant individual can begin to understand how his behavior has affected you; a person can change her hurtful ways; broken relationships can be mended; and you can begin to enjoy the connection you have desired.

As you become more skilled in the various aspects of confrontation we have talked about, you will end up finally having those conversations you have been avoiding. The problems that have been getting in the way of your relationships will become aired out and, we hope, resolved.

But something also begins to happen in a deeper way. Confrontation becomes an integrated and natural part of life. That is, you simply begin to address problems in loving, gracious, and yet direct ways with people all through your days, from casual relationships to your family and close friends. Confrontation becomes seamless, and relationship and work problems are solved sooner and better.

Finally, confrontation brings about another fruit—the most profound one of all, the fruit of spiritual growth. When we make truth our friend, God uses those conversations, both those we initiate and those we respond to, to mature us: "Speaking the truth in love, we will in all things grow up into him who is the Head, that is, Christ" (Eph. 4:15). We will ultimately experience the good things that God, truth, and relationships bring to all who seek him.

God bless you in this path.

Henry Cloud, Ph.D.
John Townsend, Ph.D.
California 2003

SMALL GROUP
DISCUSSION
GUIDE

PART 1
WHY YOU NEED TO HAVE THAT
DIFFICULT CONVERSATION

Chapters 1–2

1. The authors assert that the art of confronting well is an essential skill for those who desire success in life and in their relationships. In what ways does this assertion surprise you? In what ways have you observed it to be true? What questions or uncertainties do you have about this premise?

2. Let's talk about what it means to confront. If you were to define *confront* on the basis of your experience or expectations, what would you say it means? How does the picture change when *confront* simply means "to turn your face toward something or someone"?

3. The authors shared several fears — loss of relationship, being the object of anger, being hurtful, being perceived as bad — that can lead us to avoid confrontations. What fears would you add to their list?

4. If you feel comfortable doing so, share what you have found to be the most challenging and the most beneficial aspects of "boundary conversations."

5. What are some of the consequences of unresolved conflict in a relationship? What is your emotional response to these consequences?

6. The authors describe seven benefits of positive confrontation. Let's talk about some of the desirable results that positive confrontation can foster in a relationship. How do you feel as you talk about these results? Which results would you like to see in a relationship that is important to you?

7. Our motivation for confrontation is very important. How do you think we tell the difference between healthy and unhealthy motives for confrontation? What would you say are the warning signs of darker motives for confrontation?

Reflection Questions

1. What are the reasons you tend to avoid "boundary conversations"?

2. In which relationships or situations in your life do you long for the benefits of a stronger, more truthful connection? What would you like to see happen in each?

PART 2
THE ESSENTIALS
OF A GOOD CONVERSATION

Chapters 3–6

1. How does speaking from our own needs, our own heart, and our own experience bring clarity to a boundary conversation? In what ways do we often muddle the boundaries between "you" and "I," and what are the consequences?

2. The authors explain the importance of clarity in boundary conversations and boil clarity down to three elements: one clearly focused problem, its impact, and how you would like it solved. Why do you think it can be so difficult to actually achieve clarity?

Practice Point

Have participants pair up with another person and state their problem, its impact, and how they would like it solved. The other person then looks for lack-of-clarity symptoms, such as multiple problems, muddled impact, and fuzzy solutions.

3. Why is grace so important in a boundary conversation? What kinds of grace do we need?

4. How can the principle "When in doubt, go for grace" help you stay neutralized in a boundary conversation? What can grace accomplish that truth may not?

5. What do you think are the signs that more grace or more truth is needed in a boundary conversation?

Reflection Questions

1. *As you think about a boundary conversation you need to have, focus on one problem, its impact, and how you want it to change. Eliminate related issues until these three elements are crystal clear.*

2. *What do you find most difficult when you seek to balance grace and truth? What positive step can you take to neutralize that weakness?*

Chapters 7 – 10

1. One key principle to successful boundary conversations is to affirm and validate the person you are confronting so he or she feels valued. Describe a time when you have experienced this principle at work. In what ways did affirmation and validation make a difference in the conversation, the outcome, and the relationship?

2. What is the key to genuine affirmation and validation? What is the result when that priority is not maintained?

3. "I feel" statements are powerful and effective because they open one's heart to relationship with the other person. How would you describe the benefits and the risks of "I feel" statements?

4. Staying on track with a boundary conversation can be particularly difficult when the other person is defensive and diverts attention away from the problem. What suggestions for keeping a conversation on track can you share with the group?

Practice Point

Have participants pair up with another person and practice making "I feel" statements. The other person can listen and help clarify feelings, sort out thoughts from feelings, and flag the "you make me feel" statements.

5. Why are the words of Jesus in Matthew 7:3–5 such good advice when we're considering a boundary conversation?

Reflection Questions

1. *What is going on inside of you that you need to take care of before you consider initiating a boundary conversation? What apology from you is needed to open the door for the other person to see what he or she has done?*

Chapters 11–14

1. What do the authors say people feel when they hear the words "you should"? What impact can that have on the boundary conversation and on the relationship?

2. What alternatives to "you should" can we use in our conversations to prompt positive change while preserving the other person's dignity, choice, freedom, and equality?

3. What are some of the approaches we can take, attitudes we can have, and things we can say and do that can help move our boundary conversations from the "You got me, I'm going to get you" end of the spectrum to the "Redemptive Conversation" end? How do we know when a redemptive conversation is unlikely and another course of action would be wiser?

4. What can happen in a relationship where we want positive change to occur if we don't differentiate between forgiveness, reconciliation, and trust? What kinds of things can we say to keep those boundaries clear?

Reflection Questions

1. *Take a look at your complaints and desires. Do they tend to be more global or specific? Practice making them more specific.*
2. *Where does your specific boundary conversation need to begin — forgiveness in the past? reconciliation in the present? trust for the future?*

PART 3
SEEING HOW IT'S DONE

Chapter 15

1. Why is it important to learn to express our wants well in a relationship—not so weak that our wants go unmet, but not so strong that we drive others away? Talk for a moment about the possible consequences of not expressing wants well.

2. What feelings might we experience when our wants are not met? In what ways can those feelings impact our relationships?

3. How might a person who makes a request feel when the other person becomes defensive or engages in a personal attack in response to the request? What impact does such a response have on their relationship?

4. In what practical ways can we preserve another person's freedom—his or her ability to say yes or no to our request—when we express our wants? What must we examine within ourselves in order to do this?

> **Practice Point**
>
> Just how well do you communicate your wants to others? Choose a partner and practice expressing your wants to each other. See if the other person feels manipulated or controlled by your response when he or she declines to grant your request.

5. When our wants or needs are not being met within a relationship, what are some practical ways to meet those needs outside of the relationship that will support the healing, rather than the destruction, of the relationship?

Reflection Questions

1. *The authors say it is important to be able to express your wants inwardly to yourself before you attempt to express them outwardly to another person. What is it you want in specific relationships? Take the time to clearly identify those wants in your own mind, then practice how you would express those wants to the appropriate person.*

2. *Think for a moment about your most important relationships. What most often stands in the way of workable solutions for meeting each other's wants?*

Chapter 16

1. Most of us can name someone in our lives who behaves in a
   way that causes problems for others. What is your response to
   the possibility that God may have placed you in that person's
   life to help him or her become aware of the problem?

2. The authors suggest taking a "presumed innocent" approach
   when confronting a person who is unaware of his or her problem behavior. What do they mean by that term, and what do
   you think such an approach accomplishes? If you feel comfortable doing so, share about a time when such an approach was
   effective.

3. What can humility and empathy accomplish in conversations
   with a person who is unaware of his or her problem behavior?
   What might make us less inclined to be humble or to empathize during a behavior conversation? What can we do to
   counteract our inclination to be less humble or empathetic?

4. When someone needs to be made aware of problem behavior,
   the authors emphasize the importance of being loving but also
   being direct and specific. What are the pitfalls of being indirect
   about a problem behavior? What can we accomplish when we
   convey specific information about the behavior?

5. God created us to matter to each other. What difference can knowing how a person's behavior affects others make on that person's awareness of his or her problem behavior? What kinds of things might you say to illustrate that a particular behavior matters in the lives of those close to the person?

Reflection Questions

1. *When the truth points out a problem, it is often uncomfortable or even painful. What level of discomfort or pain do you anticipate the person you need to have a behavior conversation with will feel?*

2. *What specific objective and emotional information do you think you could share to help trigger awareness in the person you care about?*

Chapter 17

1. Requesting a specific change in behavior in order to improve a relationship is appropriate, but rarely easy. The authors present the wisdom of Micah 6:8, "to act justly and to love mercy and to walk humbly with your God," as a helpful approach to confrontation. In what ways does this wisdom prepare your heart for more redemptive confrontation?

2. The authors specify three reactions to confrontation: it is received well, there is resistance or other opposition, there is retaliation. What effect can each of those reactions have on our ability to resolve problems? What effect can each have on our relationship with the person who reacts in a specific way?

3. How do you respond when someone begins a confrontation by affirming something good about you? What conveys a person's genuine concern for you and his or her desire for an improved relationship with you? How well do you affirm others when confrontation is needed?

4. The authors present confrontation as a dialogue and not a one-sided conversation, but dialogue with a defensive person can quickly drift off track. What technique do they recommend for keeping a conversation on track?

Practice Point

Choose a partner and practice discussing an issue while your partner tries to move the conversation in a different direction. Which one of you is most adept at focusing the conversation in the desired direction?

5. What is the key to discerning when it is time to be patient with behavioral changes and when it is time to reinforce limits? Let's talk about some real life examples of where we would draw the line between patience and limits.

6. What specific suggestions for confrontation leading to behavioral change were most helpful to you? Why? How can you see yourself approaching such confrontations differently in the future?

Reflection Questions

1. *The authors agree that telling someone else they are out of line is a tough assignment with the greatest hope for a miracle but also the possibility for disappointment. After reading this chapter, what is the greatest thing you hope for as a result of a behavioral confrontation? What part of the process seems most difficult for you? How can you prepare yourself for it?*

2. *What plan do you have for after the conversation? What specifically will you ask the other party to buy into, and what will be the consequences of noncompliance?*

Chapter 18

1. What happens in a relationship when one person resists looking at issues, taking responsibility for them, or changing his or
her behavior? What range of feelings might individuals in such
a relationship experience? What might be the impact on their
lives both within and outside the relationship?

2. How important have you found feedback to be in your significant relationships? When you are receiving feedback, what
do you find most difficult in terms of your feelings and your
interaction with the other person? What blessings do you experience? When you are giving feedback, what do you find most
difficult in terms of your feelings and your interaction with the
other person? What blessings do you experience?

3. The authors emphasize that a resistant person also needs relationship, grace, and safety. In fact, they write, "without grace
and love, it is unlikely that anything redemptive will happen in
your conversation." Why are grace, love, and safety necessary?
From your experience, what makes it difficult to give these?
What enables a person to give them?

4. What do you think the authors mean when they say that "there
needs to be at least one adult present in the room for a problem
to be solved"?

5. What are the differences in attitudes, actions, and likely outcomes between a debate and a redemptive conversation? What might the person who is confronting need to do to keep a redemptive conversation from becoming a debate?

6. Which strategy for dealing with blame and counterattack did you find most helpful or enlightening? How do you see that strategy changing the character of redemptive conversations in your life? Which strategies do you feel are most challenging to apply? Why?

Reflection Questions

1. *Consider the major ways the authors say people resist confrontation: shooting the messenger, rationalization, minimization, blame, denial, projection. What are the methods most often used by the person you need to confront? Practice addressing each method of resistance that the person you need to confront would be likely to use in the situation you need to discuss.*

2. *What are your preferred methods of resistance when someone confronts you? What are you willing to do to make yourself more open to taking ownership of your shortcomings?*

PART 4
GETTING YOURSELF READY
TO HAVE THE CONVERSATION

Chapters 19–20

1. What are some of the areas of personal vulnerability that can sabotage a person's efforts to initiate or follow through on a boundary conversation?

2. In what ways might you be part of the very problem you would like to see changed in another person? What is the effect of this realization on you?

3. Why is it important to own your own stuff—motives, feelings, shortcomings, perceptions—before you attempt a serious boundary conversation? What are the hard things to face about your own stuff? What help is available in addressing these difficult areas?

4. What do the authors say can be the benefit of seeking to understand the other person on a deep level? What is the risk of doing so?

5. What specific kinds of support are important preparation for a boundary conversation? What are the barriers to such support? Where can a person find such support in your community?

Reflection Questions

1. *Think about a time when a boundary conversation went terribly wrong, when you were shocked by the direction and/or the outcome of the confrontation. What were your thoughts and feelings afterward? What, good or bad, did you discover about yourself? About the other person? About your relationship?*

2. *In what ways are you better prepared to have such a conversation today? Which areas still need work?*

PART 5
HAVING THE DIFFICULT CONVERSATION WITH PEOPLE IN YOUR LIFE

Chapter 21

1. The authors focus their chapter on confrontation in marriage around two huge statements: "the closeness of the marital relationship makes confrontation essential," and "marriage is not about making each other happy; it is about growing and helping one's spouse to grow." In what ways do these statements challenge your view of marriage? Talk about how the marriage relationship would be different if happiness were the goal versus growth.

2. What problems, needs, and opportunities does the nature of marriage create in regard to confrontation? What instructions or examples does God give us in his Word that help us understand how he intends the marriage relationship to work? What help or hope do these words offer?

3. What is "spousal equity" and what role does it play in behavioral conversations in marriage? How does one use spousal equity well? In what ways could spousal equity be misused?

Reflection Questions

1. *In what ways would your marriage relationship change if both you and your spouse viewed marriage the way the authors do?*
2. *Which of the problems specific to marriage do you feel are most important for you and your spouse to deal with? What makes it difficult for you as a couple to deal with these?*

Chapter 22

1. What key thing do the authors say confrontation accomplishes in a dating relationship? How convincing an argument do you feel they make for having boundary conversations in the dating relationship?

2. In what ways do you think dating relationships would be different if more couples were aware of and open to confronting important issues in their relationship? What can couples learn about themselves and their relationship by confronting these issues?

3. What are some of the reasons couples don't have productive boundary conversations while they are dating? What are the serious consequences of not confronting issues both to the dating relationship and to any future marriage relationship? List them.

Reflection Questions

1. *If you are involved in a dating relationship, how do you feel about your relationship in light of this chapter? Frightened? Encouraged? Concerned? Hopeful? What is at risk in your current relationship?*

2. *Which area of your relationship needs a good boundary conversation? Are you ready to take action? If not, what do you need to do to prepare?*

Chapter 23

1. What is unique about the parent-child relationship, and how do internalized boundary conversations help fulfill the goal of that relationship?

2. The authors say that any good boundary conversation with a child has four essential elements: love, truth, freedom, and reality. Why is each of these important? Talk about specific ways to communicate these elements in the midst of difficult boundary conversations with a child.

3. Children often feel unloved or uncared for when they are corrected, and these feelings are not swayed by logic or clarity. In what practical ways can a parent show love and care in such situations? What does a parent especially need to avoid in such situations?

Reflection Questions

1. *What is the most difficult part of having a boundary conversation with your child? Where do you most often falter when having these conversations? What can you do to better prepare yourself for future conversations?*

2. *When have you wronged your child through guilt, failing to admit your shortcomings, not staying connected, expecting too much, or backing down? What do you need to deal with in yourself, and what do you need to express to your child to get your relationship on a better track?*

Chapter 24

1. The authors say that the biblical principle of speaking the truth in love includes speaking the truth to parents. Parents need confrontation just as anyone else does, and no one is better qualified than an adult child who understands them, knows them, and loves them. But what is it about the parent-child relationship that makes it difficult to do so?

2. What are the differences between loving, honoring, and obeying parents? When is each appropriate? What are the complicating factors, and how can you find your way through them?

3. What is the appropriate motivation for confronting a parent? What are the risks of inappropriate motives or expectations, and what do you need to do to resolve them?

Reflection Questions

1. *What does it feel like to consider yourself as a redemptive force in the life of your parent(s)? When have you been a redemptive force? When have you avoided being a redemptive force?*

2. *What are the three greatest barriers to your confronting a parent about an important issue? Write them down and begin taking appropriate action on each one.*

Chapter 25

1. What circumstances, attitudes, and behaviors can result in parents still acting as parents to their adult offspring? Which of these things can parents change, and how? Which of these things are impossible for parents to change? What one thing can parents always change?

2. Specific and respectful communication is important in boundary conversations with adult children. What one word spells trouble when trying to set boundaries with an adult child? What does that word convey, and what are better alternatives that send a different message?

3. What are the warning signs that an issue with an adult child is getting out of control and needs to be resolved? What do you think is the primary objective of a boundary conversation with an adult child? In what ways does that objective influence how you approach the situation?

Reflection Questions

1. *Which parts of "The Essentials of a Good Conversation" would be most helpful for you to review in light of what is happening in your relationship with your adult child?*
2. *If you have been guilty of trying to control your adult child's life, which tips for letting go are most applicable to your situation? What action do you need to take to show that you want to be your child's friend, not a perpetual parent?*

Chapter 26

1. What have you seen happen in a workplace culture where people do not confront well? What are the short-term and long-term consequences to the individuals involved and to their present and future employers?

2. In what ways does the attitude that "teamwork begins with understanding how we can help make one another's load lighter" make it easier to address issues in the workplace? What are some good ways to communicate this attitude during a confrontation?

3. How does "closing the loop" with feedback—either positive or negative—help build people up and enable them to do a better job together?

Reflection Questions

1. *If you are a supervisor or manager, with which of the people on your team do you need to have a "solving problems" talk? Why haven't you already had that conversation? What do you need to do in terms of policies and personal preparation to have that conversation?*

2. *If you are an employee who needs to have a boundary conversation with a boss, what is the issue you need to talk about? In what ways are your feelings regarding the issue affecting your work? What outcome would you like?*

Chapter 27

1. Who is a person in authority? What is the role of a person in authority? Just from the nature of what is vested in the person in authority and what is required of that person, what kinds of difficulties might develop in relationship to other people?

2. Why is it important to open conversations with an authority figure with an attitude of concern for the relationship as opposed to simply dealing with the task? How would you go about doing this?

3. The authors say that a person who has difficulty working under authority may have unfinished work in becoming an adult. They describe the adolescent, child, or parent responses. What are the characteristics and limitations of these responses? What are the distinguishing characteristics of the adult response? How does an adult response support good working relationships with authority figures?

Reflection Questions

1. *What cautions in confronting an authority figure do you need to keep in mind? Do you tend toward defiance? Do you respond as a fearful child? Is clarity difficult for you? Are you operating out of a "crusade" mentality?*
2. *What are your warning signs for needing to separate from an unworkable authority relationship?*

Boundaries in Dating

How Healthy Choices Grow Healthy Relationships

*Dr. Henry Cloud
and Dr. John Townsend*

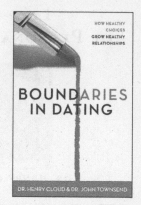

Rules for Romance That Can Help
You Find the Love of Your Life

Between singleness and marriage lies the journey of dating. Want to make your road as smooth as possible? Set and maintain healthy boundaries — boundaries that will help you grow in freedom, honesty, and self-control.

If many of your dating experiences have been difficult, *Boundaries in Dating* could revolutionize the way you handle relationships. Even if you're doing well, the insights you'll gain from this much-needed book can help you fine-tune or even completely readjust important areas of your dating life.

Written by the authors of the bestselling book *Boundaries*, *Boundaries in Dating* is your road map to the kind of enjoyable, rewarding dating that can take you from weekends alone to a lifetime with the soul mate you've longed for.

Softcover: 978-0-310-20034-5

Pick up a copy today at your favorite bookstore!

Boundaries with Kids

How Healthy Choices Grow Healthy Children

Dr. Henry Cloud
and Dr. John Townsend

What the award-winning *Boundaries* has done for adult relationships, *Boundaries with Kids* will do for you and your children.

Here is the help you need for raising your kids to take responsibility for their actions, attitudes, and emotions. Drs. Henry Cloud and John Townsend take you through the ins and outs of instilling the kind of character in your children that will help them lead balanced, productive, and fulfilling adult lives.

Learn how to

- set limits and still be a loving parent
- bring control to an out-of-control family life
- apply the ten laws of boundaries to parenting
- define appropriate boundaries and consequences for your kids

... and much more.

"Boundaries with Kids *helps us give our kids the skills they need to live realistic and full lives in meaningful relationships. Not perfect—but healthy!*"

—Elisa Morgan, president of MOPS International, Inc.

Softcover: 978-0-310-24315-1

Pick up a copy today at your favorite bookstore!

Gold Medallion Book by Dr. Henry Cloud & Dr. John Townsend

Boundaries

When to Say Yes, How to Say No, to Take Control of Your Life

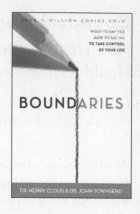

Is your life out of control?
Do people take advantage of you?
Do you have trouble saying no?
Are you disappointed with God
*   because of unanswered prayers?*

Having clear boundaries is essential to a healthy, balanced lifestyle. A boundary is a personal property line that marks those things for which we are responsible. In other words, boundaries define who we are and who we are not.

Boundaries impact all areas of our lives:

- Physical boundaries
- Mental boundaries
- Emotional boundaries
- Spiritual boundaries

Often, Christians focus so much on being loving and unselfish that they forget their own limits and limitations. Dr. Henry Cloud and Dr. John Townsend offer biblically based answers to many tough questions, showing us how to set healthy boundaries with our parents, spouses, children, friends, coworkers, and even ourselves.

Hardcover: 978-0-310-58590-9
Softcover: 978-0-310-24745-6
Unabridged Audio CD: 978-0-310-24180-5
Workbook: 978-0-310-49481-2
DVD: 978-0-310-27809-2
Participant's Guide: 978-0-310-27808-5

Pick up a copy today at your favorite bookstore!

Boundaries in Marriage

*Dr. Henry Cloud
and Dr. John Townsend*

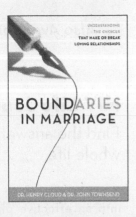

Learn when to say yes and when to say no—to your spouse and to others—to make the most of your marriage.

Only when a husband and wife know and respect each other's needs, choices, and freedom can they give themselves freely and lovingly to one another. Boundaries are the "property lines" that define and protect husbands and wives as individuals. Once they are in place, a good marriage can become better, and a less-than-satisfying one can even be saved.

Drs. Henry Cloud and John Townsend, counselors and authors of the award-winning bestseller *Boundaries*, show couples how to apply the ten laws of boundaries that can make a real difference in relationships. They help husbands and wives understand the friction points or serious hurts and betrayals in their marriage—and move beyond them to the mutual care, respect, affirmation, and intimacy they both long for.

Boundaries in Marriage helps couples:

- Set and maintain personal boundaries and respect those of their spouse
- Establish values that form a godly structure and architecture for their marriage
- Protect their marriage from different kinds of "intruders"
- Work with a spouse who understands and values boundaries—or work with one who doesn't

Softcover: 978-0-310-24314-4

Pick up a copy today at your favorite bookstore!

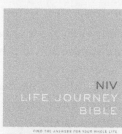